# INSHORE
## SALT WATER FISHING

◇

LEARN FROM
THE EXPERTS AT

MAGAZINE

Creative Publishing
international

Chanhassen, Minnesota

**Inshore Salt Water Fishing**
*Introduction by Barry Gibson, Editor,* SALT WATER SPORTSMAN

**Creative Publishing
international**

*President/CEO:* Ken Fund

*Executive Editor, Outdoor Group:* Don Oster
*Editorial Director:* David R. Maas
*Editor and Project Leader:* Steven Hauge
*Managing Editor:* Jill Anderson
*Creative Director:* Brad Springer
*Senior Art Director:* David W. Schelitzche
*Art Director:* Joe Fahey
*Photo Researcher:* Angela Hartwell
*Copy Editors:* Barry Gibson, Shannon Zemlicka
*Photographer:* Andrea Rugg
*Studio Manager:* Marcia Chambers
*Director, Production Services:* Kim Gerber
*Production Manager:* Sandy Carlin
*Production Staff:* Stephanie Barakos, Laura Hokkanen, Helga Thielen

**Special thanks to:** Barry Gibson, Tom Richardson, Chris Powers and the staff of *Salt Water Sportsman* magazine

**Cover Credits:** *Tarpon and Menhaden* painting by Don Ray; background pole fishing photo by Gary Kramer; front cover photos: Dave Vedder: left, Bill Lindner Photography: right; back cover photos: Bill Lindner Photography: left, Ron Ballanti: center, Bob McNally: right

**Contributing Photographers:** Joel Arrington, Ron Ballanti, John Brownlee, Hanson Carroll, Angelo Cuanang, Marc Epstein, Jim Hendricks, Richard Herrmann, Gary Kramer, Larry Larsen Photography, Bill Lindner Photography, Bob McNally, Dick Mermon, Brian O'Keefe, Doug Perrine/Innerspace Visions, John E. Phillips, Tom Richardson, Al Ristori, Neal Rogers, David J. Sams/Texas Inprint, Mark Stack/Tom Stack & Associates, Doug Stamm/ProPhoto, Walt Stearns, Sam Talarico, Dave Vedder, Tom Waters

**Contributing Illustrators:** Chris Armstrong, John F. Eggert, Diane Rome Peebles, John Rice, Dave Shepherd, Jim Singer, Mark Susinno/Wild Wings, Inc., Fred W. Thomas, Joseph R. Tomelleri, Tom Waters

Printed in China

10 9 8 7 6 5 4

ISBN 0-86573-132-2

# Table of Contents

# Introduction

Inshore salt water sportfishing is one of America's most popular pastimes, and the number of happy participants grows steadily each year. Why? It's an activity that can easily be enjoyed by just about anyone who lives or spends leisure time near the coast, it can be as inexpensive as an afternoon at an amusement park, and the fishing – or should we say "catching" – has been incrementally improving in a number of areas. And, besides being relaxing and fun, a day on the water can provide the entrée of a tasty seafood dinner.

But just what is "inshore" fishing? That's a question that many have grappled with, including those of us at *Salt Water Sportsman*. Is it best characterized by locale, such as bay, river and inlet waters – or by the size or species of the fish being sought? There's little question that flounder and seatrout are "inshore" fish, but what about, say, kingfish? Kings are normally caught well offshore, but some of the largest specimens have been taken around near-shore buoys at the entrances to busy harbors. And, deep-water dwellers such as cod and pollock have historically been taken by surf-casters in the Northeast. So, what's the answer?

There really isn't one, but for the purpose of *Inshore Salt Water Fishing* we'll define inshore fishing as the pursuit of those species that are most commonly caught in near-shore waters today. And there are plenty, as you'll see in the following pages, from Florida's acrobatic little foot-long ladyfish to Alaska's slug-it-out halibut that can tip the scales at better than 300 pounds. Nearly every species covered can be taken from beach, bridge, pier or small boat, and by a variety of techniques and tackle. Indeed, inshore salt water fishing is "everyman's" sport.

Boats, gear and accessories, too, have evolved exponentially in quality and value, making fishing easier and more productive. A brand-new fiberglass center-console boat and outboard motor, ideal for working bays and sounds, can be purchased for less than the price of a sub-compact car. Quality electronics such as LCD fishfinders, Global Positioning System (GPS) units and VHF radios can be had for little more than $100 each, providing dependable fishfinding capability, precise navigation, and safety. Tackle? Today's high-tech rod-and-reel outfits afford long backlash-free casts, and the mind-boggling array of lures on the market covers just about any species, technique, or fishing

condition imaginable. Clearly we've never had better or more affordable "stuff" with which to chase and catch inshore gamefish.

But perhaps the brightest and most promising facet is that a number of species are actually becoming more plentiful along many stretches of our nation's coastline. The recent curtailment, or in some cases outright elimination, of destructive commercial gear types and fishing practices has begun to reverse a century of abuse. Florida, for example, banned near-shore, large-scale commercial net fishing in 1994, which allowed populations of snook, redfish, pompano, mullet and a dozen others to rebound to healthy levels in just three years. California's ban on inshore gillnets in 1990 has given a big boost to the state's sport halibut and white seabass fisheries, and programs to rebuild striped bass and summer flounder along the Eastern Seaboard have yielded similar positive results.

Effective overall management, along with sensible recreational regulations and strong local, state and federal efforts to improve water quality and restore marine habitat, have helped rebuild and maintain many stocks of our important inshore food and gamefish. Proactive organizations such as the Coast Conservation Association and the United Anglers of Southern California, as well as dozens of recreational fishing publications and literally thousands of outspoken sportsmen and conservationists, can take much of the credit. They made it all happen, but nobody's letting up. There's still lots that needs to be accomplished. Join in!

As plentiful as some species are today, however – or may be in the near future – it takes the right tackle and techniques, along with a working knowledge of the targeted species' habits, to help ensure success on any given trip. That's what this book is all about. Authored by a select team of the country's most celebrated angling experts – all of whom are either SWS editors, field staffers, or regular contributors – *Inshore Salt Water Fishing* brings you tried-and-true tactics, professional insight, and decades worth of absolutely invaluable hands-on experience. These experts are the best in the business, and all are eager to help you catch more and bigger inshore fish.

Take advantage!

*Barry Gibson, Editor,*
SALT WATER SPORTSMAN

# Atlantic & Gulf Coast Fish

STRIPED BASS · REDFISH · TARPON · SPECKLED TROUT · SNOOK · BLUEFISH · BONEFISH · PERMIT · FLOUNDER

SHARKS · COBIA · BARRACUDA · BONITO · LITTLE TUNNY · LADYFISH · CREVALLE JACK · FLORIDA POMPANO

SHEEPSHEAD · TRIPLETAIL · WEAKFISH · TAUTOG · BLACK DRUM · SPANISH MACKEREL

# STRIPED BASS
## (Atlantic Coast)

Although other species may be more abundant at times, it's the striped bass *(Morone saxatilis)* that ranks first in the hearts of most inshore anglers from Chesapeake Bay (where it's called rockfish or rock) to Maine. The striper is a good-fighting fish that will hit a wide variety of lures and baits, is accessible to both shore and boat anglers, is easy to handle and provides that all-important element of mystery since it can grow to 100 pounds or more.

Some decades ago, when inshore salt water quality was not nearly as good as it is now, marine biologists stated that the striped bass was the ideal species for the industrial age. It's hard to imagine a hardier fish, other than the eel, as stripers actually seem to thrive in the worst-looking waters conceivable. New York City's East River is an example. Although water quality is a lot better than it used to be, stripers have always flourished there and in years past would even gang up at the sewage outflows. If they accumulate pollutants that affect them, it has not been noted. Ironically, the PCBs released over the years into the Hudson River turned out to be a blessing for the species, as they forced New York to stop commercial fishing in that vital spawning river. This led to a succession of strong year classes that continue to this day, making the Hudson a major supplier of East Coast stripers.

Striped bass are found along the Atlantic Coast from Nova Scotia to the St. John's River in northern Florida and in several river systems emptying into the Gulf of Mexico. They are the same species that was introduced to the Pacific Coast (p. 134) via train from New Jersey's tiny Navesink River in 1879, and now range from central California to Oregon.

The striped bass of the Mid-Atlantic and New England states is biologically the same, but actually quite a different creature from those living in other areas.

STRIPED BASS
RANGE
PRIME FISHING

The population from the Outer Banks of North Carolina, for example, is anadromous (moving into fresh water to spawn) and migrates north in the spring, returning to wintering grounds during the fall. Although adults live in salt water, successful spawning requires long rivers with the right current flow so the eggs can remain suspended but still end up in the proper river environment for survival.

The Roanoke River population in North Carolina's Pamlico Sound is considered almost entirely non-migratory. In fact, stripers found south of the sound are not only non-migratory but rarely enter the ocean. These river populations tend to migrate toward river mouths in late fall or winter, but that's as close as they come to salt water. The same applies to the northernmost striper populations in the Pacific. Stripers around San Francisco, however, live in the bay and migrate to the ocean, where they can provide surf fishing opportunities similar to those on the Northeast coast.

There now may well be more striped bass caught in fresh water than in salt because the species has been introduced into many inland reservoirs with great success. In most cases, however, stripers can't spawn successfully in these areas due to the lack of suitable habitat. Fortunately, raising and stocking striped bass is simple compared to that of most species, as they can endure wide swings in water temperatures, will eat almost anything and will even survive being released into salt or fresh water after being raised in the other type. The original inland population became landlocked when South Carolina's Santee-Cooper Reservoir system was dammed off during World War II, and the stripers still flourish today. This population has been the brood source for many of the fresh water introductions since that time.

The one area where stripers are conspicuously missing is the Great Lakes, where they might be able to reproduce naturally. Some observers feel that fishery scientists chose salmon over stripers for introduction into the Great Lakes because they could keep the former under tight control with stocking programs.

Atlantic migratory stripers winter in the ocean off North Carolina and Virginia, as well as in inshore waters such as Chesapeake Bay and the Hudson River. As water temperatures rise in spring, an inshore and northward migration starts, and spawning occurs in river systems of the Chesapeake, Delaware and Hudson Rivers in May. There is some minor spawning in Maine's Kennebec River and possibly others. Nova Scotia also seems to support a non-migratory river striper population, just as the southern states do. New Jersey is attempting to restore the Navesink River as a spawning area, but for all practical purposes the Chesapeake river systems along with the Delaware and Hudson Rivers are considered to be the producers of virtually all migratory stripers.

Large striped bass leave these areas quickly after completing spawning, and most spend summers in inshore ocean areas or large bays. Smaller stripers migrate north, which leaves spawning areas such as the Chesapeake with mainly small bass under 20 inches during most of the summer and early fall. Throughout the summer months large bass are found from Montauk in the north and south to New Jersey. The fall migration starts during September in Maine and other areas north of Cape Cod, and gets into high gear south of Cape Cod late in the month or in early October. November is usually the prime month from western Long Island to Delaware Bay, and continues into December some years from New Jersey south. The Outer Banks often produce big stripers during December, January and even into February.

Striped bass are relatively long-lived fish, with those living to 20 years or more providing the 50-pounders that are the pinnacle for avid striper anglers. The New Jersey Division of Fish and Wildlife charted the average age, length and weight relationships for striped bass captured from July to December, 1998 (below).

There is a range in striper length/weight relationships, especially as bass get larger. Pot-bellied stripers can weigh 5 pounds or more than the average, while the same applies in the other direction with skinny fish. A rule of thumb is that fork length has to be at least 50 inches to make the hallowed 50-pound mark, and requires a few more inches if the overall measurement is used.

Striped bass populations, like several other mid-Atlantic inshore species, have been cyclical over the centuries. It is uncertain whether past declines were related to natural causes or overfishing. Stripers were so abundant during colonial times that laws had to be enacted to protect them from being netted or pitchforked for use as fertilizer. It wasn't until the 1980s that serious conservation began, and it was literally forced upon the states by rapidly declining striper populations after decades of abundance. Although every state had minimum length limits, these did not mean much. The limit was a mere 12 inches in the Chesapeake and 16 inches to the fork of the tail in most northern jurisdictions. New Jersey had an 18-inch limit, but it was measured to the tip of the tail. New Jersey was the only state with a bag limit, which was 10. Commercial fisheries pounded on the striped bass not only along the migratory path, but in the spawning rivers of the Chesapeake. Given the fact that these fish were available to exploitation year-round, it was surprising that there was such great fishing for them from the 1950s through the 1970s.

Outstanding year classes were produced about every six years during this period.

It wasn't until the last of those great year classes (1970) was greatly overfished that the true nature of the crisis was finally acknowledged. The states, acting together in the previously ineffective Atlantic States Marine Fisheries Commission (ASMFC), agreed to set up regulations designed to improve the stocks rather than simply maximize their own harvests. The Atlantic Striped Bass Act was passed by Congress to put teeth into that effort by imposing federal sanctions upon states unwilling to accept the provisions of the ASMFC management plan.

The result was a steady increase in stock size from about 5 million stripers of all ages in 1982 to around 37 million by 1998. Recreational catches, which were around the one-million-pound mark during the mid-1980s, spurted to over 15 million pounds by 1997 despite strict size and bag limits. Length regulations in the Chesapeake were brought up to 18 inches while coastal anglers worked under a basic 28-inch minimum after enduring even harsher limits during the rebuilding phase. In addition to the comebacks in the Chesapeake and the Hudson River, the Delaware River was declared restored to historic levels of striped bass spawning biomass by 1998, as was North Carolina's Roanoke River stock.

By adhering to high minimum lengths and low bag limits while holding down commercial catches, the ASMFC Striped Bass Management Plan succeeded in rebuilding the population and should be able to maintain it at relatively high levels indefinitely. Fortunately, as of the year 2000, Maine, New Hampshire, Connecticut, New Jersey

## Length vs. Weight of Striped Bass*

| AGE (yrs) | LENGTH (to tip of tail) | WEIGHT | AGE (yrs) | LENGTH (to tip of tail) | WEIGHT |
|---|---|---|---|---|---|
| 1 | 10" | 0.5 lbs. | 9 | 35" | 16.2 lbs. |
| 2 | 15" | 2.1 lbs. | 10 | 36" | 19.0 lbs. |
| 3 | 20" | 3.3 lbs. | 11 | 38" | 20.0 lbs. |
| 4 | 24" | 4.9 lbs. | 12 | 40" | 22.4 lbs. |
| 5 | 27" | 6.5 lbs. | 13 | 42" | 27.0 lbs. |
| 6 | 30" | 8.5 lbs. | 14 | 44" | 35.0 lbs. |
| 7 | 32" | 12.3 lbs. | 15 | 48" | 42.0 lbs. |
| 8 | 34" | 14.5 lbs. | | | *Data from the New Jersey Division of Fish and Wildlife —1998 |

and Pennsylvania –all states along the migratory path– list striped bass as gamefish, and Massachusetts has long restricted striper sales to hook-and-line catches. On the flip side, many states remain subservient to commercial fishing interests.

## Where to Find Striped Bass

It is probably easiest to eliminate areas where striped bass are not likely to be caught! Perhaps very shallow backwater areas with no tidal movement would qualify, except that you are likely to find stripers just about anywhere inshore at some time during the year. On occasion they even appear to range well offshore, as draggers encounter them in such areas as the Mud Hole between northern New Jersey and New York. However, the vast majority of striper migration occurs in state waters (within three miles) and primarily within a mile.

It's also very difficult to pinpoint ideal striper habitat, as the fish seem able to adjust to anything. For instance, the New Jersey summer surf usually holds very little bait, but stripers stay and root around, picking up calico crabs and sand fleas.

It is important, however, that anglers keep in mind the fact that stripers are very structure-oriented once they settle into an area. Thus, rocky bottoms, points, jetties, inlet mouths, mussel beds, wrecks and any place else that attracts food sources are logical places to seek stripers. The exception would be areas where there are large schools of open-water bait such as bunkers or bay anchovies for stripers to chase.

Rips indicate a sharp rise from the bottom with deeper water on both sides and create an opportunity for stripers to lie in wait for baitfish to be drawn to them. Stripers will generally lie at or near the high point, or immediately behind it. Although not obvious at slack water, there will be agitation at the surface as the current increases, especially if it's running into the wind. The many rips across the mouth of Delaware Bay, the Sandy Hook Rip, the rips off Montauk Point, the Race between Long Island and Fisher's Island and Nantucket Shoals are among the areas that have long been famed for holding stripers.

Bridges provide similar opportunities for striper anglers, particularly those who seek fish at night. Bass feed on the uptide side of the bridge, where baitfish are delivered to them. If the moon creates an uptide shadow along a dark bridge, you'll often spot bass swimming in the shadow. Bridge lights may also create such shadow areas.

Schooling stripers are apt to be found near any inshore constriction area; a creek mouth during ebb tide would be an example. Keep in mind that stripers tend to be nocturnal in their habits and feed readily in the dark. Whether they feed in daylight or at night depends on the nature of the bait they are pursuing. As a rule, daytime fishing is best during migratory runs, while night fishing is more productive in summer during periods of hot, calm weather.

## How to Catch Striped Bass

Striped bass can be caught in many different ways under a variety of conditions. The following sections will cover the most popular baits and techniques used throughout their range.

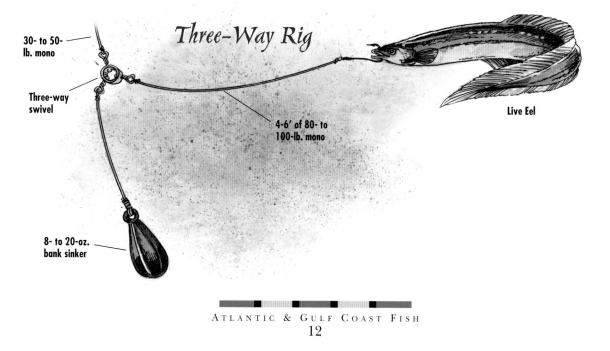

**Three-Way Rig**

30- to 50-lb. mono

Three-way swivel

4-6' of 80- to 100-lb. mono

Live Eel

8- to 20-oz. bank sinker

EELS. Eels are probably the bait most closely associated with stripers. At times there's nothing bass love more, but anglers must be aware that bass can be fussy about eels if they're keyed to feeding on something else. Eels seem to work best at night during the summer and fall. Anglers tend to avoid using them during the day because if bluefish are around, they never fail to chop these baits if given the opportunity. When blues are not a problem, eels will attract bass at any time.

Eels are best hooked through the lower jaw and out an eye socket. They stay alive for hours when rigged in this fashion, and don't have to be very lively in order to be effective. Anglers can often catch several bass on the same eel. An eel is good enough to keep on the hook if the tail curls when lifted up. In fact, during one summer period in 1999 some guides noted that dead eels were out-fishing live ones. The most important piece of equipment when using eels is a cloth to handle them with. Once hooked, they should be left flat on deck, as a hanging eel will twist up the leader and create a mess of knots and slime.

In most cases, eels are drifted through rips and over structure on three-way swivel rigs with a short dropper to the sinker and a long one to the bait (bottom left). Hook sizes vary, but 5/0 to 7/0 bait or circle hooks are popular choices.

When a strike occurs in a fast current area, no dropback is necessary. Drop the rod tip and reel tight. As with all baits, stripers hit eels head first, and even schoolies can inhale a big "snake." In shallow areas and when fished from jetties, eels are usually worked with no weight and drifted in the current, or cast and retrieved. Care must be taken to keep them off the bottom, as that's where they tend to want to go. Trophy stripers seem particularly enamored of eels, so eels are the bait of choice for targeting large fish. The author's personal best (61 pounds) was caught on an eel, and it was also an eel that fooled a 76-pounder off Montauk Point during an eclipse of the moon in 1981.

MENHADEN. Also called mossbunkers, bunkers or pogies, menhaden are another "big fish" bait. Adult bunkers may weigh 1½ to 2 pounds, yet even stripers in the teens swallow them. When stripers are feeding on schools of bunkers the surface action can be some of the most exciting in fishing, as 20-pound bass look like monsters with the splashes and boils they create.

Anglers generally use treble hooks with live

A RIGGED MENHADEN or "bunker".

bunkers, running one hook through the nose or into the back just behind the head. Striped bass have no cutting teeth and swallow fish head first, so the forward hook is all you need. While trebles are most efficient, they do result in potential gut hooking, which is not desirable if bass are to be released. As a result, guides often choose a large single hook, such as a 7/0 to 9/0 Siwash or circle hook, which provides room for the hook to work around the bulky bait. Stripers are rarely leader-shy when bait is being used, so 50-pound-test fluorocarbon, which provides low visibility plus some protection against bluefish teeth, is a good choice. Under clear water conditions anglers go to leaders as light as 15-pound-test, while in darker water anglers use black, nylon-covered wire leaders or regular wire bluefish leaders with good results.

Bunkers may be drift-fished in areas where bass are known to be present, or cast to jetty tips. Since bunkers often stay on the surface and seem to create a difficult target for stripers, anglers sometimes use a large, rubber-core sinker to keep them

BUNKER "chunks" are a frequently-used bait for stripers.

down, or even fish them on bottom with fishfinder rigs. Young-of-the-year "peanut" bunkers are often abundant in the fall and make great baits for schooling stripers. Equipment should be scaled down to accommodate the smaller bait, keeping in mind that even big bass will take "peanuts" at times. Peanuts can be easily snagged from schools on the surface, transferred to a small treble and fished right under the school. Even with all those freebies available, bass and blues will select the one injured bunker to eat first.

Far more stripers are caught on menhaden "chunks" (above) than on live baits. Chunking for stripers requires only a modest supply (one or two flats per tide) of fresh or frozen bunkers. Fresh cast-netted or snagged bunkers are always preferable, but frozen work well enough if they're all that is available.

Anchor on suitable bottom and throw a few pieces overboard around the boat (some anglers also put some in a weighted chum pot) before putting lines overboard. Most chunkers use fishfinder rigs with just enough sinker to hold bottom, with hooks sized from 5/0 to 9/0. Bunkers should be sliced like a loaf of bread, with the middle chunks being the prime bait and the tail sections utilized as chum. It is well known that many pros fish primarily with a bunker head, which seems to attract larger stripers. A bunker head fished in the surf at night is very effective. A short dropback is called for after a pick-up. Remember that when using a circle hook, simply reel tight rather than using a traditional hook set.

Chunkers in the northern part of the range tend to stay away from ground chum because of bluefish, which are frequently a problem. The exception would be in Delaware and Chesapeake Bays, where blues are generally scarce. There anglers often bring bass up in chum slicks where baits can be freelined to them. The best spots for chunking vary from area to area, but anchoring ahead of a rip is always a good bet. Mussel beds or rocky bottoms are also likely spots, especially on a drop-off or ridge. The edges of channels also frequently produce, and when stripers are especially thick all an angler needs to do is to mark fish on the depth finder, throw the anchor and start chunking.

Chunking requires a large baitcasting outfit, spooled with 20- to 30-pound monofilament or 30- to 50-pound superline. A 6½-foot heavy-action rod is a good choice; however, you can scale down in shallower water when lighter sinkers are used.

CLAMS. Clams may not be a glamorous bait, but they're hard to beat in the surf, particularly after a storm when dead surf (skimmer) clams wash up onto the beaches. This is one of the few times that stripers see clams in nature, as they are unable to open them.

A few sharp surfcasters began using clams primarily during the summer, but they are now used from spring through fall. Surfcasters normally use fishfinder rigs, while others prefer an easier-to-cast, simple two-hook set-up with hooks placed on dropper loops above the sinker. While fresh clams are preferred, as they stay on the hook better, frozen clams work also.

Frozen clam bellies have been a secret chum of Long Island bass fishermen since the 1960s. This old-time technique spread to New Jersey's Raritan Bay in 2000. In most situations clam bellies are the bait of choice over the clam meat itself, and are deadly on schooling stripers. After anchoring on a likely spot, squeeze a few bellies into the water. A chum pot should be employed at the same time so you don't have to continually squeeze bellies. Hooked bellies are then dropped into the slick on free lines if the current isn't too strong, or with split-shot rigs or on weighted fishfinder rigs in faster water.

HERRING & ALEWIVES. Ideal as early-spring baits for large stripers, herring and alewives can be harvested during the many herring runs along the coast and either fished immediately or penned for future use. Although more fragile, they're utilized just as menhaden are later in the spring and are easier for stripers to catch and swallow. Herring are particularly popular with jetty anglers and those fishing the Cape Cod Canal in May. Sea herring and hickory shad, which may be available later in the season, also make great live baits for stripers.

MACKEREL. A variety of sizes of mackerel are available as live baits in New England, occasionally as far west as Montauk in early summer. Due to their slim shape, 2-pound mackerel are easily eaten by big bass, and you need only lower the rod tip before coming back on a striper after the hit. Depending on circumstances, live mackerel can be drifted on the surface or off bottom on a three-way swivel rig (above), or slow-trolled in shallow waters. During the summer anglers in New York Bight frequently see "tinker" mackerel which make great live baits for all sizes of bass. Chub mackerel (also frequently called tinkers) may move inshore there during the summer and can be jigged and fished for trophy stripers.

OTHER BAITS. This category for stripers covers just about everything that swims or crawls where bass live. Small fish such as tautog and winter flounder were secret weapons for some pros until minimum size restrictions eliminated their use. In some areas anglers utilize cunners (bergalls) and various other small fish to attract stripers around bridges and jetties and in canals. Live squid are a good choice, and are available to

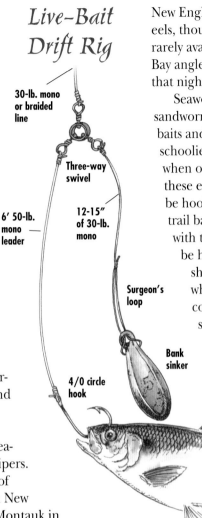

## Live-Bait Drift Rig

30-lb. mono or braided line

Three-way swivel

6' 50-lb. mono leader

12-15" of 30-lb. mono

Surgeon's loop

Bank sinker

4/0 circle hook

New England fishermen on occasion. Sand eels, though a primary food for stripers, are rarely available as live bait. Some Cape Cod Bay anglers rake them at night and use them that night or the next day.

Seaworms (primarily bloodworms and sandworms) are one of the oldest of striper baits and still work wonders, especially on schoolies. They are a top early-season bet when other predators aren't around to steal these expensive offerings. Seaworms should be hooked once in the head and allowed to trail back naturally. Bass generally don't play with them and hit at the head, so they can be hooked immediately. Soft-shell and shedder crabs are also popular baits when available. A few anglers rake calico crabs from the summer surf and select the shedders, which are tied to the hook with thread. Chumming with tiny live grass shrimp is a deadly technique for schooling stripers, but is currently not popular due to the difficulty in obtaining shrimp in quantity.

ARTIFICIAL LURES. Lures for stripers are nearly as productive as live baits since bass will hit almost anything at times. As a rule, lures don't work as well during early spring, when water temperatures are still cold and bass metabolism is low. The primary trick when lure fishing is to "match the hatch" and use a lure that resembles what the bass are feeding on.

BUNKER SPOONS. These were originally developed specifically for jumbo striped bass by

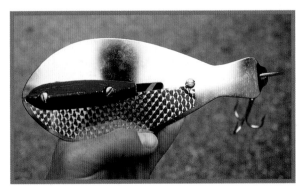

BUNKER SPOONS are a popular "big fish" lure for trolling.

utilizing the chrome reflectors of car headlights. The erratic action and size of those spoons resembles the big striper's favorite prey, a menhaden. Bunker spoons can be deadly when schooling bunkers are in the area, and are worked on wire line so they can be set at various depths.

Wire line is also the standard for most other types of striper trolling, and isn't difficult to use once you get used to it. The trick is to realize you can't make any mistakes in deploying this unforgiving line. Either Monel (softer and more expensive) or stainless steel wire in 40 or 50 pound test should be marked every 50 feet so you know exactly how deep the lure is running. For trolling at slower speeds the ratio is 10 feet of depth for every 100 feet of wire out. Many beginners opt to have their wire spooled and marked at a tackle shop. Wire is not forgiving, and backlashes lead to kinks that can cause sudden breakage. With the lure in the water and the leader cleared from the rod tip, carefully free-spool the line while applying pressure to the spool. Special wire-line rods with carboloy, silicon carbide or roller guides are needed to handle the wire and the heavy bunker spoon. Specialists using this technique prefer 9-foot or longer soft-tipped rods, which are set in holders parallel to the water. The throbbing of the spoon is reflected in the soft rod tip and determines the correct trolling speed. Many other spoons are also effective for stripers, such as those more closely imitating baits like herring.

UMBRELLA RIGS. These were developed in Montauk specifically for striped bass after Captain Gus Pitts saw a rig where fishermen were running strips of beer cans off a bar to catch pollock. Striper fishermen soon devised a more sophisticated three-armed rig with twisted #15 wire armed with cod tubes to imitate a school of small baitfish. It worked so well that within a couple of years there were many variations utilizing two metal bars at right angles with a lead drail in the middle. Tubes are still the basic lures used on spreader rigs, especially when sand eels are the main forage, but soft-plastic shad bodies have become more popular in many areas. Some anglers also trail a long tube or a plug down the middle of the rig.

PLUGS. Many styles of plugs are effective on stripers, and for some anglers casting a plug is the most enjoyable way to catch bass. When stripers are feeding on the surface they respond to the commotion created by topwater poppers, which also work well at drawing up bass holding in shallow waters but not showing. Topwater baits such as the original wooden Stan Gibbs, the Cordell Pencil Popper, and the Yo-Zuri Surface Cruiser are worked on a long-butt, soft-tip rod with a lot of wrist action and a fast retrieve to create a lot of surface action. Standard cup-faced poppers are worked slower with a more intermittent popping action during the retrieve.

Swimming plugs come in many sizes and variations, and stripers will take most of them. Surfcasters in particular like to work minnow plugs, with Bomber Long As, Gag's Grabbers "Minnow," and Yo-Zuri Crystal Minnows being particularly popular along the New Jersey coast. New England surf fishermen tend to seek bigger bass with larger plugs such as the Junior Atom and the Stan Gibbs bottle plug or darter. The IGFA all-tackle world record 78-pound, 8-ounce striped bass was caught on a plug at night from an Atlantic City jetty on September 21, 1982.

Lipped swimming plugs are employed by boaters trolling wire line to catch some of the largest stripers. More than a few 50 pounders have been trolled up during the fall on Shagwong Reef at Montauk. Plugs such as Mann's Stretch 25 that dive deep on monofilament line have become favorites in Raritan Bay among those who don't want to get into the expense of wire line outfits.

Casting these types of plugs from a boat or from shore can be particularly effective during the fall migration when schools of baitfish are moving south. Match plugs to the size and type of bait for best results.

ARTIFICIAL EELS AND TUBES. These artificial lures are standard striper baits that can be fished alone or down the middle of an umbrella rig. Large single tubes can be over 15 inches in length and often have a curvature built in that produces fish-attracting action when trolled on wire line. Tubes are rigged with a hook just behind the head and a second near the tail and can be fished with or without lead at the head. Color is a matter of preference, which changes by area often by year to year. Natural tubing has always been a favorite, while black, white, red, green and purple all work at times.

METAL & LEADHEAD JIGS. Jigs are basic for both boat anglers and shorecasters. Metal casting spoons are easy to throw and produce a tempting action with a lot of flash from the flat sides. These come in many variations, with the stainless steel Hopkins and Kastmaster spoons being among the

**Diamond jig with tube tail**

**Bunker Fly**

**Clouser Minnow**

most popular. These lures are ideal when distance is required or for casting into the wind. Many anglers prefer single-hook models with bucktail dressing. Tubes and soft plastic tails are effective trailers but can cut way down on casting distance and accuracy.

Diamond jigs are designed to be fast-sinking and to be worked in a vertical plane. They can be used for casting from shore, but have little action and tend to twist lines. Diamonds are generally dropped to bottom as quickly as possible and retrieved part-way or all the way to the surface, depending on where bass are marked on your depth finder. Remember that bluefish prefer higher, faster retrieves, so if you want to catch stripers keep the jig deep and work it slow! Fish it with a couple of quick turns off bottom, followed by several slow turns and a pause before dropping back down. Many hits are light taps felt on the pause or drop, so be ready to put the reel in gear and wind any slack line out right away.

Leadhead jigs range from 1/4 to 2 ounces and are tipped with bucktail, artificial hair, plastic bodies or tubes to imitate small baitfish. Although primarily used by casters, they can be trolled, particularly the "parachute jig," which has hair tied in both directions to provide pulsations and a larger profile. Parachute jigs are a standard for trolling the Montauk rips, where anglers continually pump wire line rods to create the proper action. A small bucktail jig tipped with pork rind has been standard fare for schoolies for decades.

Equipment for jigging stripers varies depending on the size of the fish and where they are being pursued. Deep jigging (30 to 100 feet) requires medium-heavy to heavy 6½- to 7-foot baitcasting rods, large capacity reels and lines from 15- to 25-pound-test. When jigging in shallow water or through schooling stripers, anglers go to a lighter rod and drop down to 12- or 15-pound-test lines. Anglers use longer rods (7 feet or more) and spinning reels that can hold 250 to 400 yards of 15- to 25-pound-test mono for casting jigs into the surf.

FLIES. Flies account for large numbers of schooling stripers every year, and their popularity is increasing. Just about any fly will work most times, but fly casters also have the opportunity to match the hatch when bass are feeding on small prey such as worms or 2-inch bay anchovies. As a rule, slow stripping works best for bass, which will often follow the fly to boatside before hitting. If this retrieve is not working, some fly-rod fishermen let the fly sink in the water column until they contact fish.

Nine-weight fly rods are a good all-around choice for stripers. Anglers can go up or down in size, depending on the fishing situation. A reel with a smooth, reliable drag is a must, and it should hold at least 100 yards of backing. Weight-forward lines are preferred, although intermediates are the choice when stripers are feeding on the surface.

With so many successful fishing strategies, it's easy to see why striped bass are one of the most popular inshore fish species wherever they are found.

*—Al Ristori*

# Red Drum *(Redfish)*

**D**epending upon what part of the country you're in, you may hear this member of the drum family referred to as a redfish, channel bass, red bass, spottail bass, red drum or some other colloquial name. Whatever name you use, the red drum *(Sciaenops ocellatus)* is surely one of the most popular and sought-after gamefish on the Atlantic and Gulf Coasts.

As far back as colonial times in America, the redfish was already an important part of life as a food

REDFISH RANGE IN COLOR from nearly white (above) to a vivid copper color (inset).

RED DRUM
RANGE
PRIME FISHING

source. Its range at one time extended all the way north to New England, but these days Virginia and Maryland are about as far north as you can reliably expect to find them. Redfish are found in estuarine and coastal waters south, around Florida, and west along the Gulf Coast to Texas and Mexico.

The coppery color of the fish obviously gave them their name, but they vary widely in coloration from region to region. Some reds that live in Florida Bay at the extreme southern tip of mainland Florida, for example, are nearly white. Other fish that live in darker, tannin-stained water are often a deep burnt-copper color. Most redfish possess a single black spot, or ocellus, near the base of their tail, but occasionally there are reds caught with several spots. Reds with as many as 16 spots have been recorded.

Redfish begin their lives in brackish estuaries. They are bottom feeders that prefer mud and sand bottoms and eat a wide variety of small crustaceans and fish. Young redfish tend to congregate in large schools and are often referred to as "puppy drum." These little fish are what the majority of coastal fishermen target, and they are great sport on light spinning tackle and on fly rods.

Reds move to deeper coastal waters as they grow larger, and it's possible in certain parts of the country to target these large fish. Redfish live a long time, reportedly over 50 years, and these old individuals are a real challenge to catch. The all-tackle world record, for instance, was a 94-pound, 2-ounce giant caught off of North Carolina. Such large fish are extremely rare, but 40-pounders are not uncommon.

Until the late 1970s redfish were not a primary target of commercial fishing operations, but the actions of one man helped radically alter that situation. A New Orleans chef introduced the world to the marvels of Cajun seasoning and "blackened fish." It turned out that one of his signature dishes was blackened redfish. Almost overnight, a huge demand for redfish arose, and opportunistic commercial fishermen in the Gulf of Mexico were more than happy to supply redfish to eager consumers.

Because large adult reds congregate in large schools in the Gulf of Mexico to spawn, they were an easy mark for large roller-rig gillnet boats. These boats used spotter aircraft to locate the schools, which were quite easy to see as they looked much like a giant inkblot from the air. Spotters could see the schools for miles, and the fish were easy pickings for the huge net boats.

This type of large-scale net harvest is particularly devastating to long-lived fish like redfish since they are slow to reproduce, and the boats were targeting large adult breeding population. By removing an inordinate number of the breeding stock commercial fishermen pushed the redfish perilously close to collapse.

A video taken by a National Marine Fisheries Service observer showed a single boat netting over 70,000 pounds of redfish in a single haul! The tremendous net was so full of helpless reds that additional boats had to be called in to take some of the fish into their holds.

Conservation-minded recreational fishermen cried foul and lobbied to have this destructive practice stopped. Netting was eventually halted, but not before severe damage was done to redfish stocks throughout the Gulf of Mexico. Several states took drastic action to help restore redfish stocks. Texas was first, after a group of influential Texans formed the Gulf Coast Conservation Association and began a "Save The Redfish" campaign. They also began a drive to fund a redfish hatchery.

In March of 1980, Texas enacted the first real limitation on net fishing, outlawing single-strand monofilament nets. In May of that same year, GCCA announced plans to build the world's largest redfish hatchery near Corpus Christi. And finally, at the urging of GCCA, the Texas legislature in January of 1981 introduced a bill that would make both redfish and speckled trout gamefish, thereby prohibiting sale of those fish taken in Texas waters. It was the beginning of the turnaround for redfish, and by summer 1983 the first 2.3 million redfish fingerlings had been released from the new GCCA/John Wilson redfish hatchery.

GCCA next turned its attention to the federal government, because large-scale netting was taking place offshore in federal waters off the Gulf of Mexico that were managed by the Gulf of Mexico Fishery Management Council. GCCA pressed the Commerce Department to declare a moratorium on redfish netting in the Gulf, and in December of 1986 the government closed the Gulf redfish fishery. This was an important first step in the battle to save redfish.

The state of Florida followed suit and completely halted all harvest of redfish while studying the stock situation and formulating a recovery plan. In 1988, Florida officials adopted gamefish status (no sale) and a tight one-fish-per-person recreational bag limit. They also followed suit on another front –hatcheries. Redfish fingerlings were raised by Florida biologists and released in several different locations around the state, although not on the same scale as in Texas, which has now built new hatcheries capable of releasing as many as 60 million fingerlings a year into state waters.

Miami's Biscayne Bay was the first to receive the juvenile reds, and many thousands of the young fish were released in the hopes of re-establishing them in the area. Old-timers recall the days when redfish were plentiful in Biscayne Bay, but they have been almost non-existent there recently. The Miami redfish project turned out to be a partial success at best, partly due to high predation of the fingerlings by barracuda. Still, several small schools of reds have established themselves in the northern reaches of the bay and anglers are beginning to see a lot more of them.

A different project on the other side of the state has been more successful. Fisheries biologists in Florida released over one million redfish fingerlings into Tampa Bay. These releases have been an unqualified success, in part because the Tampa redfish project took a slightly different approach to releasing the fish. They targeted specific release areas where redfish were already known to exist. Subsequent seine sampling revealed that these farm-raised fish, which were identified through an implanted bar code, were thriving in outstanding numbers.

With the help from a lot of people, redfish are now once again thriving along the Gulf Coast. Interestingly, the redfish population along the east coast of Florida northward was spared this destructive commercial harvest and has stayed stable throughout the years. In Florida, the one-fish bag limit has helped to a great extent, to the point where encountering redfish in a known area is almost a given.

On the west coast of Florida, the redfish has become arguably the most popular sport fish of all. Although snook and spotted seatrout have both held this honor at one time or another, the redfish stocks appear to be the healthiest of the three species –and if there's one thing a fisherman truly loves, it's opportunity!

## Where to Find Redfish

Redfish are found in almost every estuarine area of the Gulf of Mexico from Texas east to Florida and south to the Florida Keys. This incredible availability and the redfish's general eagerness to feed are what make them so appealing. In Texas alone, there are hundreds of shallow-water bays and lagoons ranging from tiny mud-bottomed openings to vast expanses of shallow water. All of these can harbor schools of reds, depending upon the availability of food for the fish.

Of all the Texas redfish hot spots, though, the Laguna Madre has to be the most famous. This large area of tidal flats is actually divided into two parts, the Upper Laguna Madre and the Lower. The Upper reaches of the area begin just south of Baffin Bay near Corpus Christi and the Laguna Madre extends from there all the way south to near Brownsville and the Mexican border. The city of Port Mansfield sits squarely in the middle of these two sections and is the center of redfishing activity.

The Lower Laguna Madre is very shallow, with a maximum depth of about 8 feet, but most of the flats are 2 feet deep or less, and at low tide huge areas of the flat are exposed. The flats stretch for many miles. You often need to make lengthy runs in a boat to locate feeding fish, but many schools of redfish can be found over these flats on a given day.

The extremely shallow nature of the flats of the Laguna Madre has given rise to the development of some very specialized boats for fishing it. The tunnel hull has been perfected by Texas redfish and trout fishermen because it allows them to run in very shallow water. A tunnel is designed into the hull of these boats, which feeds a column of water to the propeller enabling you to mount the outboard engine much higher on the transom. The draft of the boat is thereby substantially lessened.

Another type of specialized boats, collectively referred to as "scooters," also work well in the Texas shallows. These flat-bottomed boats are essentially just a flat platform from which to fish. They have no freeboard or even gunwales, just a flat running surface with an upturned bow and an engine-mounting bracket. Scooters are built wide for stability, and often come equipped with tall aluminum towers for spotting schools of redfish while on the run. This method of running in very shallow water while searching for wakes or redfish tails is very effective when you must cover such an expanse.

SPECIALIZED BOATS are used to navigate the shallow waters where redfish are often found, and to allow anglers to spot fish from a distance.

The Laguna Madre isn't the only place in Texas where one can expect to find reds, of course. Other bays can be productive as well, including Baffin, Corpus Christi, Aransas, San Antonio, Lavaca, Matagorda and Galveston Bays. Reds can be found consistently in many of these bays, even though some of them are commercially active and surrounded by sizeable populations of people. One nice thing about the Laguna Madre is its remote nature –you can reach areas that seem like the middle of nowhere!

One area worth noting is the deep shipping channel that runs to Port Mansfield. It often holds a considerable number of redfish and can be particularly productive under certain wind and tide conditions. It is often worthwhile to work the edge of the channel when the fish seem noticeably absent from the flats.

As you move eastward along the Gulf Coast, the habitat begins to change somewhat. Coastal Louisiana, Mississippi and Alabama all have mud flats much like those found in Texas, but they also have some extensive tidal marshes that redfish love. Louisiana has the lion's share of these marshes, which extend inland up the Mississippi River and its many tributaries. Although redfish are occasionally caught far up the river in nearly fresh water, the majority of redfishing activity takes place closer to the Gulf. It's estimated that Louisiana has 200,000 miles of fishable coastal banks and possesses 41 percent of the coastal wetlands in the United States.

The area between Shell Beach/Hopedale and Delacroix Island is a prime place to find reds, as are the brackish marshes from Venice to Port Sulfur on the west bank of the Mississippi. The waters of the Mississippi River around Venice have produced outstanding numbers of redfish, even in the midst of all the commercial traffic working the river. During times of clear water, this giant river holds incredible numbers of fish right next to downtown Venice. Lafitte is another good place to look for reds, including Lake Salvador.

The extensive marsh areas surrounding Cocodrie have consistently yielded excellent redfish catches, and large redfish (up to 60 pounds) are targeted by Louisiana anglers in several nearby passes, including Four Bayous, Barataria and Camida passes on either end of Grand Isle, along with Little Pass and Whiskey Pass near Last Isle.

Of all the areas in Louisiana where redfish are plentiful, the Chandeleur Islands are probably the most popular, or at least the most famous. This island chain runs parallel to the Mississippi River delta system from Breton Island at the southern end 60 miles to the north, ending within 20 miles of the Mississippi coast. These islands, which really amount to little more than low dunes, are surrounded by huge shallow flats where redfish abound. Wade fishing is the preferred method for catching reds here, and the fish vary in size from the usual 2- to 6-pound school fish, up to large adults weighing 40 pounds.

TIDAL MARSH AREAS are prime habitat for redfish. The large flats and marsh grasses that surround them often hold good numbers of fish.

A number of charter and hotel operators have set up mothership operations in the Chandeleurs to allow anglers to fish for several days at a time without having to make lengthy runs back to the mainland. These motherships range from relatively primitive, non-air-conditioned boats with plywood skiffs and basic sleeping accommodations to full-blown luxury barges with gourmet chefs, individual suites, well-stocked bars and state-of-the-art entertainment centers. There's a Chandeleur fishing package available for every budget. Even some of the casinos in Biloxi, Mississippi, have gotten into the act with barges and fishing packages.

Redfish also thrive in the coastal waters of Mississippi and Alabama even though neither state has much shoreline to speak of. The wide-open water of Mobile Bay contains a good population of fish on the extensive maze of tidal mud flats. The same is true for Perdido Bay, which

separates the states of Alabama and Florida. Redfishing really picks up when you move into the Florida Panhandle.

If you closely study a chart of the Pensacola area, you will notice some telltale landmarks: a point of land called "Redfish Point" and a shoreline indentation referred to as "Redfish Cove." These aren't accidental or casual names; they symbolize the prevalence of the fish in these waters.

I experienced the superb redfishing around Pensacola purely by chance. We had gone to the area to fish for white marlin offshore, but a passing cold front and high winds had made offshore fishing impossible. The dockmaster at the marina where we were staying, noticing our dejected look at being stuck onshore, suggested we try the redfish in Pensacola Bay. At first, we weren't too excited about the idea, simply because none of our crew knew the area well, and we figured our chances would be slim.

But the dockmaster reassured us, telling us how to locate the fish. "Just look for the birds." Deciding that we had nothing to lose, off we went. Sure enough, near Pensacola Pass we encountered several large flocks of pelicans and gulls frantically diving on huge schools of reddish-colored minnows. We caught pinfish for bait, and as soon as we threw the baits to the edges of the schools, we were hooked up!

My crew and I spent the next three hours catching and releasing large redfish in the 15- to 20-pound class, one after the other. All but one were too large to keep (Florida has an 18" to 27" slot size limit), and many times we had double and triple headers on. Twenty pounds is big for redfish on the west coast of Florida. It was one of the best redfish encounters I've ever experienced. It's all the more amazing when you realize that the Florida Panhandle was one of the areas hardest hit by large-scale netting, and during the height of that activity the redfish situation inshore was grim.

As with redfish elsewhere, redfish on these large flats move around a lot, and you often must search for them. These panhandle bays are not generally as shallow as the flats in Texas, so often there's no visual sign the fish are there. If birds are present they help greatly, but many times it comes down to trial and error while making a milk-run of known spots. The shorelines of Pensacola Bay, Escambia Bay, East Bay and Santa Rosa Sound are all prime places to begin your search. Redfish are also known to gang up in holes in the middle of the bays when the weather is cold, and local knowledge can help you find the fish more quickly.

Choctawhatchee Bay, located north and east of Destin, is another large body of water with a plentiful redfish population. A series of small rivers at the east end of the bay can be particularly productive. These creeks form the mouth of the Choctawhatchee River and offer a lot of fish-holding structure. The three bays that surround Panama City (West, North, and East bays) also offer countless small creek mouths, small coves and miles of shoreline where redfish can be found.

Further to the east, Appalachicola is becoming the redfish capital of the panhandle. This sleepy little fishing village has been discovered by redfish enthusiasts, and is rapidly becoming a hot new fly fishing spot, and there are now numerous fly shops and guide services.

Appalachicola Bay and St. George Sound are bordered to the south by Little St. George, St. George, and Dog Islands, which are narrow barrier islands and can provide exceptional redfish action. A number of rivers and streams empty into East Bay, creating more points and edges in which to search for fish. You can fish this area from either the town of Appalachicola at the western end of the bay, or from Carabelle to the east. Either way, these waters offer some of the best inshore fishing anywhere in Florida.

Florida's Big Bend region begins roughly at the mouth of the St. Marks River at the northern end of Apalachee Bay, and curves east and south for miles. With thousands of oyster bars, creek mouths, shallow flats and tiny islands, redfish thrive. This sparsely-populated area is sought out by intrepid redfish anglers for the sheer numbers of smaller fish that can be found here. Towns like Horseshoe Beach, Steinhatchee and Suwanee are starting points for redfishing at the southern end of the Big Bend.

Homosassa Springs is a somewhat larger and better-known place to target reds. A world-famous tarpon spot in the summer, the wintertime redfishing is superb, with mile after mile of shallow water laced with oyster bars. This maze of flats can be confusing to navigate, and hiring a guide is probably a good idea until you know your way around. Homosassa is a place where you can catch and release reds weighing in the double digits with some regularity.

Tampa Bay offers improving redfish action, thanks in part to the stocking program mentioned earlier, as do many of the heavily populated areas along Florida's west coast.

The true "hot" redfish action takes place in two southwest Florida locations: Pine Island Sound and the Ten Thousand Islands area. Pine Island Sound stretches from the city of Ft. Myers at the southern end and runs northward to Charlotte Harbor and Boca Grande. This area is bordered by numerous barrier islands to the west, including Sanibel and Captiva. The eastern side of the sound is all very shallow, with many small uninhabited islands, grass flats, potholes and oyster bars, all of which are places you might find redfish. Sight fishing is often the game here, and Pine Island Sound offers the opportunity to catch quantities of small fish and to tangle with schools of very large reds, which is rare combination to find in one area.

The Ten Thousand Islands lie south of Marco

Island and extends past the town of Chokoloskee. This area has definitely been discovered by redfish enthusiasts, especially fly fishermen. The area is well-named, with limitless bays and islands surrounded by flats teeming with fish. These flats are a sight-caster's dream. Redfish cruise along mangrove shorelines in the clear water, sometimes ganging up in schools, and offer excellent opportunities for light casting tackle.

The same is true of Flamingo, in Everglades National Park at the tip of mainland Florida. The prime redfish spots are generally closer to the Flamingo side on the north end of the bay. Snake Bight is a very large body of extremely shallow water east of Flamingo that is primarily a mud-bottom grass flat. Huge schools of small reds can be found here, particularly in the spring and fall, and (along with Pine Island Sound) this is one of the best places to find *tailing* redfish. Tailing fish feed by "standing" on their nose, thereby exposing their tail above the shallow water.

Most of the Florida west coast spots mentioned tend to produce large schools of smaller-sized redfish. However, there are several places besides Louisiana where you can find large individuals. The really big fish are most often found on the east coast. These redfish are generally considered to be a separate stock of fish from their Gulf brethren, with their own breeding and growth patterns.

The Indian River Lagoon system is home to some of the largest redfish you will ever encounter, with schools holding fish of 40 pounds around the flats near Cocoa Beach. These fish can be located visually, and it is quite a sight to see fifty large reds pushing a wake across a flat. It can weaken the knees of even the most diehard redfish fan.

The Banana River, which lies east of Merritt Island and extends north into the Kennedy Space Center, is another "giant red" hot spot. There are two restricted areas here. The northernmost section is closed to all entry; however, the southern zone is only closed to motorized boat traffic and can therefore be fished from canoes. The lack of pressure this area receives has allowed the redfish to grow quite large, and fish over 30 pounds aren't uncommon for those who are willing to paddle themselves in and out.

The Mosquito Lagoon (located north of the space center) is one of the most productive redfish spots in all of Florida. The southern end of the lagoon system contains a vast area of flats that hold both large schools of smaller fish and some larger fish. The Mosquito Lagoon has produced a substantial number of world-record redfish and other species in recent years.

To find the redfish most people consider true trophies, you need to move up the Atlantic coastline. Most of the effort for huge redfish is directed at North Carolina and Virginia. These prime surf-casting spots are home to many of the biggest redfish that swim. Because of the great size the fish attain and the ways they are fished, these giant reds could almost be talked about as a separate species from their shallow water counterparts.

The barrier islands that lie offshore of these two states form gigantic estuaries that are terrific breeding grounds for a number of inshore fish species, including redfish. As the fish mature, they tend to migrate into the ocean and along the beach, where fishermen await. The point of Cape Hatteras in North Carolina is the most popular of all of these spots, and the fall is the best time of year to encounter a trophy redfish. The fish often bite at night and in bad weather. It can be a pretty rough affair when standing on a Hatteras beach in November as a cold gale blows, but the returns can make it worthwhile.

Fly fishermen also have been taking trophy reds along the coast with regularity. Redfish over 40 pounds have been taken on fly in the Outer Banks of North Carolina. Other great places to search for the outsized redfish include Hatteras and Oregon Inlets in North Carolina; near Cape Charles, Virginia, along the lower eastern shore; Assateague Island on the Maryland/Virginia border and Hog and Smith Islands on Virginia's coast. Unfortunately North Carolina currently allows a substantial commercial harvest of redfish, jeopardizing this great fishery.

## How to Catch Redfish

Redfish are caught on many different kinds of tackle. To catch smaller fish, a 7-foot, medium-action spinning rod spooled with 8- or 10-pound-test is the best choice. At times you will need to be able to cast a lightweight bait a good distance, yet still need some power since reds are tough fighters.

So, the medium-action rod is a good compromise. Nine-weight fly rods work well for the smaller fish, and whether you use a floating or sinking line depends on where you're fishing. Bigger redfish, obviously, require bigger tackle.

Fishing for redfish is a pretty basic affair. They will strike a number of different baits and lures, so your choice depends on the size of the fish and which part of their range you're fishing. While many of the larger fish are caught by soaking bait, the smaller fish that are sight-fished can be somewhat more demanding. Redfish don't have sharp teeth, so you can get away without a leader if you're fishing over smooth mud or sand bottoms. A short piece of leader is advisable when you fish around oyster bars, rocky shorelines or manmade structure.

Redfish have notoriously bad eyesight, so accurate casting is called for. In tailing situations like you might find around Flamingo, the fish are feeding intently, grubbing around on the bottom for crabs. The most common lure used for reds in this situation is a gold colored Johnson's spoon

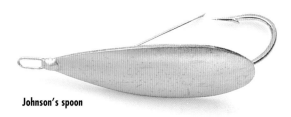

Johnson's spoon

(above) weighing ¼ or ½ ounce, often tipped with a plastic grub tail to add action. The lure is cast past the fish and then maneuvered so that it passes along the bottom right in front of the fish's nose. If you do it correctly the fish will strike almost every time. Seven-foot, medium-heavy baitcasting rods and 14- to 20-pound-test lines are used to control the fish and get them through the heavy grass.

The gold-colored Johnson spoon is popular because of its weedless design. Flies used in this situation must be relatively weedless as well. The Bend-Back, Muddler and Wobbler patterns all work well, but any puffy streamer fly will work as long as it doesn't collect weeds. It helps if the fly has a bit of flash in it to attract attention. Cast the fly past the fish and strip it slowly, right in front of the feeding fish.

When fishing for smaller schooling fish in water where you can't see them, such as along oyster bars or along the edge of salt marshes or creek mouths, lead-head jigs with plastic grub tails worked on 10-pound-test line and 6½-foot spinning rods are the top choice. To work these edges in falling water, keep the jig as close to the bottom as is practical. Another deadly technique is to work small, lipped or lipless swimming plugs close to the bottom. Baits with rattles such as Rattle Traps work well, and seem to help attract attention.

On deeper grass flats, surface poppers or plugs work great. Baits such as the Bagley's Finger Mullet or the Heddon Zara Spook are standard lures for "walking the dog," which works well. Redfish, especially larger ones, will often lay up in sand holes on a flat, so if you are drifting and see a white spot (opposite), take the time to cast to it, even if you don't see a fish. Redfish are often hard to spot in these holes.

For fishing with bait, crabs, small fish and cut bait all work very well. The largest fish, like the ones taken at Cocoa Beach, Florida, for example, can easily be convinced to eat a half of a blue crab. By casting the crab chunk in front of an approaching school, you're sure to draw some attention. Small live baits like pinfish or croakers also work well for big fish. Medium-heavy action spinning or baitcasting rods that are 6½ or 7 feet long are the best choice for live-bait fishing. Line sizes are generally 15- to 25-pound-test depending on the size of the fish that are caught in the area and the types of obstructions you may be faced with.

Surf fishermen in North Carolina and Virginia soak mullet chunks with pyramid sinkers, or use some other type of oily bait that will attract the large

**REDFISH FLIES** come in a variety of styles, sizes and colors for use in a number of different situations.

SAND HOLES ON LARGE GRASS FLATS are prime areas to look for redfish, and should be fished whenever they are encountered.

reds by scent. In this situation long (9- to 11-foot) surfcasting rods are used with heavy (25-pound-test) lines to land the fish in this area's heavy surfs and rocky bottoms.

Although redfish may get a rare case of lock-jaw and refuse to feed, for the most part they are quite cooperative and eager to eat. They will often take a well-presented spoon or fly even when they are spooked and are swimming away from a boat that has startled them. Their natural instinct to feed overcomes their flight reflex and they strike. This is not a common trait among most fish, and it's one more reason why the redfish is so popular.

Redfish are a widely distributed, tough-fighting fish that is hard to beat for the quantities available. They're also a major success story in salt water fisheries management. The future indeed looks bright for redfish. That's great news for the millions of us who love to catch them, no matter what you may call them in your neck of the woods!

— *John Brownlee*

# TARPON

Ever since the first one was caught on rod and reel in Florida around 1885, the tarpon *(Megalops atlanticus)* has been one of the most storied inshore gamefish in the world. For years prior to that catch it was considered impossible to land a tarpon at all, and many visitors to Florida tried and failed. That 93-pounder caught by H. H. Wood of New York City made international news in sporting circles, and the race to catch ever-larger tarpon was on.

It was a few years later in 1898 when the noted fishing reel manufacturer Edward Vom Hofe caught a 210-pound tarpon in southwest Florida, proving that very large fish could indeed be caught. Tarpon fever became an epidemic after these early catches, and it appears there is no cure in sight. Over 100 years later fishermen still flock to the now well-known areas where tarpon congregate on a seasonal basis to experience the unique thrill that they provide. Tarpon fishing has turned into an obsession with many anglers who plan their whole year's schedule around the tarpon runs.

It's easy to see why tarpon fishing is so addictive. The fish grow very large and are relatively plentiful. They take a wide variety of baits, lures and flies, and the fight of a hooked tarpon is one of the truly awesome experiences in the sport of fishing.

Known for their initial jumps and powerful runs, tarpon are strong adversaries not easily taken, even with modern gear. They are legendary for their ability to throw hooks because their bony mouths make hook-setting difficult. Getting a hook through a tarpon's mouth has been likened to trying to penetrate a cinder block. Combine this trait with violent, head-thrashing jumps as high as 10 feet, and it becomes clear why tarpon are able to not only throw hooks frequently, but also break lines or leaders. This ability gives rise to the mandate that one must "bow to the silver king," a technique of leaning toward the fish when you see it coming toward the surface to jump. This creates slack in the line to help keep the tarpon from throwing the hook. In spite of these challenging traits, catching a world-class tarpon remains a highlight in the angling career of many people. Tarpon of any size can put on a dazzling aerial display, then dive deep in a fight that can last anywhere from a few minutes to many hours.

## Where to Find Tarpon

Tarpon range in warmer salt water areas from Virginia to South America. They have a year-round presence in the middle portion of their range, most notably in Florida. Tarpon in the upper and lower extremes of their range tend to migrate to reach preferred water temperatures. This explains why tarpon are often caught along well-established migration routes.

TARPON
RANGE
PRIME FISHING

Tarpon are a long-lived species that can grow incredibly large. Many specimens over 200 pounds have been caught, with the current all-tackle world record standing at 283 pounds, 4 ounces. There have been a number of fish seen that would easily top the 300-pound mark, and a few of these giants have been caught inadvertently by commercial fishermen. The 300-pound tarpon is one of the Holy Grails of salt water fishing and is sought by a number of fanatic sportsmen. Texan Tom Gibson pioneered fishing for giant tarpon with his exploratory trips to Africa, most notably Ghana and Sierra Leone. Gibson has reportedly hooked several fish thought to be over 300 pounds but has not landed one. A 265-pounder is his largest to date.

Fortunately, anglers can tangle with big tarpon a lot closer to home. Although tarpon are not anadromous fish, they can tolerate rapid changes in salinity and are found in brackish and occasionally fresh water areas. Juvenile tarpon grow up in estuarine environments, usually mangrove-lined creeks and bays such as those associated with the Florida Everglades. Small tarpon (2 to 20 pounds) can be found just about anywhere this type of habitat exists.

The Tamiami Trail in south Florida is a good example of prime habitat. "The Trail," as it is called locally, was built in the early part of this century by crews dug a ditch from Miami to what would years later become Marco Island. The spoil from the ditch was piled next to the dredge to form the road bed. The ditch from this project still exists today and is full of small tarpon. This is a great place for those who like to cast from shore and want to try their luck at tarpon fishing. Similarly, the countless creeks and small bays of Everglades National Park hold mile after mile of mangrove shorelines and are prime spots to search for small tarpon.

Small tarpon are found just about anywhere that warm water and brackish estuaries exist. On Grand Cayman Island, for example, there exists a vast network of drainage ditches that were built when Grand Cayman was first settled. Local legend has it that the mosquitoes were so thick at times that cattle would suffocate from breathing them in. To solve this problem the large inland swamps had to be drained, so a vast network of drainage ditches was created. The mosquito problem was reduced substantially, and the existing ditches are now full of small tarpon. These same types of ditches exist all over Florida, and there is a group of anglers in Stuart and Ft. Pierce who specialize in catching these baby tarpon in the mosquito ditches as well as in residential canals.

Small tarpon are occasionally found in landlocked lakes such as those found in the numerous golf courses in south Florida. The fish are limited in the size they attain by the lack of food available. It is not known how the fish got into these lakes, but more than one eager tarpon fisherman has been run off a fairway by an unsympathetic groundskeeper!

As tarpon mature they move out onto open water flats, and often congregate in large schools made up of fish that weigh 30 to 60 pounds. Bays, inlets and the intracoastal waterway in Florida are all areas that have good numbers of schooling fish. These mid-sized fish are numerous along the many coastal bays on the Mexican shoreline, and a number of fishing camps have sprung up to accommodate anglers seeking both tarpon and permit in these areas. These larger fish require somewhat heavier tackle than their smaller relatives and are great sport on medium-action spinning, casting or fly-fishing tackle.

This size tarpon are also numerous in bays along the coast of Florida from Tampa south on the

MANGROVE-lined backwater areas are prime locations to catch small tarpon.

west coast and from Ft. Pierce south on the east coast. The Stuart area offers some superb inshore tarpon fishing for mid-sized fish. Local knowledge is often required to pinpoint where these schools are at a given time due to the fact that the fish in this area tend to move around. The north fork of the St. Lucie River is one area where numbers of tarpon are found on a consistent basis.

Schools of mid-sized tarpon also take up residence in the Palm Beach area during the wintertime in the shadows of the mansions along Palm Beach proper, many times stacking up beneath the docks. Similar schools are found in Biscayne Bay near downtown Miami, Pine Island Sound, Charlotte Harbor, Sarasota Bay and Tampa Bay on Florida's west coast.

The many rivers emptying into the Gulf of Mexico along the west coast also hold schools of tarpon at times. These include rivers in the Ten Thousand Islands area, such as Shark, Broad, Harney and Lostman's, along with the innumerable creeks and tributaries that flow into them. This area is a tarpon fishing nirvana that is best fished with a guide for those not intimately familiar with the geography, as it's easy to get lost.

In the Bahamas, the island of Andros has some excellent tarpon fishing, especially along the remote and undeveloped western shore. Until a few years ago these fish were rarely sought except by a few tight-lipped anglers who knew how good the fishing was. With the numerous bonefish camps springing up in Andros, more guides are making the run through the bights to target these tarpon.

Although few anglers have experienced it, Cuba is reported to have excellent fishing for tarpon. One look at a chart of the immense island leaves no doubt that tarpon exist in these waters. Many traveling fishermen salivate just thinking about the opportunity to fish the hundreds of bays and river mouths that pour into the ocean from Cuba.

Those who are seriously addicted to the "silver king" are most interested in big fish –those weighing 80 pounds and up. There are quite a few places where giants can be found with regularity. Big tarpon are most often caught in late spring and summer in the sounds of North Carolina, the inshore waters of Georgia, the entire Florida coast, and the Gulf of Mexico to Texas. The month of June is prime time for big tarpon in many of these locations.

Ground zero for summer tarpon fishing, however, is Boca Grande Pass on the west coast of Florida. This deep-water pass is the primary opening into Charlotte Harbor, and lies between the southern point of Gasparilla Island and the northern shore of Cayo Costa Island. Large amounts of water flow in and out of this pass and carry with it huge amounts of food for the tarpon that arrive by the thousands.

The first fish begin to show up in early May, congregating in the 80-foot-deep hole just off the tip of Gasparilla Island. Tarpon continue showing up in the pass, feeding on the thousands of small crabs that flow out to the Gulf from Charlotte Harbor. With the arrival of the tarpon comes the arrival of hordes of tarpon fishermen, each eager to tangle with one of these giant fish. Boca Grande has become a very crowded place to fish during this time, and each new year appears more crowded than the last. Regardless, it is still an exciting place at the height of the season due to the sheer numbers of fish in the pass. Schools containing hundreds of tarpon will roll beside a boat that may be anchored only a few feet away from the next boat.

The atmosphere in the pass is electric when the bite is on, with as many as 10 or 20 fish being fought at the same time. Good manners and etiquette are called for here, but are all too often ignored. Although it is crowded, Boca Grande still offers one of the best opportunities for many people to catch a big tarpon. When the fish are there, the town of Boca Grande becomes intently focused upon the daily events taking place in the pass, and the tarpon is the subject of most every conversation.

Other areas known for very large tarpon include the Gulf waters of Texas and Louisiana. South Padre Island, Texas, has been the site for catches of 200-pound and heavier fish. The delta area of the Mississippi River in Louisiana is also home to very large tarpon, but the fishery for large fish off of Louisiana is relatively new. Similarly, the waters off Georgia have spawned a recent run of jumbo fish. Local fishermen knew about them for years, but as a longtime Georgia resident once said of tarpon, "You can't eat 'em, so we never saw no reason to fool with 'em." The exploding interest in light-tackle inshore and flats fishing forever changed that perception.

Of all the places where you can expect to find large tarpon consistently, the Florida Keys has to be the most popular. Each year beginning in late April or early May, tarpon fishermen flock to this area to pursue the migrating schools of tarpon that will soon arrive. The migration actually begins in late winter, when the shrimp start flowing seaward out of Miami's Biscayne Bay. Government Cut, where the bay spills into the Atlantic, is home to large schools of big tarpon beginning around February. The fish gang up at the mouth of the cut, waiting for shrimp to drift by on an outgoing tide. Depending on the weather, tarpon may stay in this area for a couple of months before beginning a southward migration towards the Keys.

The fish migrate south in April as the numbers of shrimp begin to peter out. It is then that light-tackle and fly fishermen appear to intercept them along the seaward shores of islands in areas such as Elliot Key and upper Key Largo. Pods of fish move along the shore in the shallow, clear water, allowing great opportunities for sight-casting to them.

At the same time, tarpon begin to migrate southward along the Gulf Coast toward the Keys. Tarpon first appear around the southwest point of the Florida mainland at Cape Sable and work their way south along the network of shallow banks that make up the extreme western edge of Florida Bay. By mid- to late May, most tarpon have converged on the Keys and can be found in many different areas.

Once in the Keys tarpon tend to move back and forth between the bay side and the ocean side, and are often found simultaneously on both sides. Tarpon move through the cuts between islands that are crossed by the network of bridges that form U.S. Highway 1, which connects the islands of the Keys. These bridges are some of the very best places to catch a big tarpon. Bait fishermen will be found at the Indian Key, Channel 2 and Channel 5 bridges. The Channel 2 and Channel 5 bridges lie

BIG TARPON can be found in the same well-known areas year after year. They are the ultimate challenge for fly fishermen.

between Lower Matecumbe and Long Key and are major travel areas for tarpon. Much of the live-bait fishing activity for tarpon occurs here. Islamorada guides are experts at finding the fish, which often bite during different times of day and at certain tides. During this period hooking a tarpon is as close to a sure thing as you're going to find in tarpon fishing.

Farther down the Keys, the Seven Mile Bridge and Bahia Honda Bridge are two other famous tarpon hot spots. Key West harbor is another famed tarpon area. The fish actually arrive early in Key West, showing up in late winter and taking up residence in the deep shipping channels leading into the harbor and in the harbor itself. Key West guides have developed a unique method of chumming for these large fish that has proven deadly. It's not uncommon to hook a dozen or more fish when conditions are right in Key West. One such guide is said to have caught 31 fish in a row, on the same day, without losing a single fish.

The truly addicted tarpon fishermen show up in the Keys each year in search of a big fish on a fly rod. Catching a large tarpon on fly is considered to be one of the premier accomplishments in all of fishing, and with good reason. The sight-fishing nature of the sport makes it one of the most exciting things a fly fisherman can do in salt water. Fly rod fishermen will tell you there isn't anything better than presenting a fly to a 100-pound plus tarpon and watching as it engulfs the feathered offering, then takes to the air in a frantic series of jumps when it realizes it's hooked.

Fly fishermen descend upon such legendary spots as First National, Nine Mile, and Buchanan banks in the Islamorada backcountry. Here, they stake out shallow points, hoping to intercept tarpon as they swim along the edge of the shallow flats. Many oceanside flats hold migratory fish in the upper Keys as well. The frustrating thing for many anglers is that the swimming pattern that tarpon choose can change on a daily basis. In the lower Keys, the Marquesas Keys hold a special magic as a tarpon destination, being relatively close to Key West yet surprisingly remote. The numerous islands that make up the backcountry in the vicinity of Big Pine Key hold substantial numbers of tarpon for those knowledgeable enough to navigate this intricate shallow-water system.

Those who aspire to be in the true "big league" of tarpon fly fishermen end up in Homosassa Springs on Florida's west coast north of Tampa. The Gulf waters off of Homosassa are home to a unique group of tarpon that are considered to be among the largest found anywhere. These fish are not longer than those caught in the Keys or elsewhere, but tend to be much larger in girth. Fish of 150 to 200 pounds are not uncommon in Homosassa, and several fish over 300 pounds have been documented.

The fact that no angler has taken a tarpon over 200 pounds on a fly rod and the quest to do so attract many of the most serious salt water fly fishermen in the world to this sleepy little Florida town each summer. It is here that world-renowned fly fisherman Billy Pate caught the largest tarpon ever taken on fly, a 188-pound monster, in 1982. It is surely only a matter of time until the 200-pound barrier is broken, and most experts agree that it will happen at Homosassa.

## How to Catch Tarpon

Tarpon will take a wide variety of natural baits, both live and dead, as well as an amazing assortment of artificial lures and flies. They can be very accommodating fish, yet there are just as many times when they will refuse any and all offerings. Tarpon fishing can indeed be a maddening endeavor. However, the feeling you get when you do finally catch a tarpon makes it worth all the frustration you may have had to endure.

For catching smaller-sized tarpon, keep in mind that these voracious little fish will strike eagerly most of the time when you find them in a mangrove-lined canal, bay or landlocked body of water. For fish up to 20 pounds, light casting tackle spooled with 12- or 15-pound test is a good choice. Lighter gear can be used, but if you are casting up against a mangrove shoreline you need stout enough tackle to horse fish away from the bushes after they're hooked.

Artificial lures work well in this situation, with small MirrOlure, Rapala, or Boone minnow plugs often bringing strikes. Small white bucktail jigs are another good choice and should be worked relatively slowly with a pronounced jigging motion. Small silver or gold spoons also work well, as will most small streamer flies such as Whistlers or Clouser Minnows.

Big tarpon will strike many of these same plugs and jigs too. It's just a matter of scaling your tackle up to meet the size of the fish. When fishing for really big tarpon on plugs, it's a good idea to replace the standard treble hooks with stronger 4X trebles. Medium-heavy casting tackle with lines in the 15- to 20-pound class are needed for these bigger fish. A number of fish are also caught by slow-trolling large, lipped swimming plugs like the Magnum series from Rapala. Jig fishermen have developed a deadly technique for fishing Boca Grande Pass that involves fishing vertically with very large soft-bodied grub-tails rigged on oversized leadheads.

All tarpon, no matter what their size, have a very hard, bony mouth, and their jaws are supported with an equally hard, raspy surface that will cut through line in a hurry. Because of this fact, no matter what lure or hook style you are using, sharp hooks and quality leader material are a necessity. For small fish, 20- or 30-pound-test leader material will suffice. While monofilament leaders have traditionally been the choice, serious tarpon fishermen are increasingly turning to fluorocarbon because of its low light refraction qualities and abrasion resistance. Many tarpon experts are convinced that fluorocarbon leaders elicit more strikes.

When fishing for large tarpon with live bait, 20- to 30-pound lines spooled on either spinning, casting or conventional style gear are the top choice. Live-bait fishing is popular around the bridges and usually involves anchoring while drifting live baits on floats. A typical setup is to tie a short double line section with either a Bimini Twist or a Spider Hitch, then attach about 5 feet of the leader with either a swivel or a knot. Although in the past live bait fisherman insisted on 100-pound-test leader material, most now prefer using 80-pound, or occasionally go as light as 60-pound. There is more and more pressure on tarpon in these areas than ever before, and lighter, less visible leaders have become necessary to elicit strikes. Many guides have switched over to using fluorocarbon exclusively.

As with many other salt water species, circle hooks have gained popularity among tarpon fishermen due to their propensity for lodging in the corner of the fish's mouth (below). Circle hooks greatly reduce gut-hooking, particularly when live-bait fishing. The Owner Mutu Light 5314 Series has become a favorite among tarpon experts; others prefer the conventional Mustad 9174 J-hook, or the live bait series from Eagle Claw. Hook styles are a matter of personal preference, and circle hooks take a little getting used to if you haven't used them before. They do not require a traditional hook-setting motion, as they are designed to set themselves when you come tight on the fish, catching in the

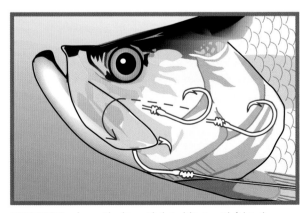

CIRCLE HOOKS reduce gut-hooking with their ability to catch fish in the corner of the mouth.

corner of the mouth. Circle hooks tend to come razor-sharp out of the box.

A standard bait hook should be honed to a very sharp point so that it will penetrate the hard jaw bone, and several vigorous hook sets are advised when setting on a tarpon when using standard hooks. No matter which style you use, remember that landing big tarpon takes stout, large hooks normally in the 5/0 to 8/0 size range. It takes a lot of pressure to force a big tarpon up after it has sounded, and your hook, as the first point of connection, must be up to the task.

TARPON will take a variety of fly patterns.

Tarpon eat a number of different baitfish, as well as a variety of crustaceans. Pinfish, mullet, squirrelfish (a Boca Grande specialty), croakers, sardines, menhaden, herrings, bunkers and pogies all make splendid live bait offerings. As with most live bait situations, the bait you choose should be the one that the tarpon are feeding on in the particular area you are fishing.

Some of the biggest tarpon caught each year are hooked by soaking dead bait on the bottom in a known tarpon-producing area. While it may not be the most glamorous style of tarpon fishing, casting out a crushed mullet head on a bottom rig is definitely a productive method.

Fly casting for large tarpon requires heavy fly gear consisting of 11- to 13-weight rods and large-capacity reels capable of holding at least 200 yards of backing. Weight-forward floating lines are preferred for shallow-water fishing, while sinking mono-core lines are used where it's deeper. Sixteen-pound tippet is standard, and although 20-pound is now IGFA legal, many traditional tarpon fly fishermen won't use it.

Fly fishing for tarpon usually involves sight casting to cruising fish, although fish can be caught by blind casting or dredging (fishing weighted lines in deeper water). When sight casting you have to be able to cast quickly and accurately. Schools of tarpon glide along just under the surface, often showing no signs of their presence until they are near the boat. Tarpon do not normally deviate from their chosen path. A fly cast to a tarpon must land close to the fish, where it will move into the fish's field of vision when stripped.

Sixty to 80-pound shock tippet is a must when fly fishing, and hooks must be very sharp. Tarpon flies are typically simple, non-imitating streamer patterns tied on 2/0 to 5/0 long shank hooks. Tarpon flies come in a bewildering array of colors and patterns (above). The best advice is to check with a local fly shop or guide in the area you'll be fishing to see what is working the best.

No matter what type of tackle you choose, fishing for tarpon is one of the highlights of inshore fishing. Tarpon come in all sizes and will eat an incredible assortment of baits, plugs and flies. They are truly great fish, but a word of caution before you decide to try tarpon fishing for yourself. Years of experience have proven beyond a shadow of a doubt that tarpon fishing is habit-forming!

—*John Brownlee*

# SPOTTED SEATROUT (Speckled Trout)

**T**he spotted seatrout, *(Cynoscion nebulosus)* or speckled trout, is among the most popular marine gamefish in America. More seatrout are caught by more anglers than any other salt water fish in the South, especially along the Gulf of Mexico and Florida.

The popularity of seatrout is easy to understand. First, they are indigenous to the inshore salt water throughout the entire South, on both the Atlantic and Gulf Coasts. Further, they are a hard-hitting, hard-fighting inshore sportfish that can be caught with a wide variety of natural baits and

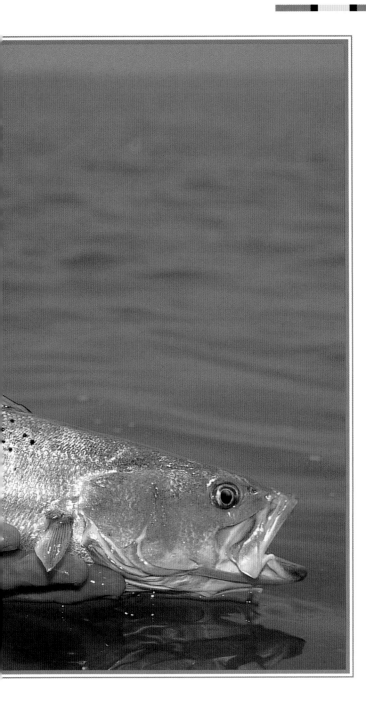

popular gamefish, but the spotted seatrout is at the top because of its wide geographic availability and abundance.

Spotted seatrout are readily available to boaters, surf anglers, waders and even jetty, pier and bridge fishermen. The seatrout is among the best table delicacies available to sportsmen. Fried, broiled, poached or baked, the seatrout has few peers on the end of a fork.

Spotted seatrout are often confused with weakfish, since their size, shape, coloration, feeding habits and environmental preferences are nearly identical. In fact, in some areas both species are caught simultaneously. Weakfish, however, are more common in northern waters of the western Atlantic from North Carolina to Massachusetts, although at times (chiefly in winter) they're found in South Carolina through northeast Florida.

The easiest way to differentiate spotted seatrout from weakfish is by their spots. Spotted seatrout have fewer and much larger spots than weakfish. Spots are so small and abundant on weakfish that from a distance they appear gray, thus the nickname "gray trout." In parts of the south weakfish are also known as "yellowmouth trout" due to the yellow coloration inside the mouth. As with the other members of this family, specks have a soft mouth and can be lost on hard hooksets or "horsing" of a hooked fish.

Seatrout are typically found in large schools. Seldom, in fact, do anglers catch only a single fish from a productive area. For this reason it's wise to move hooked fish away from a "hole" or other spot where trout congregate to avoid spooking remaining fish in a school.

artificial lures. In addition, the average size is good with 2-pound fish common, fish to 5 pounds frequently boated and ones to 10 pounds occasionally caught. The IGFA world record spotted seatrout is a 17-pound, 7-ounce fish caught from the Indian River near Ft. Pierce, Florida in 1995.

Spotted seatrout belong to the same family that includes weakfish (p. 90), the silver seatrout, the sand seatrout and white seabass (p. 126) found in waters off of California. Many members of the genus *Cynoscion* are

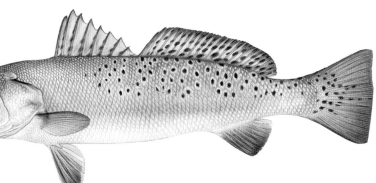

# Where to Find Spotted Seatrout

Spotted seatrout are distributed liberally throughout the Gulf of Mexico, around Florida, and up the Atlantic Seaboard as far north as New York. In Florida, the famed Indian and Banana rivers on the east-central coast are well known for giant seatrout, with many 10-pounders caught annually. This area also is home to a number of IGFA world line-class trout records.

SPOTTED SEATROUT
■ RANGE
■ PRIME FISHING

Perhaps the best seatrout fishing is available along the hundreds of miles of Gulf of Mexico waters, from Florida through Texas, in many of the same areas redfish (p. 18) are found. Some places in this area have long, rich histories regarding seatrout fishing, such as the remote, beautiful Chandeleur Islands located about 30 miles off Louisiana's southeast coast. The Texas coast also boasts many miles of prime spotted seatrout shallows. San Luis Pass, for example, at the lower end of Galveston Island is a top spot for wade fishermen seeking seatrout. So is the 100-mile-long bay-like area known as Laguna Madre. There, guides who specialize in seatrout have made a name for themselves among anglers searching for big, beautiful, heavily-spotted seatrout.

Conservation measures and protection from netting have really helped seatrout populations in the northern Gulf Coast. Every summer anglers catch fish pushing the 10-pound mark. There has been a surge in fly-fishing interest, and shallow-water seatrout fishing, especially with fly gear, is growing along the entire coast. Texas, for example, has always had good trout fishing but guides note it is only getting better and should continue to improve because of conservation. The seatrout story is much the same along the Upper Gulf Coast in Louisiana, Alabama and Florida, where the species is now considered a sportfish, and conservation measures are protecting them from commercial over-harvest.

Water conditions play a vital role in where trout are found and how they may be caught. Tide phase is the most important thing anglers have to take into account, though there is no set rule about which areas to fish during each tide phase. Two nearby productive trout spots that look identical to fishermen can be completely different to seatrout. One may have trout only during high tide, while the other place has trout just at low tide. Only through fishing each spot during all tide phases and during different seasons of the year will an angler know when trout can be caught there consistently.

Water clarity is very important to successful seatrout fishing. Generally, the clearer the water, the better the action. If there's been abundant rain, and creeks and bays are muddy, work water close to the open ocean during rising tides. This "outside" water should be clearer than that found inshore. Also, live baits are generally more productive than artificials in murky water.

Seatrout also require highly saline water. Thus, an inshore hot spot that had produced great trout action may suddenly have poor fishing if abundant rain has "freshened" the bay or estuary. Some anglers even check saline content with special meters to learn if water is suitable for trout.

Another thing that is good to keep in mind when targeting seatrout is that, like most fish, they have two driving forces in life, safety and food. Seatrout feel safe when they're in large schools, holding in deep water, or around cover (bridge abutments, pilings, etc.). Their choice foods (shrimp, silversides, mullet) are found in salt creeks and near oyster bars, river ledges and other forage spawning sites. The angler who spends his time fishing such seatrout "safety" and "food" spots will not have long to wait between strikes.

Seatrout are also notorious for inhabiting shallow grass flats, particularly in the Gulf of Mexico, where turtle grass beds often extend for miles. But while huge, endless expanses of grass can hold trout, places with sand holes (opposite page) often are best.

Sometimes seatrout hold right in a sand hole; at other times they'll be on the grassy edges watching for baitfish and shrimp that mistakenly cross the barren sand. Sometimes two or three adjacent sand holes are best, and the biggest trout often hold on grass patches adjacent to these sand holes.

Many veteran fishermen say big trout hold in grass, facing the sand, because they're better camouflaged and can ambush prey more easily in the barren sand. They're kind of like a lion hiding in a jungle near an open savanna. Anything coming out of the jungle to the savanna is easily spotted and caught by the lion or, in this case, by seatrout near an open sand hole.

While a large, isolated sand hole or two in a broad grassy area may be the ultimate spot for finding seatrout, it is often large areas of "broken" bottom that hold the largest numbers of fish. As a rule, when fishing an unfamiliar area anglers should run across solid grass flats, looking for scattered sand holes before shutting down to fish. Even in deep or off-colored water, locating a few faint "white spots" on a grass bottom is worthwhile. Anglers should wear polarized sunglasses and a brimmed cap to maximize their ability to find such spots.

When water temperatures drop in winter, big trout tend to move far offshore to deep water where the temperature is more stable; or they migrate inshore to deep creeks, canals, channels and power-plant discharge areas. Power-plant fish become well educated, and trout stack up in these areas. Some fishermen employ "free-lined" shrimp in the winter for big seatrout that have migrated to these warm-water discharges. Fishing at night can be especially good, as it's less crowded, the fish aren't as spooky, and the biggest trout are often night feeders.

Most night fishermen work areas around docks, piers and bridges that have lights reflecting in the water. The lights draw small baitfish and shrimp, which in turn attract trout. Some innovative night anglers hang camp lanterns with ropes from bridge catwalks and piers above the water. This tactic works particularly well on bridges and piers that have no other lights.

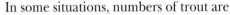

## How to Catch Spotted Seatrout

More seatrout have been caught on live shrimp than on all other types of natural baits and artificial lures combined. Small live mullet, croakers and pieces of cut bait are used effectively in some locales, but shrimp are the bread-and-butter bait of seatrout anglers everywhere.

Many experienced anglers use shrimp almost exclusively when fishing for big trout, when the water is cold or the fish are deep. Big trout are wary and often tough to catch on lures or even live shrimp if there is a lot of terminal tackle dragging the bait down.

One important key to effective live-bait fishing for trout is to keep lines, leaders and terminal rigs simple and as light as possible. Small size #4 or #6 treble hooks and size #2 to 1/0 Kahle hooks are popular with natural-bait anglers throughout the seatrout's range. Anglers use the lightest sinkers and split-shot possible to get baits to the proper depth. One of the simplest and most deadly of all seatrout tactics is simply "free-lining" live shrimp in a running tide. Light spinning tackle generally is employed. A hook is tied to the line, and the shrimp is hooked under the "horn" to keep it lively. The shrimp is cast out and allowed to drift naturally with current. No weight is used because it inhibits the free swimming motion of the shrimp. A sliding float can be used to keep bait above the weeds.

In some situations, numbers of trout are

SAND HOLES on grass flats are productive areas to find seatrout.

caught with the aid of specialized fishing floats called "popping corks." These have proven to be one of the most effective rigs for catching trout with live shrimp. A popping cork (opposite page) is a 3- to 5-inch long, commercially-made float that looks much like a top-water chugger plug without the hooks. It's positioned on the fishing line above a live shrimp or jig and is generally fished in water less than 8 feet deep. The best method is to cast the popping cork to a likely shallow spot, then yank the rod hard a time or two, making the float "pop" loudly. The surface popping simulates feeding seatrout, attracting trout to the lure or bait hanging below.

It is likely that every avid seatrout fishermen has at least some plastic-tail jigs in his tackle box. Indeed, few lures are so perfectly matched to a fish species as the "grub" jig is to the spotted seatrout. Some fishermen, in fact, state flatly that the grub jig was designed specifically for seatrout fishing and subsequently gained a reputation for catching redfish, blues, mackerel and a myriad of freshwater species.

Dozens of tackle companies manufacture plastic-tail jigs, and the bulk of them are good. But specific brand loyalty is very localized among trout casters. Some "hot" lures sell well in very small geographic regions, usually because they produce fish so well there. Popular jig weights for fishing seatrout are ¼- and ⅜-ounce, but some ½-ounce jigs also should be in every trout angler's tackle box for those times when fish are extra deep or when tides are particularly strong. At times, lightweight ⅛-ounce jigs are needed for very shallow water or slack tides.

Fan-casting rigged grubs or tandem grub jig rigs is very effective in locating schools of trout, and will often turn on fish that are reluctant to strike other lures. These two-jig rigs are the norm in some famed seatrout areas such as Lake Calcasieu, Louisiana. Anglers should try different grub colors and lure actions until they discover the right one for that day.

Calcasieu seatrout guides often fish a red grub tied in tandem with a white one, or a green one with a brown grub. Usually one color works best, and when they discover which one it is, the guides switch both jigs to that one.

Pink probably is the most popular plastic-tail jig color since it most closely resembles the hue of shrimp – the favorite food of seatrout. White,

yellow, green, silver and combinations of those colors are commonly used for seatrout. A grub jig tipped with a whole, fresh shrimp is also an outstanding taker of trout.

Minnow-imitating plugs also have their place as seatrout lures, and a healthy selection of different sizes, styles, weights and colors of such artificials belongs in every seatrout fisherman's kit. The MirrOlure is a mainstay of seatrout plug casters. Fast-sinking, slow-sinking and floating models are all good under the right conditions, with popular colors being red and white, blue and white, silver and silver and blue.

Seatrout on shallow flats, particularly big ones have a passion for floating plugs such as Bang-O lures, big Rebel minnows, Zara Spooks and MirrOlure Top Dogs. In addition, top-water chuggers and plugs with propellers fore and aft are good lures to try.

Another outstanding trout lure option is the soft plastic jerkbait, made famous in largemouth bass circles. These soft, slender jerkbaits are preferred by many veteran trout fishermen because they imitate needlefish, which are a prime seatrout forage. Bright-colored jerkbaits or ones having built-in sparkles and flash are excellent. The Culprit Jerk Worm and Lunker City Slug-Go are favorites of trout anglers. When rigged Texas-style

**Slug-Go**

and twitched, they are completely weedless, have outstanding action and are tough to beat in water less than 4 feet deep. The lure is rigged with a 2/0 to 5/0 "wide-gap" hook, and can be fished with a low-stretch superline for better hooksets. Soft plastic jerkbaits are among the most deadly of light-tackle lures for heavyweight seatrout.

Seatrout do hold in deep holes, channels and canals where deep-diving lures are needed to ferret them out. Though "lipped" diving plugs or crankbaits are not especially popular with seatrout anglers, they are excellent for casting and trolling around deep seatrout structure. The Heddon Sonar (a metal vibrating bait) is also an outstanding seatrout artificial when jigged in deep holes. Small spoons such as the Johnson Sprite, Hopkins, Krocodile and Kastmaster are all good for those times when trout are feeding deep on small, shiny minnows.

Seatrout are outstanding fly-rod fish that readily strike streamers and poppers, especially when they are located in shallow, clear water. As seatrout feed primarily on shrimp and small baitfish, few lures resemble such food better than a fly or popping bug. Streamers and poppers are versatile and can be tied many different ways to resemble any type of natural trout forage such as shrimp, glass minnows, needlefish or mullet. Shrimp and crab fly patterns intended for bonefish are excellent choices for seatrout.

Large streamers are popular with fly fishermen, and most streamer patterns will take some spotted seatrout. Those made of bucktail, marabou, saddle-hackle and synthetic materials such as FisHair take fish, and expert anglers will switch from one streamer type to another until one produces. Accomplished salt water fly fishermen prefer streamers with a bit of Mylar or Flashabou tied in with winging. Streamers having flashy bodies made of Flashabou Tubing, Flashabou Minnow Body or Everglow Tubing (fluorescent colors) are also deadly at times.

Seatrout streamers should be tied on size #1 to 3/0 quality stainless hooks. Some streamers should have weighted bodies when it's necessary to sink flies fast; others should be made on smaller, lighter hooks with winging of bucktail for buoyancy. The best streamer colors are yellow, white, pink, blue, brown, green or combinations of those colors, since they most closely resemble the colors of real trout forage.

Fly rods for seatrout run from 6- to 9-weight outfits, with an 8-weight being a good all-around size. Weight-forward, floating lines are preferred for windy areas, and the reel should have 100 to 150 yards of backing. Big seatrout can make good runs, and you never know when a big redfish, tarpon or other heavyweight may swallow a streamer intended for trout. Well-made salt water fly reels with smooth drags are best for seatrout.

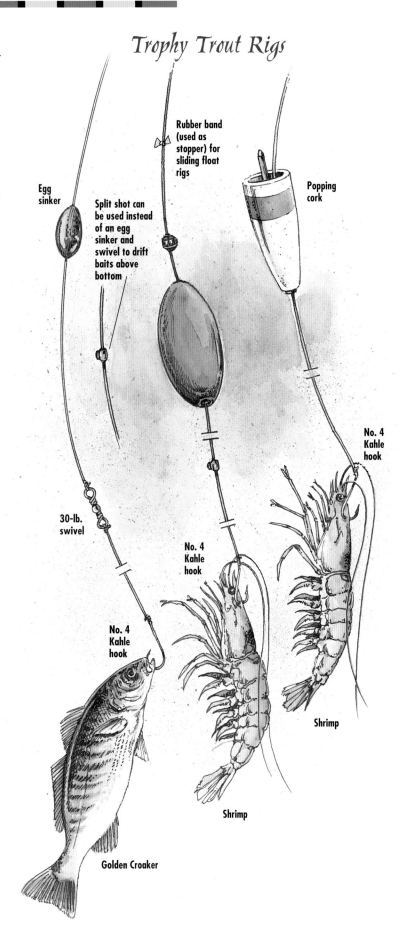

*Trophy Trout Rigs*

Egg sinker

Rubber band (used as stopper) for sliding float rigs

Split shot can be used instead of an egg sinker and swivel to drift baits above bottom

Popping cork

No. 4 Kahle hook

30-lb. swivel

No. 4 Kahle hook

No. 4 Kahle hook

Shrimp

No. 4 Kahle hook

Shrimp

Golden Croaker

Light spinning tackle is the most popular option for taking trout throughout much of their range, although light baitcasters are in vogue on the Texas, Louisiana and Mississippi coastlines. Many veteran trout fishermen favor 7-foot graphite rods with fast tips and cork handles to transmit light takes from trout. Longer rods also help cushion the fight of trout, and help prevent lures from pulling free from their delicate mouths.

In many regions 8-pound-test monofilament is the preferred trout line, though 6-pound test is good in ultra-clear water. Anglers fishing in dark water or around heavy cover such as dock pilings and shell beds may opt for 10- or 12-pound line. Some anglers opt for low-stretch superlines which transmit strikes extremely well and allow for sure, quick hooksets, especially in deep water or when long-distance casting is in order.

Although seatrout don't have razor-edge teeth like mackerel or bluefish, their canines and smaller teeth can fray line during the course of landing a fish. So in light-line situations anglers are wise to employ a short length of heavy monofilament "shock" leader, 20- to 30-pound-test is preferred. Many anglers double the 2-foot end of light line with a Bimini Twist or Spider Hitch, then attach a shock leader with a Surgeon's Knot. The lure is then attached to the shock leader.

A tip for night fishing for seatrout originated on the Georgia coast, where there are many dedicated seatrout fisherman. Some night fishermen there work the same oyster bar drop-offs and creek mouths during the same tide phases that produce during the day. But at night they place a gas lantern in a large, metal, floating washtub and anchor it near a productive oyster bar or creek mouth. Trout fishing is better in these areas at night because the lantern attracts shrimp and baitfish and the size of the fish caught is generally larger.

Many top guides concur that big trout are night feeders; one guide stated that 90 percent of his trout weighing 10 pounds or more are caught

NIGHT FISHING may offer your best chance at a big seatrout.

after the sun sets. To target big fish look for sand flats and mangrove edges that drop into water about 5 feet deep, particularly in places where there are a lot of baitfish, such as mullet.

Topwater plugs that can be cast a long way are a top choice for night fishing because they are easy to see and can be launched a long distance for shallow, easily-spooked trout. Larger trout are often more scattered than smaller fish, and they are not often found in the same waters as 2- and 3-pounders. Most guides agree that anglers looking for big trout should avoid schools of smaller ones, fish at night and should try using large topwater plugs to increase their chances for a trophy.

While catching trout in shallow water is fun and often productive, the bigger trout are most often taken in a completely different area. "Rocks are where I get some of my largest seatrout, these are fish in the 7-, 8-, and even 10-pound range," said one veteran seatrout guide. Trout hold around rocks because they offer food and cover and provide a way for fish to get out of strong running current. They are also excellent areas for trout waiting to ambush bait.

Although many anglers fish easily spotted rip-rap areas and inlet jetty rocks, many areas that hold trout are completely submerged. Finding areas where rocks are on the bottom in prime trout country is tough, and such spots are learned through fishing experience and many lost baits, hooks, sinkers and fishing line.

An example of one such area is a mid-river "sunken island" that has a vertical wall dropping from 12 feet into a river channel 40 feet deep. For one guide this area has produced a tremendous number of seatrout weighing 7 pounds or more, because, he says, "It's deep and there are rocks on the spot."

Many rock jetties that attract trout are shaped like a pyramid; it is usually not necessary to fish a bait deep along the rock bottom to catch fish. Trout can lay out of the current around high peaks of jetty rocks, so fish baits along their edges. On most jetties this will be from 4 to 8 feet deep, depending on the tide level and current speed. Anglers should try to keep their bait near the tips of the rocks, and can count on getting hung up a lot when they first start fishing this way. Through experience you can learn how deep to fish baits in certain areas according to tide phase and current.

Big trout are also caught around the legs of large range-markers or tripods. These large ship-channel markers are usually positioned on a channel edge near deep water and have a number of supports, or legs. Currents push through them, and bait comes right past the legs, where seatrout wait in ambush. Some of these tripods also have rocks around their bases and holes, or wash-outs in the bottom nearby. Usually trout are in the back eddies around range markers and lie out of the tide flow waiting to strike baits. Fish in current near these back eddies. It's also important to fish a bait just off bottom around range markers, as they often hold big fish.

Many anglers believe water temperature has a lot to do with catching seatrout. Some say the best trout action is had when water temperature is 65 to 75 degrees. But most every veteran angler has stories of catching the biggest fish during the hottest or coldest weather imaginable, which tempers the water temperature theory. Nevertheless, many trout guides and experts like March to April and October to November as the peaks for seatrout.

Oddly, not many guides and trout experts like the full or new moon phases, mainly because tides are too strong to present baits and lures effectively. Favorite times for trout are three days before the full and new moons, and about one week after them. Guides prefer to fish early in running-tide phases, when the current is moving but not too swift.

There is something special about spotted seatrout that excites anglers. Maybe it's their widespread distribution, their dime-size black spots along sleek silver flanks or the way they swat lures and baits. The fact they're among the most delicious fish available doesn't go unnoticed either. Whatever the reason, seatrout are different from all other gamefish, and so, too, are the tactics needed to consistently catch them.

—*Bob McNally*

# SNOOK

ort Lauderdale, skiff guide John Glorieux had explained in detail how many snook – big snook – I'd see in a "typical" summer's morning fishing the calm, clear, Florida beach areas with him.

But I still wasn't prepared for the spectacle of 1,500 snook that hovered just off bottom in 10 feet of water below our 18-foot flats skiff. It was shortly after an August dawn and a slight ocean haze covered the sun, which somewhat impaired our water vision through polarized sunglasses. But there were so many fish, packed so tightly, that their dark black shapes stood out starkly in the otherwise clear-blue ocean water.

"Wait, don't cast yet, those are just cudas," he cautioned as he threw more live baits over the rising cloud of snook.

With more baits tossed into the water and the ever-increasing frenzy of feeding cudas, blue runners and jacks, individual snook began crashing topside, too. Soon we saw the dark lateral lines of heavy snook at the surface wildly chasing bait. Their forked tails quickly sliced the water; their long sleek bodies cut circles into the pilchards, and their wide menacing mouths slammed shut noisily over frantic sardines.

"There! There! Now some good fish are tearin' up baits. Oh! That's a 30-pounder! Get 'em! Get 'em! Cast! Cast! Cast! Now!"

This, in a nutshell, is why snook fishing fever has become so intense in Florida. Catch-and-release restrictions have greatly increased snook populations throughout the state. Inshore gillnetting in Florida has been made illegal, so incidental commercial harvest of snook has been halted. Add to this an increase in baitfish populations and a string of consecutive mild winters (water temperatures below 70 degrees stress snook, and below 60 they can't survive). The result is that snook populations are on the increase. All of this has inshore anglers excited, since by any measure the snook is one of the world's premier sportfish.

Biologists list a dozen snook species worldwide, six in the Atlantic Ocean, six in the Pacific. But the common snook *(Centropomus undecimalis)* is the most abundant and most important species for anglers. The common snook is indigenous to the

MANGROVE SHORELINES are the preferred habitat of snook.

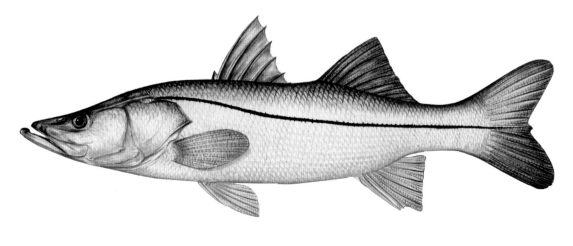

western Atlantic Ocean. The world IGFA record for common snook was caught out of the Parismina River on the east coast of Costa Rica, weighed 53 pounds, 10 ounces and was just 54 inches long. The all-tackle world record snook weighed 57 pounds, 12 ounces, caught from the Rio Naranjo, near Quepos on the Pacific Coast of Costa Rica. This all-tackle record fish is actually a black snook, which run larger, but are a notoriously fickle fish to catch.

The swordspine snook, tarpon snook and fat snook also occur in the United States (chiefly Florida), but are comparatively rare and average 6 to 10 pounds, considerably smaller in size than the common snook. Twenty- to 30-pound fish are regularly caught in Florida, Mexico, Belize, Honduras, Nicaragua and Costa Rica. The common snook record in Florida is 44 pounds, 3 ounces, but fish to 50 pounds have been reported. Snook weighing 60, even 70 pounds have been well documented in the South American part of their range and are often seen in fish markets, where 5-foot fish are occasionally displayed for sale.

All snook species have a similar appearance: a long, silvery, thick body; elongated, a tapered head with large mouth (no teeth); a divided dorsal fin; and a very pronounced black lateral line extending from the top of the gill plate behind the head to the caudal fin. Once an angler sees a snook, or better yet catches one, he will always be able to identify the fish as no other looks like it or fights like it.

## Where to Find Snook

Florida offers the most available snook fishing for inshore anglers. A wayward snook can be caught almost anywhere in the state due in large part to the conservation efforts. The best snook fishing occurs along the so-called "snook line," which extends from about Cape Canaveral on the east coast to Port Richey on the west coast. Snook are abundant on both coasts south of that line, including parts of the Florida Keys.

Snook spawn in passes and inlets during strong, full-moon and new-moon tides of spring and early summer. Fish jam in channels and cuts and near beach areas where tidal flows support their eggs long enough for fry to hatch. In decades passed, anglers descended on such huge concentrations of snook and unfortunately kept most of the

SNOOK
RANGE
PRIME FISHING

giant "linesiders" they caught. This focused, intense fishing was devastating to snook populations. This situation changed with closed fishing seasons in Florida, and although the season is closed in spring, catch-and-release fishing in the passes and inlets is superb.

While snook are an inshore fish of the first order, they occasionally hold in open ocean water. Big snook are caught every year around wrecks and reefs off both coasts of Florida, and scuba divers report huge schools of heavy fish around artificial reefs. Many big snook are caught from reefs in the Marco Island, Florida, area, for example.

Backcountry fishing is classic snooking, and anglers should bone up on their casting skills. Snook are found around most mangrove shores throughout south Florida, especially on the southwest coast. Fish will be almost anywhere mangroves grow, but points of treelines with strong current pushing into or alongside them are preferred. Often the very best mangrove edges have water at least several feet deep. Sometimes a distinctively deep trough will be made by tide and current and will run tight to a mangrove edge. Such places are natural highways for snook to follow, particularly during low tides. Shell bars, holes or isolated patches of grass in backcountry area can also be snook magnets.

Snook also like to cruise beaches, holding just outside the lapping wave line looking for baitfish, shrimp and crabs washed in by tides and currents. Flood tides are especially good, since it washes food out of the sand and draw snook looking for a meal. Unlike snook found under a pier or boathouse, which may refuse perfectly presented lures and baits, snook on the beach are there to feed.

Beach fishing is superb for snook in the warm months (March to November), and peak fishing occurs at beaches around west coast passes during the spawn. Falling tides are the best choice for beach anglers when fishing near the passes. There is also good fishing before and after the spawn, often for fish that are considerably less pressured than "inside" mangrove and bridge snook that know the the drone of an electric motor and can be tough to catch.

The peak of beach snook fishing also coincides with Florida's summer closed-harvest season on the species. This restriction was set up to protect

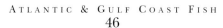

fish during the spawn and runs from June 1 through August 31. Snook harvest by anglers (two per person, per day, minimum size 24 inches) begins September 1, and fishing throughout south Florida during this time is a often crowded. The state snook season is also closed from mid-December through January, but snook fishing from the beaches is not good in winter months. Anglers should check regulations before fishing, which can change from year to year.

The best beach fishing of the year for heavyweight linesiders happens in autumn, during the east coast mullet run. Nearly all predator fish feed on the mullet that migrate down the coast as water temperatures drop; these species include tarpon, jacks, redfish, sharks and of course, snook. All of these species can be found holding around the mullet pods, picking off stragglers.

Anglers interested in catching numbers of big snook on lures but not eating them are better off fishing during the closed-harvest season. There are a lot of places to tap into this type of snook fishing in Florida.

## How to Catch Snook

The method for catching big snook in south Florida passes (both coasts) is to drift with live baits, usually pinfish or mullet, in deep water. Live shrimp work well, but are often eaten by other fish. Many anglers believe the bigger the baitfish the bigger the snook, and at times 10-inch mullet are employed, particularly on the east coast. The key is to get the bait deep but not hung on bottom, as there are often huge rocks and rubble in the passes where snook take up residence. Fishing the passes is usually a bait-drifting game, and anglers seldom anchor. Drifting can be difficult in swift currents, and can make it tough to fish with other fishermen trying the same tactic.

In remote passes, anglers chum with live baits such as sardines, pilchards or mullet, which can turn snook to feeding and result in fast action. Snook will hit lures in passes where vertical jigging spoons or leadhead jigs work well. Use a jig just heavy enough to maintain contact with bottom. Pinfish and mullet-imitating sinking plugs can tempt snook in passes and inlets when cast up current. Lures should be fished slow and allowed to drift deep with occasional twitches during the retrieve.

Anglers walking a beach at dawn and dusk –when swimmers are few and fish most abundant– can catch plenty of snook, and many large linesiders are landed this way. Often, snook can be spotted on shallow beach areas, and casts can be made to individual fish. Sometimes small schools of juvenile snook are seen, and a live bait, plug, jig or fly will trigger a violent strike. It's important to note that beach fishing is not a big-rod surf fishing game. Standard snook tackle (6½-foot medium-heavy spinning or baitcasting rods spooled with 14- to 20-pound test) is used for beach fishing, as you are generally not casting great distances. In fact, fish are often seen just feet from a wading angler. For best results any long casts should be made parallel to the beach, ahead of a knee-deep wading angler, rather than far out and away from shore.

Beach fishing from boats can be very productive also, particularly in the shallow Gulf. Sight-casting similar to that done for "flats" species is often possible. Some anglers use specialized flats skiffs that have towers allowing anglers to get well above the water level to spot fish in the surf. A stealthy approach, accurate cast and properly presented lure or bait are needed for this technique, as snook that see you first are very difficult to catch. Caution should be taken when beach snooking from a boat as the waves are rolling and the water extra shallow. For this reason, some anglers use boats simply to ferry to isolated beaches where the snook are abundant and undisturbed. The trick is to anchor the boat, then wade and cast to cover a lot of beach in a hurry on these choice spots that rarely see fishing pressure.

Throughout the backcountry, anglers who chum with live bait can expect to attract and catch active snook. Southwest Florida guides have this system down to a science. Bait can often be found around channel markers, caught with a cast net, and kept in a boat's live well until needed. The boat is anchored up-current of a likely mangrove point or cut, and a couple handfuls of bait are tossed to the spot. Then anglers will hook a bait through the back or lips, and cast to the likely spot. It does not take long to learn if snook are nearby, and a lack of quick action leads to a search for a new spot.

Guides also score well on "inside" linesiders by anchoring near sand holes on grass flats similar to those that speckled trout use (p. 39). Such sand holes are easily spotted by anglers wearing polarized sunglasses. They are devoid of grass and usually are

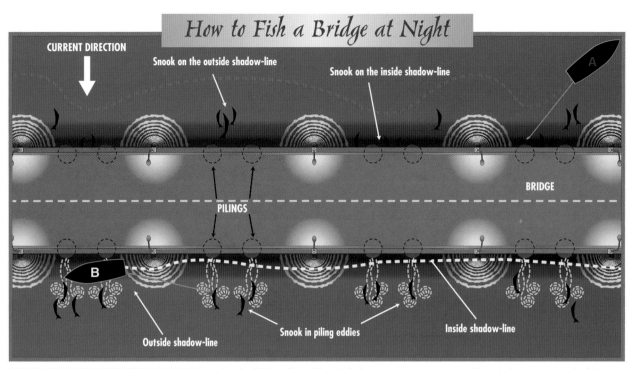

## How to Fish a Bridge at Night

CURRENT DIRECTION

Snook on the outside shadow-line

Snook on the inside shadow-line

A

BRIDGE

PILINGS

Outside shadow-line

Snook in piling eddies

Inside shadow-line

B

STARTING ON THE UP-CURRENT SIDE OF THE BRIDGE, anglers should (A) troll parallel to the bridge in a weaving pattern that allows the lures to contact all of the shadow-lines produced by the lights on the bridge. On the down-current side, (B) troll tight to the bridge, which allows the lures to be swept out to the fish.

slightly deeper than surrounding flats, showing up as a light spot on the bottom. They are natural ambush spots for many inshore gamefish species, including redfish, seatrout and tarpon. But in southwest Florida, snook are the prime sand hole residents. Often the best sand holes are near mangrove points, or shell bars, with a good tide flow crossing the hole and moving toward the mangroves. Anchor up-current of the hole and chum with live bait, then cast baits to the hole and its perimeter.

Few fish have a stronger reputation as night feeders than snook. Almost any summer evening, a casual glance around almost any good-sized south Florida highway bridge with lights shining down will reveal the large, green shadowy figures of cruising snook. Dock and marina lights draw baitfish and snook at night also. Many hard-core summertime snook fishermen sleep all day so they can use their skiffs all night.

Much like snook during the daytime, night snook in lights can be tough to fool into striking, but with tenacity and good, fresh live bait, an intrepid angler should score. Fish hovering in the edge of a light beaming into the water are the best targets. Make long casts with as light line as you dare (8- to 10-pound test), using minimal terminal tackle, and target the fringe areas of the light for best results.

Excellent night beach fishing also can be found in summer. The lights from hotels and condos draws bait, which will increase your odds in locating snook when fishing these areas.

Some serious snook-chasers work mangrove backcountry spots at night. It's difficult business, and an angler better know the way there and back in the often–confusing country. Global Positioning System (GPS) units have made this type of fishing a bit more realistic for the average angler. Be prepared, however, as the bugs are often bad, and tossing lures around mangrove edges at night is a sport only a lure manufacturer could invent. However, a well prepared angler can have great backcountry snook fishing at night all summer in south Florida.

In late fall as water temperatures drop, many snook begin migrating out of the backcountry to the passes and inlets. They also move to the headwater areas of rivers, where deep water is warm and inviting to baitfish and snook. Usually by Thanksgiving, and certainly by Christmas, snook are in the deeper stretches of south Florida rivers, and fishing for them can be exceptional. Others, particularly big snook, retreat far up the rivers into freshwater areas, where they adjust just fine. Heavyweight fish weighing 12 to 20 pounds can be found far up the rivers and can offer small boat fishermen good action, especially from the Marco Island area south into the Everglades.

During warming trends in winter, snook become more active and will move downriver toward the open parts of harbors, bays and river mouths. Power-plant outflows can offer especially good winter snooking. The number of fish using these areas tends to increase as water temperatures become colder. Look for snook to move into shallower water after consecutive days of warm weather.

Trolling is also a popular method for catching fall and winter snook in headwater river areas, river mouths, passes and inlets. Trolling allows diving plugs to run deep and is a good way to cover a lot of water until fish are located. One of the most popular snook lures for trolling is the odd-shaped Spoonplug, a lure made famous by North Carolina bass angler Buck Perry, the man who started the structure-fishing craze for fresh water fishermen. In very cold winter weather, lethargic snook living in deep river holes and outside bends in the stream bank can only be taken on slowly fished jigs or live baits.

**Heddon Zara Spook**

Snook tackle is not too specialized and is much the same as that used to catch redfish, tarpon or striped bass. Medium-heavy baitcasting, spinning and fly gear is useful for all types of snooking. Big snook sought in tight quarters around line-cutting obstructions like mangroves and docks may require heavy action rods, heavy line and heavier leaders. Some fishermen who dangle giant mullet and pin-fish tight to pilings around dock lights for giant linesiders have been known to use 50-pound-class offshore trolling tackle to subdue their targets quickly. Such line-cutting spots are no place for light-action spinning rods and 6-pound test. However, just such gear can be fun for snook in clear water along a beach or on an open flat sand hole. At times light gear will produce more and larger fish because light lures and/or live baits can be presented delicately without spooking fish.

A snook fisherman's gear and tackle arsenal should look something like an all-around fresh water bass fisherman's gear. There should be long

bait-casting rods with suitable reels and lines testing 12 to 20 pounds for larger plugs, medium-action baitcasting outfits for jigs and live bait fishing and medium-action spinning gear spooled with 8- to 10-pound test. Carrying a combination of these rods is best for all-around snook fishing, and allows for quick changes to try new baits, lures and line sizes as conditions dictate.

Where you are fishing dictates lure choices, and at times snook hit almost anything cast to them. But much of the time special lures are most productive, and live bait is often the best choice.

Classic snook lures include the 97MR-18 and 65M MirrOlures, and Heddon Zara Spooks. Other "walk-the-dog" style lures such as D.O.A. Bait Busters and Tough Guys, Trader Bay's Trader Raider, Snook Slayer and Sea Dude work well. Large, soft-plastic jerk-baits like Lunker City's original Slug-Go, Culprit's Dart Baiter and Berkley's Power Slug are big fish producers. Good colors for all lures are silver, white, blue and green.

Fly fishermen (using 7- to 9-weight outfits) can enjoy multiple hookups with snook, and many standard salt water patterns work well, including the McNally Smelt, Clouser patterns, and large, well-made popping bugs.

A favorite pattern of many Florida guides is a very simple streamer designed for striped bass, measuring about 4½ inches long. It has two long white saddle hackles that extend well beyond the hook bend. A good tuft of white "FisHair" is tied in above the hackles to add forward bulk to the streamer, a bit of green FisHair is added for winging. The fly is finished with a bit of pink marabou or FisHair for a throat. The streamer has no body and no name and takes only minutes to tie.

Combine all the features of the snook and you have one of the great inshore salt water species available to anglers. Unfortunately, their United States range is more limited than that of many other salt water species, but the high population numbers where they are found make them a great sportfish.

—*Bob McNally*

# BLUEFISH

BLUEFISH
▓ RANGE
■ PRIME FISHING

**W**ithout a doubt bluefish (*Pomatomus saltatrix*) are among the most voracious fish in the world, and are rightly regarded as one of the premier gamefish. Although their primary range is from North Carolina to southern New England, they're caught north to Maine and south to Florida and even the Gulf of Mexico. They are also found in various other areas of the Atlantic, the Caribbean, the Indian Ocean and Australia.

Historically regarded as a cyclical species, bluefish have gone through vast changes in abundance over the years. This is particularly true in the fringe areas of their range, such as north of Cape Cod, where they disappeared for so long at times in the past that no one knew what they were upon reappearing. The relative abundance of bluefish today has been present since the 1960s and shows no sign of diminishing.

The recreational catch of bluefish, as calculated by the National Marine Fisheries Service (NMFS), peaked in 1980, when it was estimated at 153,468,000 pounds – far more than that of any other salt water fish in the entire United States. At that time surveys also showed that blues were the number-one target of anglers in both the North Atlantic (Maine to Connecticut) and Mid-Atlantic (New York to Virginia) areas. By the 1990s catches were only a fraction of that figure, but were still more than enough for most anglers fishing in the prime areas from Rhode Island to New Jersey. Release rates have escalated sharply; more than 50 percent of blues hooked are currently being released.

Sport fishermen seeking other species such as striped bass, weakfish, flounder or sea bass avoid bluefish because these fish not only interfere with catching, but cut through mono leaders and destroy lures with their razor-sharp teeth. It's not unusual for blues to chop off pieces of other fish that a fisherman is fighting.

Fortunately, bluefish aren't quite as bloodthirsty as described by the great fishery scientists Jordan and Everman a century ago in their classic *American Food and Game Fishes*: "The bluefish is a carnivorous animal of the most pronounced type. It has been likened to an animated chopping machine, the business of which is to cut to pieces and otherwise destroy as many fish as possible in a given amount of time. Going in large schools, in pursuit of fish not much inferior to themselves in size, they move about like a pack of hungry wolves, destroying everything before them. Their trail is marked by fragments of fish and by the stain of blood in the sea. It has even been maintained that such is the gluttony of this fish that when the stomach becomes full the contents are disgorged and then again filled. It is certain that it kills more fish than it needs or can use. The amount of fish they consume or destroy is incredibly great. It has been estimated at twice the weight of the fish in one day, and one observer says that a bluefish will destroy daily, 1000 other fish."

There is no question that bluefish are extremely aggressive and certainly kill more than they consume, as pieces are lost in the course of bit-ing into fish too large to be swallowed whole. The concept that they kill simply to kill, however, doesn't hold up. A three-year study of bluefish feeding characteristics conducted in a large tank at the Sandy Hook Marine Lab decades ago proved that while blues would go into a feeding frenzy when baitfish were introduced, they fed only until sated. After that the baitfish, sensing no immediate danger, would join in the blues' swimming pattern.

An aspect of that study of particular interest to anglers was the discovery that introduction of larger prey fish to the tank would stir those sated blues again. Bluefish anglers have found the same thing to be true, as a popping plug will often be hit when standard baits and lures become ineffective.

The concept that blues simply charge into a school of bait to maim as many as possible was also disproved in the tank. Rather, they zero in on a particular baitfish and will literally push aside others to get at the selected victim. Unlike gamefish that lack sharp teeth, blues can handle large prey by chopping them in pieces rather than swallowing them headfirst. That's why tail hooks are most effective on lures and why stinger hooks are used with large, live baits. This feeding behavior also often provides a clue to the blues location, as the cut prey fish release oils that form a slick on the surface that can be both seen and smelled.

Bluefish are primarily day-feeders, and sight seems to be the primary means of locating prey. They do hit lures at night, particularly during the full moon period, when night plugging can be far superior to day sport. Blues also have a tendency to feed by scent at night, as party boat skippers found out long ago while putting out slicks of menhaden (bunker) chum.

There have long been rumors of 30- to 40-pound bluefish from North Africa. But even after sportfishing has penetrated even the most remote regions of the world, the IGFA record remains the 31-pound, 12-ounce chopper trolled up in Hatteras Inlet, North Carolina.

Males and females are the same general size, and individuals live for 10 to 15 years, with a few aging to 20 years or more. There seem to be at least two stocks of bluefish that migrate along the Atlantic Coast. The southern group moves up the Florida coast in March and April and reaches North Carolina. Those that winter off North Carolina move north in April, behind schools of mackerel, and start moving inshore as water temperatures go over 50 degrees. At first blues are rather lethargic and spend most of the time right on the surface (where they can be spotted finning) where water temperatures are highest. They tend to go deeper in the water column as it warms, yet regularly return to the surface when feeding on surface-dwelling baitfish.

Spawning occurs offshore during early summer, and the fry take up residence in coastal estuaries, where they grow rapidly. Some reach 10 inches or more by fall, when they start a southern migration. Young-of-the-year blues are called *snappers*, and many young fishermen in New York and New Jersey get their first taste of the sport of fishing by casting small lures on spinning tackle for these aggressive little blues.

By their second year, blues will weigh over 2 pounds. They continue to add about 2 pounds per year, until the average drops to about 1½ pounds when they're six years old and weigh about 10 pounds. A ten-year-old blue weighs around 15 pounds (about 32 inches fork length), which is considered very large. Twenty-pounders are considered real trophies at over 36 inches fork length and nearly 20 years old.

A BLITZ can occur any time bluefish are feeding on large schools of baitfish.

## Where to Find Bluefish

As blues move up the coast during their spring migration, they spread into all sorts of salt waters. They feed in the ocean, yet many enter bays and tidal portions of rivers. While smaller blues tend to dominate in most inland areas, trophy-sized blues are commonly hooked in the Hudson River off Manhattan and the Statue of Liberty.

The initial run of bluefish seeks the warmest surface waters and even warmer inshore areas, while others continue arriving well into early summer before settling into favored areas such as the Mud Dump and 17 Fathoms in New York Bight. Schools of blues range from the surf to far offshore, where fishermen trolling for bluefin tuna or chumming for sharks in June are frequently inundated. Blues have been known to chop up expensive baits and cut off lures up to 65 miles offshore. At such times it becomes more a matter of where to avoid catching blues than where to find them!

As a rule, blues are where the bait is found. Since they require a lot of food, the logical place for them to be is where easily attacked schools of bait are gathered. This explains why large schools of blues are often found feeding far from land on sand eels, anchovies, young-of-the-year mackerel or anything else they can eat. Because most baitfish aren't tied to structure, bluefish locations may not be the same the next day if the bait moves on.

When schools of bait aren't available, blues often settle in on rough bottoms where they can always scrounge up a meal of cunner (bergall), sea bass or ocean pout. Areas such as 17 Fathoms, the Farms, Shrewsbury Rocks, the Rattlesnake and the Mud Dump in New York Bight, along with the Cartwright Grounds south of Montauk Point, are good areas for summer and fall bluefish. Many other rough bottom areas can be similarly productive. Look for lobster pot buoys, which are placed right on the areas that anglers should be checking out.

The fall run of blues is a reverse of the spring migration except that more fish tend to stay inshore. Surfcasters often get into blasts of bluefish, and the choppers tend to feed voraciously on schools of finger mullet, peanut bunkers, sand eels and bay anchovies. Falling water temperatures fail to discourage feeding blues, which often linger into December in New York Bight and may provide surf blitzes on the Outer Banks of North Carolina anytime from Thanksgiving through January.

## How to Catch Bluefish

There are few techniques that won't produce bluefish at times, as fishermen seeking other species often find out. Blues will attack anything from squid and killies being drifted on bottom for fluke (summer flounder) to high-speed lures being trolled for tuna, as well as everything in between. However, there are several means of targeting blues that are particularly effective.

CHUMMING & CHUNKING – The sense of smell seems to be as powerful with blues as with sharks, which makes chumming an ideal means of attracting them to an area. Chum is made from ground-up fish, the oilier the better. That means menhaden (bunkers) are at the top of the list as a chumming material, though mackerel and herring will do.

Party boats in New York Bight specialize in chumming for blues, and they employ heavy-duty grinders into which bunkers are fed to produce smelly ground meat, which is scattered continuously over the side to form a slick. Private boaters can buy bunker chum frozen in 5-gallon buckets or slightly smaller tins. After the top is removed, chum buckets are turned over into a bag or some other holder in order to provide a steady slick as the chum thaws. Hooks are then baited with pieces of bunker, mackerel, butterfish or practically any other fish and drifted back in the slick on a 5/0 to 7/0 bait hook (or the equivalent size circle hook) with a short wire leader and small swivel. Baits should be cut so that they don't spin in the water and hooked once just under the skin at the front end of the bait. Trimmed fillets are good, but chunks cut by slicing the fish like a loaf of bread provide the greatest yield from your baits. Bunker backs are prime baits that can be created by making a downward cut behind the head to the backbone, and then turning the knife to slice to the tail. The weight of these various baits affects how fast they sink and can change their effectiveness. Change bait size if the fish suddenly stop biting, to try to present the bait to different fish.

If the blues are fussy, switch to a heavy mono or fluorocarbon leader and a longer-shank hook. When the free-floating bait is picked up, put the reel into gear right away and come tight. Split shot may help at times, but it's generally best to avoid any extra weight, as the hook and swivel are usually enough to pull your bait below the slick. Strip off several yards of line at boatside to give the chunk a chance to sink

## Popular Lures for Bluefish

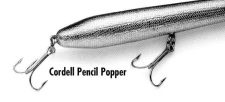

**Cordell Pencil Popper**  **Bomber Long-A**  **Hopkins Spoon**

a bit before free spooling. It may be necessary to help the line off the reel in order to achieve the natural presentation (rather than a bait dragging through the water) that is the key to success with this technique, whether for blues, tuna or tarpon. Let the bait out a couple of hundred feet, and then repeat the drift. Once the fish start hitting at a particular point in the drift, you'll probably be able to duplicate those strikes for a period of time.

At times it pays to chunk up extra bunkers or mackerel and drift a few pieces back into the slick. In shallow waters it is possible to skip the chum and just spread bunker chunks around the boat. Baits can be free-spooled, or you can set chunks on bottom with fishfinder rigs.

Although chumming and chunking will usually bring blues up, there are occasions when they won't rise much off bottom. This situation calls for a heavy split shot or a small sinker. Over rough bottoms it often pays to drop to bottom and raise the bait up a couple of feet.

Light conventional tackle is best in this situation with 15- to 25-pound-test line preferred. Some anglers will go to spinning rods for casting a light bait, which allows for a slower drop.

JIGGING – Bluefish are normally aggressive fish and will frequently hit jigs even when there is no natural bait around. However, jigs are deadly when blues are actively feeding, particularly if sand eels are present in large quantities. During the 1980s there were so many sand eels that party and charter boats in New York Bight didn't even bother taking chum, as all they needed were diamond or banana jigs. When schools of blues are located, jigs are dropped to bottom and retrieved at high speed. Although in general jigging isn't quite as dependable as it was in the past, it is often the best bet in the daytime, when blues are feeding on large schools of bait. Bridgeport diamond jigs with treble hooks were the standard decades ago, until a famous party boat mate came up with a "better mouse trap." He

designed the Ava diamond jig, which featured a single hook on a swivel. The single hook worked just as well as the treble and was a lot safer to remove, while the swivel prevented blues from gaining leverage to twist it out. This rigging is now standard on many brands.

Since this time, the only basic improvement has been the addition of tube tails to diamond jigs. This has proven to be very effective for the tail-biting bluefish, as it keeps blues well away from the leader. Mono or fluorocarbon leaders should always be used, with 60-pound test being a good choice. If the blues are particularly large, go to 80- or 100-pound. Heavy leaders are also helpful in that they permit blues to be lifted aboard rather than gaffed, which avoids blood on the boat and is necessary for releasing them unharmed. In general, it is not advisable to net blues.

Medium-heavy baitcasting outfits are preferred for jigging and are spooled with 15- to 20-pound-test on large capacity reels. Spinning rods are often used as they are effective for the high-speed retrieves that blues prefer, but they are more likely to cause line twist when blues fight.

Night fishermen may want to try diamond jigs with a glow coating that can be charged with a light source. These jigs work quite well at night, when ordinary diamonds aren't usually effective. Leadhead jigs are also effective for blues, though most anglers prefer to throw something that is less easily destroyed. Blues tear up not only the bucktail or other dressing, but also the thread used to tie the material to a leadhead jig. Anglers will go through a lot of plastic shad bodies or other such jig dressings when blues are on.

When jigging, try running ahead of any fish that you read on the depth finder or see working before dropping your jig to the bottom. Remember that when fishing blues, there are usually many more fish underneath those you see on the surface. The only exception would be when deeper waters are cold at the beginning of the spring run. Then it's best to cast the jig away from the boat and retrieve it just under the surface, as most blues will be in the warmer surface waters.

TROLLING – Bluefish are easily trolled throughout the season. When they first arrive in the spring, the best technique is to slow-troll on the surface with small plugs or diamond jigs. Once the water column starts warming and they go deeper, wire line, downrigger or planer-board trolling becomes the best technique. Umbrella rigs fitted with tubes are particularly effective when trolled on wire line, especially when sand eels are present. Umbrella rigs with 6- to 8-inch plastic shad bodies have become very popular in recent years, but the blues' feeding habits make these rigs expensive to troll, as they bite off the action tails as well as tear up the body during the fight. When blues are marked at certain depths, simply adjust your lures accordingly and troll at a slow but steady pace of 2 to 3 knots.

Many other lures are effective for trolling. Small plugs such as the Bomber Long A, Gag's Grabbers Minnows and Yo-Zuri Crystal Minnows work well in early spring, when blues are on top. Larger plugs such as the MirrOlure 113MR and Rebel Jawbreakers pull blues up from the depths later in the year. A big problem with plugs, however, is getting thrashing blues off the hook without getting a hook in yourself. Bunker spoons (p. 15), although usually intended for big striped bass, are also a top choice for jumbo blues.

Wire line trollers prefer a 4/0 reel and a fairly heavy action 6½- foot rod with tungsten carbide or silicon carbide guides. Fifty to 100 yards of Monel or stainless wire in 40- or 50-pound-test is backed with dacron or mono. The exception to this set-up would be when using bunker spoons for jumbo blues. In this situation, anglers use specially designed rods from 8 to 11 feet in length with a flexible tip so they can see the action of the spoon.

CASTING – A variety of casting lures are effective on blues, and many anglers prefer popping plugs for spectacular surface strikes. Topwater poppers, such as the Yo-Zuri Surface Cruiser, Mega Bait and Cordell pencil popper are favorites. If blues are feeding on the surface, they often get stirred up even more by a popper, even if it doesn't resemble anything they're feeding on. Anglers who have had their fill of catching frenzied blues will take the hooks off a popper and enjoy the heart-stopping surface action without having to bother unhooking toothy blues. Blues will often pull the lure under and refuse to give it up for several seconds at times.

Long spinning rods are hard to beat for casting lures to bluefish. That's especially true with popping plugs, which are retrieved fast and require high gear ratio reels to work without tiring the angler. A 7- to 8-foot fairly stiff spinning rod with a softer tip for casting and a reel that will hold at least 200 yards of 15-pound monofilament makes a good outfit for plugs that run 1 to 2½ ounces.

LIVE BAIT – If there's one thing a bluefish can't resist it's a large, live bait. Menhaden (bunkers) and eels are like candy to them. However, anglers usually intend those baits for other species and try to avoid feeding them to choppers, which generally cut off the rear end and may not get anywhere near a hook. As a result, live eels are not practical for blues. Bunkers are only practical if they are rigged with both a wire leader and stinger hook, which will hook blues hitting from the tail.

FLY FISHING – Blues are suckers for a wide variety of flies, and it's rarely necessary to "match the hatch." Fly fishermen don't throw valuable flies at them, and will use a trace of wire in order to avoid a high level of bite-offs. Double-hooked flies are most effective for these tail-nippers, but blues are usually so abundant when located that missing a few bites is no big deal. A 9-weight outfit with a reel capable of holding at least 100 yards of backing will take care of most situations.

SURF CASTING – There are few experiences in fishing more thrilling than a bluefish blitz in the surf, as choppers often drive frenzied baitfish right up on the sand in their desperate attempt to get away. In this situation anglers cast all types of lures just a short distance from the wash, where it's usually difficult not to hook up. Although the action usually moves along the beach and should be followed, there are times when anglers can stand in one spot for hours and catch blues on almost every cast. Metal lures with single hooks such as the Hopkins and Acme Kastmaster are favored. Popping plugs can be great, except for the necessity of dealing with the treble hooks. Poppers are very effective for working the surf blind, since they frequently stir up single blues that are not actively feeding. Bait fishing will goad blues into biting even when they don't appear to be present. Finger mullet are a popular choice, but pieces of any oily fish (especially menhaden) will do the job.

Love 'em, or hate 'em, blues can provide great action wherever they are found.

—Al Ristori

# BONEFISH

The bonefish *(Albula vulpes)* inspires incredible devotion among those anglers lucky enough to have caught a few. Lots of people give up fishing for anything else after being afflicted with bonefish obsession, or at the very least bonefishing becomes their primary choice of angling pursuits.

Many years ago I was fishing in a sailfish tournament in Mexico and found myself in a buffet line next to the legendary boatbuilder John Rybovich. Our conversation naturally rolled around to fishing, and I was eager to hear tales of his travels because he had fished many of the world's finest offshore waters. But when I asked him his favorite species to pursue, he said without hesitation, "bonefish." He told me that of all the fishing he had

done, he enjoyed stalking a quiet flat for bonefish more than anything else.

Fast-forward a few years. I'm at a charity fund-raising auction in Palm Beach with a dentist buddy, an accomplished offshore angler in his own right. Bob Branham, the legendary south Florida bonefish guide, had donated a day of bonefishing to the auction, and my friend wanted to know if it was worth buying. I told him a day with Branham was one of the best he would ever spend on the water. He said he would buy the trip if I would accompany him. A free day of bonefishing? No problem.

We arrived at Crandon Park near Miami's Biscayne Bay on the morning of our trip, watching the tops of the palm trees sway in a steady 20-knot breeze under solidly overcast skies. My dentist friend was certain this was all a waste of time, but I told him to be patient. I had seen Branham pull off double-digit bonefish catches for his clients on days like this, and knew it could be done.

The first flat we stopped on was no larger than a quarter-acre, and the water was milky brown from several days of wind and rain. Branham grinned at our skeptical expressions and told my buddy to cast to a white spot that was barely visible ahead of the boat. He had tossed a handful of shrimp chunks into the spot moments before, and no sooner had our shrimp landed than we were both solidly hooked to a double header of 7-pounders! We caught eight that day, and my dentist buddy was hooked for life. Another bonefish convert!

It's not hard to understand why such conversions are commonplace. Fishing for bonefish combines all of the best aspects of hunting and fishing into a single experience. Bones swim in water so shallow you would swear their bellies must be aground, and most of the time the fishing is visual, taking place while polling across the flats in a skiff. Catching bones consistently means developing skills at stealth and stalking, and then there's casting. Supreme accuracy is the rule if you expect to consistently score with bonefish.

Those who are patient enough to develop these skills are rewarded with the unique thrill that only a hooked bonefish can provide. There is little else in fishing that compares to the initial run of a fleeing bone. It often seems impossible that a fish of this size (5- to 7-pound average) could swim so far so fast. Runs of over 100 yards are common on light tackle. Watching your line rip through the skinny water at high speed is enough to weaken the knees of even the most seasoned flats veteran. Indeed, the hunt itself often causes acute cases of marine "buck fever" among the less experienced, who, after finally hooking a fish, promptly break it off or get "spooled," unprepared for the initial run.

Bonefish nearing 10 pounds are considered big, and fish in the double digits are exceptional. The current world record for bonefish stands at 19 pounds, and was caught in the waters off South Africa in 1962.

The bonefish is a nervous sort, constantly on the move and aware of every little sound in its vicinity. This means that most of the time you must cast at a rapidly moving target. About the only time it slows down for very long is when it stops to bury its nose in the mud to root for crustaceans, its primary food. This *tailing* behavior can happen abruptly, and one of the truly exciting events on the flats occurs when several silvery tails suddenly rise from the surface in an area of water you would have sworn was barren of life only a few seconds before.

Bonefish possess extraordinary eyesight, and are voracious feeders, sometimes creating huge *muds* where a school roots en masse on a muddy bottom. The fish have an adipose eyelid that acts as a transparent cover so that they are not blinded when feeding face-down in clouds of mud. This works to the fisherman's advantage when casting to a tailing bone, as it is still able to clearly see things around itself even in milky water.

## Where to Find Bonefish

Bonefish are a decidedly tropical species, and south Florida is at the extreme northern end of their range. Bones can be found on tidal flats throughout the Florida Keys, the Bahamas, the Caribbean, and Central America, as well as around the world in the Pacific Ocean. They are truly a worldwide fish. How-

BONEFISH
▨ RANGE
■ PRIME FISHING

ever, just because an area has flats that look right doesn't mean you will necessarily find bonefish there. One of the trickiest parts of bonefishing is predicting where and when the fish will be on a given flat, or if they will be on a particular flat at all. Tidal flow, water depth, water temperature and availability of food all combine to make a flat attractive to bonefish.

In the Florida Keys, arguably the most popular bonefish spot in the world, the fish move around a lot depending upon the season. In the wintertime, large schools of bones may roam the oceanside flats, hugging the shorelines in search of a meal. Spring and fall bring what is perhaps the best bonefishing of the year, with water temperatures still cool enough so that the bones stay high on the flats. In mid summer, the fish work their way into slightly deeper water to escape the heat of the day, and bonefishing becomes an early-morning or late-afternoon affair.

Islamorada is generally considered the heart of Keys bonefishing, and has an incredible number of flats to choose from. The backcountry flats around Shell Key hold some of the biggest bonefish in the world. A number of world records have come from Islamorada, including quite a few fish over 15 pounds, and 12-pounders are taken with relative frequency. It should be noted that these fish that live in what the locals call "downtown" Islamorada waters are notoriously difficult to get to eat. It takes skill and patience to master catching these giants. Fortunately, Islamorada is home to some of the best flats guides to be found anywhere, and marinas like Bud-N-Mary's, Papa Joe's, Lorelei and Holiday Isle can steer you to a number of guides that can put you on big fish.

The lower Keys also offer outstanding action on the flats that surround Big Pine Key, including the waters of the Content Keys, and the bayside keys west towards Key West. Oceanside flats along the shore of Key Largo can offer great bonefishing too, when winds and weather cooperate. The flats near the Ocean Reef Club in northern Key Largo, at the southern end of Biscayne Bay, can hold huge schools of bones in the wintertime.

Biscayne Bay is at the extreme northern range of the bonefish, but this beautiful body of water that extends both north and south of downtown Miami may be one of the most overlooked destinations of all when a bonefish trip is planned. The flats south of Key Biscayne are home to surprising numbers of bonefish, and the average bone is around 7 pounds. The sheer amount of habitat available is staggering the first time you see it, and it always seems disconcerting to turn around and see the skyscrapers of Miami in the distance. It is amazing that such a pristine body of water (now a national park) exists in such an urban setting.

For anglers willing to travel outside the country to pursue bonefish, the islands of the Bahamas offer amazing fishing, and a number of bonefish camps exist there. The most famous of all bonefish flies, the "Crazy Charlie," was invented here by Bahamian guide Charlie Smith, who prowled the vast flats of the Bahamas in the early days of bonefishing.

BONEFISH FLIES come in a wide variety of colors and patterns, with the best ones imitating shrimp, crabs or small minnows.

## How to Catch Bonefish

Fishing equipment for bonefish usually consists of a 7-foot, fast-action spinning rod spooled with 8-pound-test line. The rod should be capable of casting a light bait like a shrimp a considerable distance, and the reel should hold at least 250 yards of line. A short section of double line is formed using a Bimini twist, and a 1/0 hook, often an Eagle Claw Bait Keeper, is tied to the end of the double line. A small split shot is pinched onto the double line about 12 inches above the hook to take the bait down.

A shrimp is the bait of choice, but small crabs, clams, or mollusks of any type will work, especially when the fish may not be too finicky, as is often the case in other countries. Bonefish have been caught on everything from hermit crabs to sliced conch chunks. If you prefer artificials, bonefish can often be convinced to take a light (⅛- or ¼-ounce) swimming jig hopped along the bottom with natural (shrimp or crab) colors preferred.

Many people fish for bonefish exclusively with fly rods, and bones are perhaps the perfect quarry to pursue with a fly. Fly fishing for bonefish is an extreme challenge, since you must present the fly accurately and work it just right to get them to take it. Long, tapered leaders are the norm to prevent the fish from spooking when they see the fly line, which is sometimes as long as 14 feet. It's a matter of opinion as to how to tie these leaders, but the most important factor is getting it to turn over. The leader must turn over during the cast,

allowing the fly to land as softly and as far from the fly line as possible, to consistently catch bonefish.

There seem to be as many bonefish flies as there are stars in the sky, and everybody has a favorite. Small hooks are the norm. Flies like the Gotcha and the Crazy Charlie resemble small crustaceans and are often a good choice to start with. Numerous shrimp imitations and epoxy head flies are also available. The best advice about flies is to check with several knowledgeable fishermen in the particular area you plan to fish and get their recommendations, as effective patterns tend to be very localized.

Seven- to nine-weight fly rods are most often chosen, as are floating lines to minimize the chances of the fly hanging in the bottom. You must learn to make long, accurate casts very quickly, as bonefish don't often give you a second chance. Accurate casts of 60 or 70 feet are often necessary, sometimes longer. To become truly proficient at catching bonefish on any kind of tackle you must practice, and it will often take years to become proficient at taking bonefish. This is not the type of fishing that can be mastered overnight.

Once you do get it down though, you will discover what people like my dentist friend have known for some time — there is nothing in fishing quite like poling quietly across very shallow water, searching for bonefish, then making a presentation that may or may not result in a hookup. It is fishing at its best, where practiced skill and luck combine to let you interact with one of the most fascinating creatures in the sea.

—*John Brownlee*

# PERMIT

The permit may represent the toughest challenge inshore fishermen face, for while it is frequently encountered on the flats, it is often a very frustrating fish to catch. This is especially true when fly fishing. Inshore fly rod catches of permit are so rare that even the most veteran fly caster can usually tell you precisely how many permit he has caught on a fly in his lifetime.

Permit *(Trachinotus falcatus)* grow to over 50 pounds. (The current all-tackle record is 56 pounds, 2 ounces.) They have large, powerful tails, and offer a truly exciting light-tackle opportunity. It's hard to forget the first time you hook a permit. Its initial run and powerful, dogged fight is reminiscent of other members of the jack family. The permit, however, is often considered the most beautiful and prized member of the jacks.

The shimmering silver sides of a permit often flash at you like a brilliant diamond as it approaches the boat. Other times you see nothing but a black streak from the tail or fins, usually after the fish has passed and is well out of casting range. Either way, an encounter with a permit on the flats is a breathtaking experience.

Although permit are distributed over a wide geographical range, they are primarily caught in a relatively limited number of places. In the U.S., the flats and reefs in southern Florida are where you

PERMIT
■ RANGE
■ PRIME FISHING

will find this highly-prized species. The Caribbean shorelines of Mexico, Belize, and Honduras, and the Bahamas are also top destinations for anglers targeting permit. While permit are found both inshore and offshore, permit purists scoff at catches made in deep water, instead reserving their admiration for shallow-water victories. In nearly all situations when fishing for permit, the main technique involves poling a skiff silently across the flats to get within casting range.

## Where to Find Permit

Like bonefish (p. 56), permit are a species that root around on the flats in search of small crabs, shrimp and other crustaceans hiding in the marl. Thus, crab or shrimp is the bait of choice. When using artificials the same applies, so crab and shrimp imitations work best. Because permit possess larger, "deeper" bodies than bonefish, they are often found in deeper water areas and on the edges of the flats rather than up on the flats. At times, however, permit work their way into surprisingly shallow water.

When searching for permit, most fishermen scan the surface for telltale wakes made by the tails and dorsal fins of the fish. Unlike bonefish, permit rarely leave "muds" where they are feeding, so wakes are often your first clue that permit are in the area. Because of the difficulty in catching permit, few flats fishermen specifically target them. They are most often encountered while fishermen search for bonefish, tarpon or other flats species.

The permit's tail is what most often alerts the flats fishermen to the fishes presence. Permit tip up on their noses to dig for food like other bottom-feeding flats residents do. Their tails have a unique look. Unlike bonefish tails, which tend to be a translucent silver color, permit tails have a black anterior margin that no other tailing flats fish possess. When you see a black glistening tail waving at you, break out a crab.

Many knowledgeable flats guides believe that permit prefer a hard or rocky bottom, the type of area where sea fans proliferate. However, permit are also encountered in channels between flats, on sand ridge flats and along beaches, so there exists no hard and fast rule about the types of bottom they like. There are some specific geographic areas where the fish are found with regularity, though.

The Florida Keys are at the top of any permit angler's list, with the lower Keys and Key West area as ground zero. Lower Keys areas including the Marquesas Keys, the Content Keys, Ramrod Key and the Barracuda Keys all consistently produce outstanding catches of permit. The best times to catch permit are in the fall months, from late summer until the winter cold fronts cool the water and drive the fish from the flats. Warming spring waters bring them back in great numbers. Most of these keys have plentiful hard bottoms and shallow mud flats combined with an ample supply of crustaceans, which makes for perfect permit habitat.

At certain times of the year, particularly in mid-summer, permit will "lay up" in deeper water just off the flats in areas where there's current, waiting for an unlucky crab or shrimp to float by. There they sit with their backs and fins out of the water, often near floating weeds. In this situation, unlike most other times, they tend to take baits readily. Many guides call this phenomenon "blooping," and it offers most anglers their best shot at catching a permit.

Permit are also found with regularity over different types of flats. Several areas of the Bahamas, for instance, offer world-class permit fishing over white sand or marl bottoms, a far cry from the darker habitat you generally expect to find in the Keys. The best advice is to cover a lot of water, try to determine what type of bottom the permit are keying on, and then look for similar areas.

## How to Catch Permit

Permit require no special tackle. Eight- to 12-pound-test spinning tackle is perfect for casting crabs, bearing in mind that lighter line throws easier than does heavier line. Permit have no teeth to worry about, so all that is needed in the way of terminal tackle is a couple of feet of double line, formed via a Bimini Twist, tied directly to the hook.

Most permit fishermen like a 2/0 or 3/0 hook, with the Eagle Claw or the 9174 Mustad live-bait hook perennial favorites. More people are using circle hooks for permit too, with the Owner 3/0 Mutu Light the hook of choice. Crabs should be small, about the size of a silver dollar, with the claws broken off. The crab is hooked though the shell to one side, just inside the point of the shell. Take care not to break the shell by trying to force the hook through. Instead, press the point of the hook against the underside of the shell, where it's generally softer, and work the point back and forth until it goes through. Also, the point of the crab's shell shouldn't extend out farther than the hook point. If it does, break off the tip of the shell with pliers.

When fishing with crabs for permit that are cruising, cast the crab upcurrent to a spot close enough that the fish can easily see it, but not close enough to spook it. You want to work the crab across the surface until the permit sees and pursues it, then stop reeling and let the crab sink. If the permit are tailing, you want to drop the crab as close as possible to a fish without hitting it. It is imperative to get the crab close so that the permit, which is feeding intently below, will see it. Countless opportunities to catch a permit have been lost because of an errant cast.

It is fly fishing for permit, however, that offers possibly the greatest challenge in inshore fishing. Very few people have caught permit on a fly, and with good reason. Barroom stories of flies perfectly presented and worked, yet refused, are commonplace, and if the truth be told, most people don't have the patience for fly fishing for permit. Most stick with the more reliable and cooperative bonefish.

It is safe to say that anglers targeting permit for the first time should go with a guide to get a

**Del Brown's Merkin**

**Nat Ragland's Puff**

feel for what what type of water and the bottom in which the fish can be found, and to learn the intricacies of how to present a bait to a permit. These are things that only years of experience on the water can teach, and learning them in several trips is often well worth the expense.

When fly fishing for permit, anglers usually opt for a 9-foot, 8- or 9-weight rod. A long, tapered leader with no shock tippet will work fine, unless you plan to fish a very light class tippet. In that case you would want to tie on a relatively light shock tippet. There are few permit flies that one can call reliable, but the two most famous are Nat Ragland's Puff and Del Brown's Merkin (above).

If you are lucky enough to actually hook a permit on any type of tackle, a hard hook-set isn't necessary. Simply raise the rod tip and the hook will embed itself as the fish takes off –and it will take off with blinding speed! Keep your rod tip raised high as the fish runs to ensure that the line stays at a high angle, away from the myriad of snags present on the flats. If the permit runs off into deeper water, you will need to lower the rod for additional leverage and move the boat toward the deeper water to avoid

obstructions that occur on the edges of the flat (below). You will also need to lower the rod as the permit nears the boat, as it will lay broadside to the boat and offer substantial resistance near the end of the fight.

Permit can be taken with a net prior to release, but most people "tail" permit by simply grabbing them just forward of the tail and lifting them out of the water. Bear in mind that you may have to let go once in a while because these are strong fish, and can sprain a wrist if they are still green when grabbed. Tail-landing is strongly recommended because landing nets invariably rub off a great deal of the permit's protective slime layer and do unnecessary damage to the fish.

Although some people say they're good to eat, nearly all permit are released. Also, the fact that permit school up offshore to spawn makes them vulnerable to overfishing. Permit are a hardy fish with excellent release survival rates, and as long as you handle them carefully and minimize their time out of the water, they should swim away fine. That way another angler just might experience that rare thrill of catching a permit.

*—John Brownlee*

**RIGHT**          **WRONG**

MOVE QUICKLY to position your boat off the edge of a flat when fighting a permit or other gamefish. There is often sharp coral on the edge of the flats that can break lines quickly once the fish reach deep water.

# SUMMER & SOUTHERN FLOUNDER

You sure wouldn't know it to look at them, but both summer flounder and southern flounder are aggressive predators, and have the teeth to prove it! Although flounder spend a good deal of their time buried in the sand, lying in wait for unsuspecting baitfish to wander within range, they aren't shy about chasing down a meal. They have even been known to take a lure on the surface.

Like all marine predators, both of these flatfish seek out areas that give them the biggest advantage over their prey. In the case of southern flounder, this means shallow depressions where current or wave action makes baitfish more vulnerable. Shallow, mud-bottomed pockets or "holes" near creek mouths, outflow pipes, drainage ditches and along grassy marsh banks are favorite haunts of flounder. These areas are especially good on an outgoing tide, when baitfish are being flushed from the flooded backwaters. Some of these spots can be quite shallow, perhaps less than 5 feet deep, making southern flounder ideal targets for small-boat, wade and shore fishermen.

Although some people take issue with the number of bones present, the meat on both species is white and firm, with a delicate flavor. This, along with the fact that both species are relatively abundant and easy to catch, makes them a favorite species along the East and Gulf Coasts.

SUMMER FLOUNDER
RANGE
PRIME FISHING

SOUTHERN FLOUNDER
RANGE
PRIME FISHING

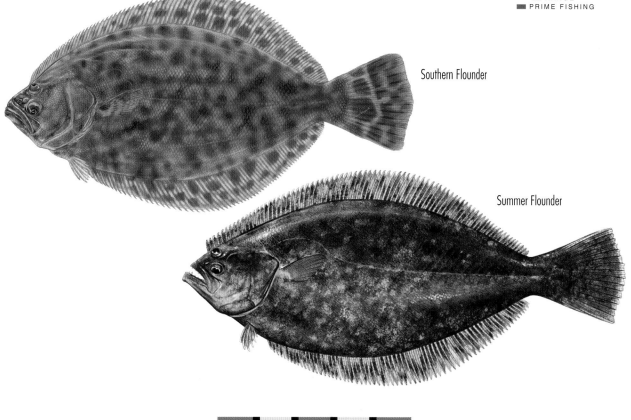

Southern Flounder

Summer Flounder

## Where to Find Flounder

Summer flounder *(Paralichthys dentatus)*, better known as "fluke" in the northern part of their range, inhabit areas of strong current. They range from North Carolina up through Massachusetts, and can weigh up to 20 pounds (the world record is 22 pounds, 7 ounces). An immensely popular recreational species in the Mid-Atlantic and Northeast, summer flounder are making a comeback along many parts of the coast, largely due to wise management measures that have reduced overfishing.

Unlike southern flounder, which can be caught year-round, fluke are only seasonally available to inshore anglers. They move into shallow areas in spring and fall, but in midsummer and winter retreat to much deeper waters (40 feet plus), where they can be hard to locate. In May and June (prime time along much of the coast), good-sized summer flounder can be caught in less than 10 feet of water over sand, or mud bottomed areas washed by strong current. Areas around river and creek mouths are prime spots to check early in the season.

Structure is another key ingredient for locating flounder. Any place a smooth bottom abuts some rocks, dock pilings, bridge abutments, a jetty or a sunken wreck is a great spot to fish for fluke. In open water bays, sandy pockets surrounded by eelgrass also hold fluke, with current making such spots even better.

As is the case with southern flounder, beach areas are also favorite haunts of summer flounder. This is especially true in the early season, when flounder gather close to shore to feed on baitfish caught in the surf, making them easy targets for surfcasters. Look for them on the edge of sandbars and in troughs between bars.

As waters warm in July, the biggest fluke move to progressively deeper zones, sometimes taking up station on steep drop-offs and ledges in 40 to 60 feet of water, where they can be difficult to catch. Anglers who want to try for fluke at this time of year should concentrate on the edges of rocky, deep-water structure. Come September, flounder often gang up inshore again before departing deeper water with the onset of winter.

Southern flounder *(Paralichthys lethostigma)*, whose range extends from Virginia down through Florida and along the Gulf Coast to Texas, also hold near shallow inshore structure such as oyster rocks and bars, grass beds, artificial reefs, sunken wrecks, channel markers, bridge abutments, jetties, rocky riprap and dock pilings. Since baitfish also collect in these spots, look for the flounder to take up position on the down-current edge of the submerged structure, waiting for bait to be swept past.

Along the Gulf Coast, southern flounder can be caught along exposed beach fronts. Here, they take up station on the edge of sandbars or holes, picking off bait tumbled about in the surf. Oil and gas drilling rigs in shallow, open bays are other good places to find flounder. As in most situations, the fish typically hold on the down-current side of the rig pilings. As the current increases, they position themselves farther down-current of the structure, and vice versa.

## How to Catch Flounder

Both southern flounder and summer flounder can be taken on a wide variety of baits and lures. Small (⅛- to ½-ounce) bucktail jigs are extremely popular in southern waters. A variety of soft-plastic baits such as shad bodies, paddle tails, and curl-tail grubs rigged on similar-sized jigheads also produce. Popular colors include chartreuse, yellow, hot-pink, white and green with a red tail. Some anglers "sweeten" their jigs by adding a piece of shrimp or squid to their jig hooks.

Jigs should be cast out and hopped back over the bottom. Work the jig through deep holes and along the edge of drop-offs. You can also drift over a likely holding area while bouncing the jig over the bottom straight below the boat. In either case, the key is to keep your jig on the bottom.

For big flounder, nothing beats natural bait. Finger mullet, pilchards, pinfish, shrimp and mud minnows, fished live or dead, all make excellent flounder baits. Simply cast them out on a standard fishfinder rig or three-way bottom rig and let them swim around or sit on the bottom until a big flounder homes in on the scent. When you feel a pickup, give the fish plenty of time to scale and swallow the bait (some anglers wait as long as two minutes) before setting the hook.

Natural bait also takes its share of summer flounder, favoring the larger ones just as with southern flounder. Favorite offerings here include sand eels, live killifish (mummichogs), silversides,

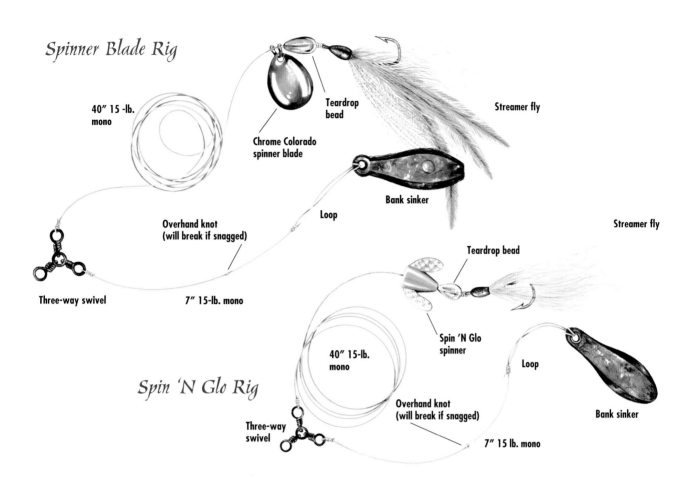

**Spinner Blade Rig**

40" 15 -lb. mono

Teardrop bead

Streamer fly

Chrome Colorado spinner blade

Bank sinker

Streamer fly

Overhand knot (will break if snagged)

Loop

Teardrop bead

Three-way swivel

7" 15-lb. mono

Spin 'N Glo spinner

**Spin 'N Glo Rig**

40" 15-lb. mono

Loop

Bank sinker

Three-way swivel

Overhand knot (will break if snagged)

7" 15 lb. mono

seaworms and squid. Small, live bluefish in the 6-inch range also make outstanding baits, and seem to target really big fluke. Live baits should be fished on a three-way swivel rig, a sliding egg-sinker rig, or a fishfinder rig. Some anglers do well by impaling their live or dead bait on a large bucktail jig to give it scent and hop it over the bottom.

Natural baits can also be fished on two-hook spreader rigs or high-low (dropper-loop) rigs. Often, a combination of baits or lures is used on these multi-hook rigs in order to determine the fish's preference. Spinner-blade and Spin 'N Glo rigs are also very effective, as flounder are attracted by the action and flash of the lure (above).

Summer flounder can also be taken on a variety of artificial lures, including bucktail jigs in the ½- to 3-ounce range; soft-plastic grubs, shads and soft jerkbaits and diamond jigs, small metal spoons and plastic squids. As is done when fishing for southern flounder, these lures are often rigged with

a squid strip, sand eel or section of fluke belly for added scent and taste.

The standard method for fluke fishing is to drift along a drop-off or channel edge, or over a series of sandbars or holes until the fish are located. As you drift, hop the rig lightly over the bottom. If using natural bait, allow the fish several seconds to swallow the bait before setting the hook. With artificial lures, set the hook as soon as you feel a tap. If you miss the fish, immediately free-spool your bait back to the bottom.

When you do hook up, mark the spot and repeat your drift, as fluke often gang up in the same area. Anchoring can also be effective once a concentration of fish has been located. At times a matter of 10 feet can make the big difference between success and coming up empty. Again, the most important thing to remember is to keep your bait or lure on the bottom and keep moving until fish are located.

—Tom Richardson

# Winter Flounder

Unlike its cousins the summer flounder and halibut, the winter flounder (*Pseudopleuronectes americanus*) is more of a scavenger. It lacks sharp teeth, and is therefore unequipped to prey on baitfish. Instead, winter flounder are content to lie on the bottom, waiting to suck in seaworms, grass shrimp and bits of vegetation and detritus with its small mouth. Despite its sedate manner, it remains a popular recreational target among Northeastern anglers, and is one of the first available inshore species to herald the arrival of a new season.

their eggs, could be responsible for low levels of abundance in certain locales where these fish were once numerous.

## Where to Find Winter Flounder

True to their name, winter flounder prefer cooler water than summer or southern flounder (p. 65). From fall through spring they take up residence in shallow, mud-bottomed areas that are perfect for the small-boat angler. Prime time to catch them is just after the spawn, which occurs at different times along the coast and is dependent on location and water temperature. In New Jersey and New York, blackbacks can be caught as early as late February, while the bite north of Cape Cod usually doesn't start until April.

The range of this mild-mannered flatfish extends roughly from North Carolina north through Maine. Normal size runs 1 to 4 pounds, with a 6-pounder being considered a real trophy.

Winter flounder, also known as "blackbacks," make delicious table fare and are highly prized as a food fish. Some areas, such as Dorchester and Quincy Bays in Massachusetts, winter flounder once drew anglers from as far away as New York. These flounder aficionados would make pilgrimages by the busload to fill their coolers with the tasty flatfish.

Sadly, pollution and commercial overfishing depleted stocks throughout most of their range, although they are showing signs of recovering in some areas. It is also thought that powerplant cooling intakes, which suck in juvenile flounder and

WINTER FLOUNDER
■ RANGE
■ PRIME FISHING

The fish feed most aggressively just after the spring spawn, for a period of several weeks. After they spawn, as the waters warm into summer, they move to deeper zones, then return to the shallows in late autumn. In the cooler waters north of Cape Cod, flounder often feed well in moderately shallow (20 to 30 feet deep) areas through the season. Prime areas to seek out these fish include mud-bottomed coves, bays, estuaries and salt water ponds in 6 to 15 feet of water. In the early season, when waters are coolest, pick a warm, sunny day with a high tide occurring around noon. As the tide begins to ebb and the sun-warmed water flows off the flooded shallows, flounder take up station in areas where the current will bring food to them. Prime spots include the entrances to coves and ponds, channel edges, mud flats, the edges of mussel bars, "narrows" between points of land and shallow bottom depressions. When searching for flounder, give each spot at least 15 minutes to produce before moving to another locale.

## How to Catch Winter Flounder

While you can catch winter flounder by slow-drifting through an area, anchoring is the preferred method. The key is to anchor just up-current of, or directly above, a known "flounder hole" and set baits on the bottom. It often helps to "walk" rigs back with the current by intermittently lifting the rod and free-spooling line. If the rig isn't right on the bottom, you will not catch blackbacks.

Like most species of fish, winter flounder respond well to chum. Experts employ the use of a small, wire-mesh chum pot or onion bag, which they load with mussels, cat food, tuna or some other type of odor-filled, oily bait and lower it to the bottom directly below the boat. The idea is for the current to carry the scent of the chum back to the fish, which then follow it to the hooked baits. Some anglers even go so far as to rig a miniature chum pot made from a perforated film canister above their hook (right). Another trick is to scatter pellets of gerbil or hamster food or canned corn kernels about the general area as an attractant.

Favored flounder baits include small pieces of seaworm, mussels and clams. Curing mussels and clams helps to toughen them and keep them from falling off the hook too easily. In a pinch, night crawlers work as flounder baits, although they tend to bleach out quickly in salt water. For some reason, winter flounder seem to be attracted to the color yellow, so most flounder fishermen rig a small yellow bead ahead of their hooks. Others even go so far as to dye their mussel and clam baits with yellow food coloring.

Although fishing for winter flounder is not rocket science, it does require a fair amount of skill to locate the fish and detect their subtle bites. The standard flounder rig consists of two long-shank flounder-style hooks rigged on a spreader or a high-low dropper-loop rig. Sinkers should be as light as possible so that bites can be detected more easily. Increase the weight of the sinker as the current and depth increase, and vice-versa.

Light spinning or baitcasting gear in the 6- to 12-pound range is sufficient for handling these fish. Rods should be in the 6½- to 7-foot range and have a very sensitive tip to detect the flounder's subtle bites. Low-stretch superlines may provide an edge in detecting bites because of its greater sensitivity and small diameter, which creates less of a belly in the current.

A sensitive touch is needed in this game. If you feel a flounder nibbling at the bait, give it a few seconds to eat before setting the hook with a swift upward flick of the wrist.

—*Tom Richardson*

### Chum Pot Rig

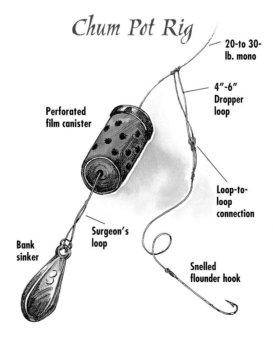

20-to 30-lb. mono

4"-6" Dropper loop

Perforated film canister

Loop-to-loop connection

Surgeon's loop

Bank sinker

Snelled flounder hook

# SHARKS

LEMON SHARKS are a common inshore species.

Of all the species available to the inshore fisherman, it would be hard to name one that you can count on seeing with more regularity than the shark. Sharks of one species or another inhabit virtually every body of salt water that exists, but many people overlook them as a prime source of angling adventure. That's too bad, because sharks can provide outstanding light-tackle action – a fact that a growing number of fishermen are beginning to appreciate. And while it used to be that almost every shark caught was killed (the "only good shark is a dead shark" mentality), sharks are now released most of the time.

People used to fear sharks mainly because of ignorance and terrifying tales of attacks on helpless swimmers –tales that were passed down from generation to generation and were surely exaggerated. It therefore became a sort of moral imperative among some fishermen to rid the world of these evil fish.

Over the years our knowledge about sharks has increased dramatically. Starting with the early television shows featuring Jacques Cousteau, sharks have been demystified to the point where people now are fascinated by them rather than fearful of them. So much so, in fact, that shark dives, in which swarming sharks are fed amidst a throng of excited scuba divers, have become a very popular tourist excursion. People now seem to have developed an insatiable curiosity about sharks and a desire to interact with them.

Also increasing are the number of people who prefer interacting with sharks at the end of a fishing line. Fortunately, that's pretty easy to arrange, as sharks, which have historically been an incidental inshore catch, have become a primary target. Inshore guides that used to fish for sharks only as a last resort – a day-saver if you will – have focused on sharks as a directed fishing opportunity.

Sharks offer a lot to those who pursue them. They will eagerly take both natural bait and artificial lures, they can be sight-fished in many instances, and they get big and sometimes offer a tremendous fight. Not all sharks offer the same amount of pull on the end of the line, though. For instance, the ubiquitous nurse shark – arguably the most common inshore shark – isn't much of a fighter and is rarely targeted as a primary species. Yet for a younger angler a big nurse shark can offer a thrill (right). Most nurse sharks, however, end up on the line of anglers fishing for something else.

Nurse Shark

Most anglers first encounter a shark by accident, often when they have already hooked another fish species and the shark makes a meal of it. Once, in the Bahamas, I was fishing for yellowtail snapper over a large coral head. My son was only about six at the time and was delighted with the swarm of yellowtail swimming in the chum cloud under the boat. He hooked a particularly fat one on his 8-pound-test spinning gear and was working it towards the boat when a barracuda of around 15 pounds appeared from nowhere and engulfed the doomed snapper. But before anyone even had a chance to speak, a 100-pound Caribbean reef shark charged from underneath the boat and ate the barracuda! My son had gone from a 2-pound snapper to a 100-pound shark in a matter of about three seconds, and when the shark took off, the line came off my wide-eyed boy's reel at an alarming rate. It was a very short fight as he had no leader, but quite exciting nonetheless and an excellent demonstration of the food chain in action.

## Common Inshore Shark Species

The following are some of the most common inshore shark species available and methods for catching them. Although you may encounter a number of other shark species, the methods for catching them are pretty much the same wherever sharks are found. Most of these methods can be applied in a wide range of shark fishing situations.

The smaller sharks you might hope to encounter on flats, for example, are prime targets for light tackle. These include bonnethead, small blacktips and small lemon sharks. They are most often found on shallow flats, cruising for a meal by swimming on or near the surface where they leave a telltale wake, often showing their dorsal fin. Such a situation can be sight fishing at its best, not unlike fishing for bonefish or permit.

The bonnethead shark (below) is the smallest of the hammerhead sharks, which are common on the flats of the Florida Keys, and are widely distributed throughout the western Atlantic Ocean. Bonnetheads feed primarily on invertebrates, including crabs, shrimp and snails. People fishing for bonefish often mistake an approaching bonnethead for a bonefish because of its small size. However, when bonefish activity is slow a bonnethead can take up the slack in action. Because bonnetheads tend to

Bonnethead Shark

eat what bonefish eat, casting a shrimp or crab will usually bring on a strike. Eight-pound test-line is perfect for the average bonnethead and they are a lot of fun on 8- or 9-weight fly fishing gear. Small streamers also work well, as do most of the crustacean imitations that are used for taking permit and bonefish.

Because of their impressive dentition, fishing for all species of sharks involves the use of a wire leader. It is not just the shark's teeth that offer a sharp, line-cutting obstacle, but also the skin, which is very rough –much like sandpaper – and can chafe through monofilament line in a hurry. Even if you hook a shark on mono leader material with the hook placed cleanly in the corner of its mouth, the line will often rub against the skin, causing it to break.

Blacktip sharks (right) are also commonly encountered on the flats, but these sharks are often considerably larger than bonnetheads. Although they are generally not considered dangerous to man, more than one flats fisherman has felt a bit uneasy when wading in the vicinity of a large blacktip. Blacktips are known for quirky, sudden movements when hooked and are truly a thrill on light tackle. Tackle for catching blacktips consists of medium-heavy action spinning or casting gear to hold lines from 12- to 20-pound-test, or 9- to 12-weight fly rods.

Blacktips will respond to most types of artificial baits and enthusiastically pursue live baits. One of the most effective and fun ways to catch them is on topwater

Blacktip Shark

plugs. On a recent trip to the Chandeleur Islands off the coast of Louisiana, we encountered numerous blacktips in the 60- to 80-pound range. As is their normal habit, they were cruising just beneath the surface leaving a noticeable wake that was visible for some distance. We would pole the skiff to within casting distance and cast a MirrOLure 84MR Top Dog surface lure in front of the cruising shark. By walking the plug across the surface we could entice a strike every time. As soon as the shark spotted the plug it would immediately attack with a violent roll on the lure. Like many sharks, the blacktips would streak off in the shallow water, proving the conviction of many inshore fishermen that sight fishing for sharks can offer one of the biggest thrills on the flats.

If you prefer fly fishing, popping flies work well to get a shark's attention, and any type of large streamer works well. With

CUDA FILLETS work well for attracting lemon sharks.

streamers it's simply a matter of getting the fly down to the level of the shark so he can see it, and then working it rapidly so the fish will strike. Since blacktips are generally eager to feed they may attack a fly as soon as they see it regardless of how you are working it, but a steady quick retrieve is probably the best choice. Flies with solid eyes, which help them sink, are a good idea if you are fishing in water deeper than a foot or two.

For those anglers who want to tangle with a large shark in shallow water it's hard to beat lemon sharks. Lemon sharks (Photo p. 70) are a commonly-found inshore species that range from New Jersey to Brazil and can reach lengths of up to eleven feet. While fishermen soaking bait on bottom catch them on a regular basis, guides in Key West, Florida, have developed a specialized method of taking lemons on fly. A big lemon on a fly rod is an incredible experience. Following this technique to attract lemons will also work with conventional tackle.

Start by catching several small barracuda on the flats and cutting the fillets off each side of the fish but not removing the meat (below). Put the cuda overboard on a rope as chum and allow the boat to drift with the wind over the flat, usually in 3 to 5 feet of water. The scent of a cuda fillet attracts lemons in no time, and it's not uncommon to have several appear at once. They will often swim right to the boat, making the presentation of the fly, lure or bait a cinch. Large streamer flies are the norm, the same type of fly you might throw at a sailfish or tuna offshore. If it resembles a half of a chicken, as the old saying goes, it is probably all right. Stout, 12-weight fly rods are the gear of choice.

Bull Shark

Bull sharks (above) are very common and provide a lot of pull, even on heavy tackle, due to their sheer size. Although they don't get as big as some of their relatives, such as the tiger shark, bull sharks are stocky, powerful fish and have been known to attack humans. They are especially dangerous to anglers wading in murky water. Soaking dead baits in areas known to produce bulls is the best method for catching them.

I was once wade-fishing with a friend on the western shore of Tampa Bay, and the snook were feeding like crazy. He had his two-fish limit on a stringer trailing behind him in the waist-deep water, and suddenly felt a strong tug on the stringer line. Alarmed that one of the fish was escaping, he wheeled around and tugged back, only to find himself face to face with a 200-pound bull shark! He escaped injury, but the shark had a fine snook dinner that afternoon.

Tackle for shark fishing varies considerably depending upon the species you're targeting. Small species like bonnethead sharks are tremendous fun on small spinning tackle or fly rods, while large bull sharks or lemon sharks require rods and reels more stout in nature. The best bet is to match the tackle to the size fish most commonly caught in the area you are going to fish. You will always need a length of metallic leader to guard against cutoffs. Single-strand stainless leader wire works fine, but Steelon braided wire is best because it is flexible. A flexible single-strand wire from Malin called Boa Wire offers the thin diameter of conventional stainless wire with the flexibility of a braid, and you can even tie knots in it.

Many different species of shark can be caught inshore where the waters are murky by soaking bait on the bottom. Some very large sharks are caught this way in surprisingly shallow water, including bull and spinner sharks or species such as sixgill and sevengill sharks on the West Coast. In bays and estuaries, look for creek mouths and moving water or concentrations of baitfish. A dead bait soaked in one of these spots will usually produce quickly if sharks are in the vicinity.

As you would expect, anglers should use extreme caution when landing sharks. Unless you have experience handling them, cutting the leader as close to the hook as is safe and releasing them is the best option. Losing a finger or worse is not worth the 50-cent hook you are trying to retrieve. Sharks can be extremely violent when brought on board and can bite in a split second. Gloves are a must for gripping the sharks' raspy skin and for handling the leader while trying to cut them free.

There are many shark species found around the U.S. coastline that are not mentioned here, but by remembering a few shark-fishing basics you can add a new dimension to your inshore fishing. By experimenting with different combinations of metallic leader material, baits and tackle and by trying areas where it seems likely sharks would be, you too can experience the excitement of catching sharks – on purpose!

—*John Brownlee*

# COBIA

Cobia can be caught year-round along many eastern and Gulf Coast states and can be taken many different ways by anglers fishing from boats, piers or even beaches. Moreover, cobia are big, strong and tough, as well as a superb-tasting table fish.

Cobia have a large, broad head and a wide mouth with eyes placed far to the sides. They are usually chocolate brown to almost black along the back, sides and head. (Some light-colored fish have noticeable dark lateral bands along the flanks.) The belly varies from a dirty gray to almost snow white.

The cobia *(Rachycentron canadum)* is a unique fish in that fisheries biologists have set it in a scientific family by itself, Rachycentridae. In many coastal areas the large size of cobia, their shape and their slow-swimming attitude often cause people to mistake them for sharks. They are also frequently seen in small schools or *pods* that swim just below the surface in many of the same areas that sharks inhabit. Unlike sharks, cobia have no large teeth. Instead, they have fine ones much like striped bass do.

Cobia are known by a multitude of different names such as lemon fish, ling, cobio, cobra, crabeater, flat-head, black salmon, sergeant fish, black runner and black kingfish.

## Where to Find Cobia

Spring runs of cobia are noteworthy. The fish migrate from south to north along the southeastern U.S., with prime fishing beginning in the Florida Keys in February. As the cobia run progresses up the Atlantic Coast (following the warming weather and water temperatures), angling action increases at different locales along the coast.

Cobia have an affinity for objects that cast a shadow, and a two-ton manta ray throws a massive shadow. Further, as mantas swim, their large wings churn up bottom sediment, which disorients baitfish, crabs and other forage on which cobia feed. Thus, spring-run cobia are commonly found with migrating manta rays. Cobia also can be found swimming with bat rays, stingrays and even turtles near the surface. It's also common to find cobia holding around channel markers, buoys, oil platforms and anchored ships.

The Gulf Coast "run" is well documented, too. Peak inshore fishing occurs at varying times throughout the spring (below) with April and May being tops. Farther up the coast cobia are found around near-shore oil rigs in water just 20 feet deep, off the coast of Louisiana in June.

Cobia are found world-wide in warm to tropical waters. They're common along the East Coast of the United States from Chesapeake Bay to Florida, and along the entire Gulf of Mexico coast. Cobia average 15 to 30 pounds, although 50-pounders are common. The largest cobia caught in U.S. waters and recognized by the IGFA, is a 128-pound, 12-ounce giant taken off Pensacola Beach, Florida, in April 1995. The IGFA all-tackle cobia weighed an incredible 135-pounds, 9-ounces, caught from Shark Bay, Western Australia, in July 1985.

COBIA
RANGE
PRIME FISHING

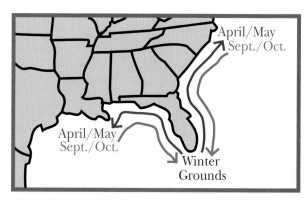

COBIA MIGRATION ROUTES

April/May
Sept./Oct.

April/May
Sept./Oct.

Winter
Grounds

Throughout their range cobia can be found offshore near wrecks, reefs and natural ledges where water temperatures remain warm through winter months. Cobia also frequent such locations when near-shore water temperatures drop. So while there are south-to-north migrations of cobia near-shore in spring, there also may be some offshore-to-inshore movement as well.

During spring runs cobia often cruise along beaches, where anglers casting from small boats, piers, jetties, breakwalls and even on the beach itself catch them. In areas such as South Carolina's Port Royal Sound, big cobia commonly move several miles inshore from the open ocean with moving tides. This movement makes the fish available to anglers fishing from small skiffs and jon boats, and at times to bridge and dock fishermen.

After the spring run of cobia has finished, huge cobia are caught sporadically around inlets, sounds and river mouths, and over near-shore reefs and ledges. However, the best summer and early fall fishing for cobia is found around open water ledges, wrecks and oil rigs, sometimes far offshore.

## How to Catch Cobia

Tackle for cobia can run the gamut from large surf-fishing outfits to medium-light baitcasting and spinning combinations to boat tackle used for trolling to heavy fly rods. Because cobia size can vary from 10 pounds to 100 pounds, tackle used to catch them can range from light to heavy. Line sizes from 12- to 50-pound test are used depending on the situation. For cobia hugging tight to channel markers and oil rigs, anglers use heavy line and stout rods to "horse" the fish from line-abrading obstructions. Cobia on reefs and those that migrate with manta rays require similar heavy tackle. But when cobia are found in open water, with no line-cutting problems at hand, lighter tackle can be employed.

Heavy monofilament leaders (50- to 100-pound test) are better than wire, since wire spooks fish, prevents good lure and bait motion and is not needed, as a cobia's teeth are neither large nor sharp.

A HUGE COBIA taken off the Florida coast.

Many varieties of lures score for cobia, including surface chuggers, darters, big crankbaits, swimming plugs, spoons and jigs. Fly-rod fishermen use streamers and bugs, which readily take fish. Cobia are also suckers for live baits, especially eels, so large, black plastic worms (6 to 12 inches) made for largemouth bass fishing are deadly as they perfectly imitate eels.

Cobia are becoming more popular with each passing year and should be on the "must try" list for all inshore anglers.

—*Bob McNally*

# GREAT BARRACUDA

A SURE SIGN a cuda is in the area (inset) is a clean cut just behind a fish's head as you reel it in. Anglers wanting to catch barracuda should have a rod rigged with a leader and should cast the area after getting "chomped."

The great barracuda (*Sphyraena barracuda*) could be the Rodney Dangerfield of inshore fish; it just gets no respect. Dismissed as a nuisance for their habit of attacking hooked fish that you actually want to land and cleanly separating head from body just behind the hook, cuda are nevertheless being pursued as a target species by an increasing number of inshore fishermen.

It's easy to see why more people are targeting this species, as barracuda are plentiful in inshore waters from the Carolinas south through Florida, and around the Gulf Coast as well as the east coast of Mexico. Indeed, barracuda thrive in tropical salt water environments around the world, making them accessible to a great many people.

Scientists believe that around 20 species of sphyraenids exists around the world; three of these are most often encountered by inshore fishermen.

GREAT BARRACUDA
▨ RANGE
■ PRIME FISHING

These are the great barracuda, the sennets (northern and southern) and the Pacific barracuda (p. 122). The ranges of these three fish overlap somewhat, meaning cudas can be encountered in

one form or another from Brazil to New England at certain times of the year.

The great barracuda is the largest of the species, running 5 to 15 pounds, but much larger fish are often seen and caught. The world record is 85 pounds.

I once converted a dedicated largemouth bass fisherman to salt water after taking him to a shallow-water wreck and encouraging him to cast an artificial lure over it. After a few lackluster retrieves I urged him to reel the lure in as fast as possible the next time. He didn't believe anything existed at this particular spot, but to humor me he began a rapid retrieve on the next cast. Ten feet from the boat a 30-pound cuda skyrocketed from the water, crashing down on the lure from 10 feet up in the air. My speechless friend caught and released that monster and never looked at a fresh water bass the same way again.

## Where to Find Barracuda

Barracuda live on flats, in channels and around structure in almost every type of inshore environment. Those who have come to appreciate the cuda as a gamefish are well aware of the difficulties and rewards involved with catching them. Cuda, especially great barracuda, are known for spectacular jumps when hooked, and their strike is both violent and exciting.

Fishing for barracuda is usually an opportunistic affair. You do, however, need to be ready when you come across them. The Florida Keys is perhaps the best place to target inshore barracuda, as the fish tend to aggregate on the flats in the winter months, making them easy to spot. Cuda are often mistaken for bonefish by novice flats fishermen, but whereas bonefish are almost always moving, cuda tend to rest motionless for long periods of time. Because of this propensity to lie still they are easy to cast to, but getting them to eat is another matter.

## How to Catch Barracuda

Barracuda eat a wide variety of smaller fishes including puffers, pinfish, sardines and small jacks, and these all work well as live baits. But the needlefish may be the cuda's favorite menu item, and has given rise to the ubiquitous tube lure as the artificial of choice. Tube lures (right) imitate the action of a needlefish and are made from lengths of surgical tubing rigged with two or more hooks.

Most knowledgeable cuda fishermen prefer bright colors for their tubing, usually red, fluorescent green or yellow, but some traditionalists still prefer a neutral tone. The tube lures sold commercially are usually about 12 inches long, but some anglers prefer much longer tubes of up to 3 feet.

To make your own tube lure simply buy a length of tubing and cut one end diagonally, then run lengths of stout wire (#7 or larger) through the tubing, rigging one 6/0 hook at the diagonally-cut end. The other hook is rigged about halfway up in a notch cut into the side of the tube. You can use either treble or single hooks. (Singles are much easier to remove from fish.) The wire from both hooks is then attached to a large barrel swivel.

Tube lures work best when curved, so if the tubing you buy has a natural curve to it, don't try to straighten it out. And store your tube lures rolled up. The erratic action this provides drives barracuda nuts. Cast a tube lure to a sighted fish or into a known cuda hangout and retrieve it along the surface as fast as you can reel. If there's a hungry cuda around, chances are it will find the tube irresistible.

Other lures work well too, including shiny plugs, spoons and flies. Cudas are attracted to shiny objects (hence the oft-repeated warning against swimming with them while wearing shiny jewelry), so silver spoons or silver-sided topwater plugs often elicit strikes. Long streamer flies resembling needlefish or ballyhoo, cast far and retrieved fast, can provide exciting fly-rod action. Some type of wire leader is a must, and braided wire works well for casting lures or flies due to its flexibility.

Live bait also should be presented on wire leaders, but barracuda are notoriously fickle about taking live baits with hooks in them.

There are also times when barracuda will refuse any and all offerings, and will follow artificials in a pack but still not take. As a rule, as you approach a cuda or likely cuda area, it is on the first few casts that most of the action will occur. Long casts are better because once the cuda see the boat, their attitude often changes for the worse.

Barracuda are surprisingly good to eat when prepared properly despite the foul stench they emit when handled. However, they should probably be released due to the possibility of ciguatera poisoning. Ciguatera is a sometimes-deadly nerve poison that is passed when a person eats a fish that contains the toxin. When handling and releasing a barracuda, always be wary of its teeth, hold the fish firmly behind the head and use a glove and pliers to remove the hook. Never try to remove a hook with your fingers, as a cuda can remove one in short order.

With its fast initial run and spectacular leaps, the barracuda is truly a worthy gamefish. It's also easily found in a wide variety of locations. Cuda can offer lots of inshore-fishing excitement on light tackle and are deserving of our respect.

—*John Brownlee*

# ATLANTIC BONITO & LITTLE TUNNY

Atlantic bonito and little tunny (the latter often referred to as false albacore or "albies") are each small members of the tuna family. Both species are found off Florida and the Gulf Coast states year-round, and migrate north along the East Coast each summer, when bait concentrations and water temperatures are at their peak. The northern boundary of their range is Cape Cod, Massachusetts. Because of their similar migration patterns and feeding characteristics, the two species are often written about and sometimes caught together.

**ATLANTIC BONITO & LITTLE TUNNY**
▓ RANGE
■ PRIME FISHING

Atlantic bonito (*Sarda sarda*) are somewhat sleeker and more torpedo-shaped than little tunny, and can be distinguished by the thin, horizontal stripes that run along their upper flanks and by

their set of widely spaced teeth. They also have dark vertical bars along the sides which fade almost immediately when the fish is landed. Little tunny (*Euthynnus alletteratus*), on the other hand, have no real teeth to speak of, and their bodies are rounder than that of a bonito. They weigh up to 20 pounds, and are easily identified by the wavy markings along the top of their back and by the three black "thumbprints" on either side of their belly. Another major difference between the two species: bonito are delicious eating, while albies are not and are often released.

## Where to Find Bonito & Little Tunny

Anglers that spend any amount of time on the water have more than likely run across a school of bonito or tunny at some point. Both are schooling fish, and are often seen on the surface as they make

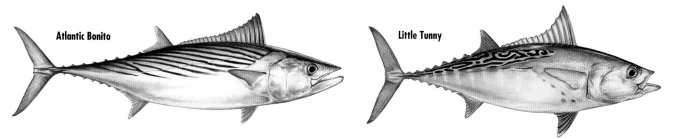

Atlantic Bonito

Little Tunny

slashing attacks through schools of tightly packed baitfish. They are keen-eyed and super-selective and tend to move rapidly from one spot to another, so anglers must fire off quick casts when in pursuit.

In the southern portion of their range, from North Carolina down through Florida and along the Gulf Coast, bonito and albies are often found around anchored shrimp boats. Here they feed on the bycatch of small fish and crustaceans tossed overboard. In this situation the fish can be extremely easy to catch. Simply hook a dead baitfish or bait chunk and free-line it behind the shrimp boat. A similar situation can be set up with a chum line to get the fish feeding behind your boat.

Other likely spots to find these fish throughout their range include inlets, points, jetties, rips, sandbars, banks and beachfront drop-offs. The key is to find a place that holds an abundance of baitfish, particularly baitfish influenced by current or wave action. Inlets are therefore especially good places to look for bonito and tunny, which gather near the mouth to feed on baitfish being swept out by the outgoing tide. On the incoming tide fish sometimes move deep inside the inlet. Along beaches and rips the fish often establish a pattern or circuit, popping up in predictable spots. In this case, blind casting and waiting for the fish to come to you is more productive than chasing them around.

## How to Catch Bonito & Little Tunny

If you find bonito or albies feeding on the surface, do not charge up to the school at full throttle and begin hurling lures. This will only serve to put the fish down and incur the wrath of other anglers in the area. The best approach is to idle just within range and cast to the outside edges of the activity. Here the fish will be looking to pick off injured or disoriented baitfish. Because schools are often moving, try to motor ahead of them, cast 10 to 20 feet in front of the lead fish and let your lure or fly sink a few feet before beginning the retrieve.

If you fail to hook up on the first few casts, try to figure out what the fish are eating. This is important, as bonito and albies frequently key on a particular type of baitfish and refuse to eat anything that looks the least bit dissimilar. To learn what's on the menu, watch for baitfish leaping clear of the water

FAST ACTION can occur during a little tunny or bonito feeding blitz.

as they're being chased or search for injured bait in the vicinity of the last blitz. You can also look below your boat, since baitfish will often school up around the hull of a drifting boat. A boated fish will often regurgitate its last meal, giving you a detailed view of the local prey. Once you determine what the fish are eating, tie on something that matches its length, profile and color. If this does not help with hooking up, retrieve your lure or fly at various depths and speeds. Slow retrieves, dead-drifts or simply letting the lure or fly sink are often the best option to get strikes.

If you have absolutely no idea what the fish might be eating, the best strategy is to go with a small metal spoon, a small white jig or a small white fly. Continue to change lures until you find the one that works. Keep in mind when chasing schools that there are times when they will refuse everything you show them. An example would be when they are feeding on minute baitfish. In this situation, tie on your favorite type of fly or lure and make repeated casts, letting the lure sink below the school.

Bonito and tunny can be taken by trolling small swimming plugs, flies or spoons. This can be a very effective technique when the fish are popping up sporadically in a rip line or feeding below the surface. Keep your lure or fly swimming in the first waves of the rip line, where the fish are likely to be waiting for bait to be swept over the shoal or ledge. Troll slowly back and forth along the length of the rip. If the leading edge isn't holding fish, try the down-current side before moving on.

Trolling can also work in open water when the fish are holding off structure. If you know fish are in the area, try trolling a fly, plug or spoon close to the boat, right behind the prop wash. The theory is that bonito and albies, like all tuna, are attracted by the turbulence of the prop wash, which appears to look and sound like a feeding blitz. The same theory applies to the wakes of other passing boats, where fish often appear in the whitewater, feeding on baitfish that were stunned or injured by the turbulence.

In areas where fish are popping up sporadically and you may have to move on short notice, drifting is often the way to go. Shut down the engine upcurrent of the area where you expect the fish to rise, turn the boat broadside to the current and cast as you drift along. Once you've located the hot zone, circle back and repeat the drift.

Drifting takes the cooperation and courtesy of the other boats in the area to be successful, especially in congested areas when fish are concentrated. Anglers need to be patient and give each other room to cast. In addition, you should always stay in your drift lane, even if a pod of fish pops up nearby. Otherwise, the situation could deteriorate into what is commonly known as a "bonito rodeo," where the sudden movement of boats quickly sends the fish down. To avoid this situation always keep an eye on the surrounding boats and be prepared to move away if someone hooks up right next to you. If another angler's fish does happen to run under your boat, reel in and raise your engine until the line is clear.

Albies and bonito will often frustrate you by disappearing just as you get within casting range, only to pop up 50 yards away. Although the fish seem to move about at random, careful observation may reveal a pattern. Stick around and watch, and you'll often see the fish appear in the same spots time and again. This is particularly likely in areas where the fish are herding bait against a beach or rocky shoreline and along shoals or ledges.

If you detect such a pattern, anchor up along the fish's route and continue casting. Even if you don't see fish feeding on the surface, you stand a good chance of intercepting the school as they cruise by. Patient anglers using this tactic often catch more fish than anglers who chase after schools. Remember, the longer a lure or fly is in the water the more likely you will catch fish.

Another effective technique is to chum while anchored. Surprisingly few inshore fishermen north of the Carolinas bother to chum for bonito and albies, even though the technique has proven effective in many southern states. When anchored in a likely spot simply tie a mesh bag full of ground fish or other attractant and let the current and scent do their job. Meanwhile, chop some fresh or frozen baitfish into small cubes and scatter a handful behind the boat every few minutes. If you have a live well and can net some small baitfish, toss three or four live baits into the slick as well. Once the fish appear behind the boat, dead-drift a live bait, chunk, fly or soft-plastic lure back with the chum. To hold the fish's interest, continue to throw out a few chunks or live baits every so often.

A good spinning or baitcasting outfit for handling these tiny tuna would include a 7-foot, fast-action rod and a reel spooled with 200 yards of 8 to 12 pound-test monofilament. For fly fishermen, a 7-, 8- or 9-weight outfit is a good choice. Fly reels should have a super-smooth drag and hold at least 200 yards of backing. Many fly fishermen prefer floating or intermediate-sink lines for this type of fishing, but a fast-sink line may be better for getting your fly quickly below the surface and reaching fish that are feeding in the depths.

Leaders are unnecessary, as a bonito has sharp, pointy teeth that are conical and will not cut fishing line. Most of the time anglers tie the lure or fly directly to the line; however, when the fish are acting line-shy, a 1- or 2-foot section of fluorocarbon can sometimes turn the trick.

When it comes to lure and fly choices, it's a good idea to have a wide variety on hand, since you never know which one the fish will prefer. Proven lures include 2- to 4-inch metal spoons such as the Deadly Dick, Acme Kastmaster, Hopkins No=EQL, Swedish Pimple and Acme Need-L-Eel. Small 1/8- to 1/4-ounce white bucktail jigs also work well at times, as do a variety of soft-plastic lures. A white, 6-inch Slug-Go can be deadly when twitched on the surface, and is a great lure for weedy situations. Lastly, be sure to pack a few small minnow plugs such as those made by Yo-Zuri, Rapala and Rebel, which are particularly effective when trolled.

Fly fishermen should stock their boxes with plenty of patterns to match every type of inshore baitfish, especially sand eels, silversides, bay anchovies and juvenile menhaden. Proven patterns include white Bonito Bunnies, Surf Candies, Baby Bunkers, Hardbody Shiners and Clouser Minnows.

Flies are effective at imitating the small, thin baitfish on which albies and bonito feed, and it's hard to beat a fly's translucent look and swimming action. Anglers using spinning and baitcasting gear can reap the benefits of flies by using a dropper loop tied in ahead of a plug, jig or spoon.

—*Tom Richardson*

# LADYFISH

Ladyfish are no ladies, at least not in the way they strike lures, attack baits and fight in a no-holds-barred, wild-leaping fashion. While rarely weighing more than 4 pounds, a ladyfish performs aerial acrobatics on light tackle at least as well as a tarpon or snook of similar size. Few inshore fish are faster, including bonefish or barracuda.

If the ladyfish does have a shortcoming, it would be its size. The world record is 6 pounds and was caught from Jupiter, Florida, in 1997. Most ladyfish caught are in the 1- to 2-pound range.

Although ladyfish sometimes are confused with bonefish (no doubt because of their silvery color and torpedo shape) and small tarpon, they're easily differentiated. Ladyfish have an oversized hinged mouth, whereas bonefish have an underslung mouth similar to that of a drum. Ladyfish also have extra-large eyes and smaller scales than a bonefish or tarpon. They jump repeatedly, rather than making long blistering runs as bonefish do and unlike tarpon, ladyfish do not have a long filament extending from the back of the dorsal fin.

Ladyfish (*Elops saurus*) have been caught from New England to Brazil, but are most abundant in the tropical and subtropical waters of the western Atlantic Ocean, chiefly from the Carolinas through the Gulf of Mexico. Similar looking but different species of ladyfish occur in the Pacific and eastern Atlantic oceans, where they've been documented to weigh from 10 to over 20 pounds. The African coast is touted as having the largest ladyfish; there, a 20-pounder hooked on light tackle surely produces an awesome fight.

Most fishermen hook ladyfish incidentally while fishing other targeted species such as seatrout, redfish or flounder. They can be a nice change of pace, however, because ladyfish fight better than most fish that anglers specifically target. Ladies strike hard, run far quickly and are adept at switching directions at any moment – all while leaping, twisting and turning with wild gyrations that frequently toss hooks or sever leaders.

Ladyfish will hit most live (or dead) bait from shrimp to mullet, and readily hit jigs, plugs, spoons and streamer flies. They're an outstanding fly-rod target, particularly when lightweight 4- to 6-weight outfits are employed.

Anglers that specifically target ladyfish often try chumming around shoals and oyster bars during running tides. Inlet jetties and bulkhead areas also hold ladyfish in good numbers. Fish-cleaning areas near marinas are also prime spots for catching ladyfish. Night fishing around dock and bridge lights in summer is another excellent way of locating numbers of ladyfish, which will often hit flies and plugs. Live shrimp are a surefire bait.

Ladyfish are generally not considered a good eating fish, and most are released unharmed. Marlin and tuna anglers occasionally keep ladyfish for use as offshore trolling baits.

—*Bob McNally*

LADYFISH
RANGE
PRIME FISHING

# CREVALLE JACK

**C**revalle jack *(Caranx hippos),* or jack crevalle as they are commonly called, are among the toughest-fighting fish in salt water. Indeed, few inshore fish can hold a candle to the bull-like runs jacks make. Although they rarely jump, they dive and run hard in a rod-pulsating fashion.

Crevalle are extremely aggressive, especially when surface-feeding schools are hammering baitfish. Feeding jack schools can at times cover an acre or more in size. At such times they'll strike almost any lure, fly or bait cast their way. They often go hard for topwater chugger plugs when they are on the surface to feed. Jacks are relentless in their pursuit of baitfish, often herding menhaden, mullet and other small fish into tight schools, then attacking in unison from all sides and underneath. Jacks are so voracious in their attacks that they've been known to literally run schools of baitfish out of the water and onto land.

This great light-tackle gamefish commonly weighs 1 to 6 pounds, with large specimens weighing 20 to 30 pounds readily available. The IGFA record is 57-pound, 14-ouncer, caught in August, 1957 near the mouth of the Mississippi River in Louisiana.

Jacks have a rounded, blunt-nosed head and white to gray flanks, darkening along the dorsal. They often have a clearly visible, bright yellow outlining along the underside of the belly to the lower tail, which is deeply forked. Dark spots on the tip of the gill cover and near the base of the pectoral fin differentiate it from other jacks, such as the horse-eye. For years crevalle jack were believed to inhabit the Pacific Ocean, but biologists now believe that is a distinctively different jack species.

## Where to Find Crevalle Jack

Crevalle probably have "saved the day" for more salt water anglers trying to impress friends with their fishing prowess than any other species. From spring through early fall crevalle can be found throughout the south Atlantic and Gulf Coasts, in the lower reaches of tidal rivers, bays, lagoons and sounds and along inlet jetties and break walls. In winter, most crevalle migrate to warmer waters, either heading south or deep offshore.

CREVALLE JACK
▨ RANGE
■ PRIME FISHING

Big jacks aren't found in huge schools like smaller ones, and they can't be counted on to feed at a certain spot, during a certain tide, day after day. When big fish do school, they are more commonly found in the open ocean, in broad sounds or river mouths. Jacks in the 20- to 40-pound range frequently are found in tight pods of three to ten fish. The real giants, however (there are reports of 70 pounders), tend to be solitary and difficult to target.

Strong tides, swift currents and rips where baitfish are tossed around and disoriented are choice crevalle fishing spots. Inshore channels, holes, deep water bulkheads, inlet jetties, offshore ledges, reefs, rock outcroppings and wrecks can be counted on to hold jack schools when surface water temperatures are 70 degrees or more.

## How to Catch Crevalle Jack

Jacks in a feeding frenzy are a sight to behold, even for veteran anglers who have caught more than their share of crevalle. When they're really "hot," jacks leap out of the water at scurrying baitfish, slam and knock bait into the air, and boil water into such a froth that it can look like a river's rapids. Almost any lure or bait dropped into the melee immediately draws a strike. Topwater plugs and streamer flies are especially fun to cast at such times. Some anglers even remove the hooks from surface plugs when big crevalle schools are located, so they can revel in having fish strike a lure six to ten times during a single retrieve.

Jacks weighing over 15 pounds are more wary than small fish, but can be coaxed to strike by fishing lures at top speed, or with aggressive surface retrieves. Over the years anglers have noted that crevalle jack have a curious liking of yellow-hued lures. Yellow bucktail jigs tipped with fresh whole shrimp are rarely refused by even the biggest, most educated crevalle. Live baits, such as mullet, menhaden, croakers and pinfish are also top jack baits.

Crevalle jack are great sport on anything but the most stout offshore tackle. Because most encountered are 3 to 6 pounds, medium-action spinning and baitcasting gear is advised, with lines from 6 to 12 pounds. Fly fishermen employ 6- to 8-weight outfits. For bigger jacks weighing 15 pounds or more, much heavier tackle is called for, as jacks of such size are dogged fighters. A small trace of heavy monofilament "shock" leader is advised: 20-pound-test for small fish, 50- to 80-pound for bigger ones, as jacks do have teeth.

Clear water is best for catching jacks on artificial lures. Spoons, plugs, jigs, surface chuggers, streamer flies and bugs all produce crevalle. Fast, erratic retrieves are effective. The famous "Florida whip" retrieve, in which an angler "whips" the rod tip constantly and severely through the course of bringing in a lure, is great.

Almost any small live bait or shrimp also work well. Menhaden and mullet are excellent baits. Cut bait and squid bait strips also are effective.

Crevalle do not have sharp teeth and can be netted and handled safely. Grip the fish from around the back of the head (thumb on one side, forefinger on the other) and press firmly on the gill plates. (Be careful not to put fingers into exposed gills.) Jacks are momentarily calmed by this grip, which facilitates easy hook removal. Crevalle meat is dark and bloody and often has parasites; thus jacks are not generally considered a choice food.

—*Bob McNally*

# FLORIDA POMPANO

There are several species of pompano available to inshore anglers, but the Florida pompano *(Trachinotus carolinus)* is the most widely distributed, and certainly the most sought after. Pompano are a member of the jack family, and are often confused with the highly-prized permit. Unlike permit anglers, though, most pompano fishermen seek their quarry because the fish has no peer on a dinner plate. Indeed, it is one of the most expensive food fish available, and is without question one of the most delicious.

Florida pompano normally run from 1 to 3 pounds, and the world record is an 8-pound, 1-ounce monster caught from a northeast Florida beach by a surf angler. While it's likely that more Florida pompano are caught in the Sunshine State than in all other locations combined, the species is distributed from New England to Brazil, and is widely caught throughout the Gulf of Mexico.

Pompano have a rounded or blunt nose with a

FLORIDA POMPINO
RANGE
PRIME FISHING

gray-green back, silvery sides and a yellow underside with a hint of yellow in the fins. The tail is forked, the body deep but relatively narrow across the back. Pompano can be differentiated from small permit by the lack of a dark patch under each pectoral fin. Permit (p. 61) also average larger in size (commonly 10 to 25 pounds),

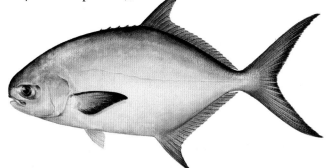

have a more deeply forked tail, a deeper body, and longer, wispier dorsal and anal fins. Still, there is confusion between the species and no doubt some juvenile permit are caught, killed and eaten by pompano fishermen every year.

Pompano fishing has improved steadily in recent history, which many anglers believe is due to the restrictions placed on the commercial gill netting that took a heavy toll on the species in the past.

It is so good, in fact, that some people believe pompano fishing has never been better.

## Where to Find Florida Pompano

Pompano angling is mainly a spring-fall fling, but fish can be caught year-round. The most consistent times for pompano are April through June and September through November. Good fishing can be found on both the Atlantic and Gulf Coasts, with the Gulf side probably offering better all-around action and certainly more light-tackle possibilities. Most Atlantic Coast fishing is done from the surf or from piers, which usually requires heftier tackle. In the Gulf, light-tackle beach casting is popular, especially at daybreak, when the water is calm. Pier fishing also produces pompano in the Gulf, and the generally shallower, calmer water (compared to the Atlantic) allows more opportunity for light rods and small diameter lines.

Pass fishing for pompano is also very productive in the Gulf of Mexico. Most Florida Gulf-side passes offer excellent pompano fishing during moving tide phases. Anglers have noticed a huge increase in pompano numbers well up into Gulf-side bays and rivers since gill-net bans went into effect. Winter fishing has been on the increase in some areas, likely for the same reason.

## How to Catch Florida Pompano

Runs of pompano are legendary, and when fish are "in" it seems everyone along a stretch of beach, on a pier or in a pass is catching fish. For this reason, anglers should not be shy about joining others who are catching pompano, but should be courteous about their approach.

Pompano have an unusual habit of jumping or "flipping" that offers a unique way of locating fish for anglers running beach areas in boats. One trick anglers use is to turn around and watch the boat wake as they're running. As the boat crosses fish they leap out of the prop wash and over the wake like a silver-white Frisbee. It is not known why they jump in this fashion, but it's an easier way to locate fish, than stopping to cast at every likely spot.

Once you spot several pompano launch out of a boat's wake and belly-flop back into the water, circle back, put out the anchor and start fishing.

Pompano are shellfish eaters, and chumming with crushed shrimp, fiddler crabs, clams or barnacles is very effective. Deep holes along clear-water beaches, areas near channel drop-offs, passes and around bridges are all likely spots to try. Pompano can be caught during all moving tide phases, with full and new moon phases being particularly good. Pompano can be caught with a wide variety of tackle, from heavy surf and pier outfits to ultralight models and 4-pound line.

Keep in mind that most pompano weigh under 3 pounds, and the majority of fish are in the 1- to 2-pound range. Fishing for for this size pompano calls for light-action graphite spinning rods and matched skirted-spool reels. Drags should be smooth, especially if light line is employed, as even small pompano fight plenty hard.

The exceptions to this light gear rule are surf and pier fishing (usually in the rougher Atlantic), as heavy lead sinkers are needed to hold and reach bottom in running tides. Often, long-distance casts, 2-ounce pyramid weights and 15- or 20-pound-test lines are needed for this situation, and suitable rods and reels are needed as well. Fresh sand fleas (mole crabs) are the most popular bait in the surf and off piers, and are threaded onto a size #1 Kahle hook.

Light-tackle spin fishermen do well with sand fleas, using a # 1 Kahle hook and a sliding 1/4- to 1/2-ounce sinker on a fish-finder rig. Jigs in a wide variety of bright colors are favored. Yellow, red, orange, chartreuse, white, green, blue, root beer and multicolor models with Mylar, Flashabou or CrystalFlash can all be good. Nylon jigs are usually preferred by most experienced pompano chasers, and short dressings trailing just beyond the hook point are the mark of these specialty lures to thwart short strikes. Jighead weights run from 1/4- to 5/8-ounce, depending on water depth and current. For heavier jigs, line size should increase, and some anglers favor low-stretch superlines with a 12-pound monofilament leader.

Though fly fishing for pompano is not very popular at this time it should be, particularly in the clear waters along Gulf beaches. Here, fish move en masse to sheltered bays where flies score surprisingly well. A 4- or 6-weight fly outfit is plenty adequate. Shrimp, crab, epoxy and lead-eye flies can do well on pompano, just as they do on permit.

—*Bob McNally*

# SHEEPSHEAD

S heepshead fishing is a peaceful, quiet, simple kind of fishing that lets an angler enjoy the sun, sights and sounds of being on the water. But consistently catching sheepshead is about as difficult as doing so with any of the more touted inshore species. This is because sheepshead are known as the "kings" of all salt water bait-stealers.

The sheepshead (*Archosargus probato-cephalus*) is a member of the porgy family, and are common along the inshore waters of the western Atlantic Ocean from Nova Scotia to South America. Sheepshead are easy to identify. They have a silver-gray body with five or six wide and prominent dark vertical bars running down the flanks. The dorsal has a number of pointed spines, so angler should be careful when handling these fish. The mouth is unique in that it has large teeth (right) that look much like those of a sheep, thus the name sheepshead.

SHEEPSHEAD
▇ RANGE
■ PRIME FISHING

While the teeth are not sharp on the order of a bluefish, cuda or mackerel, anglers should keep their hands away since the powerful jaws are used for crushing shells, barnacles and crabs. The teeth and specialized shell crushers inside the fish's mouth turn a hook point quickly, which is why sheepshead are very difficult to consistently hook and land. Even the best sheepshead anglers miss several fish for every one they catch.

Sheepshead commonly weigh 2 to 4 pounds. Fish to 10 pounds are caught seasonally, especially in Florida, where the state record is 15 pounds. The world record is 21 pounds.

## Where to Find Sheepshead

Sheepshead are shellfish feeders, and are found in areas where they can find oysters, crabs and barnacles. Old pilings, channel markers, shell bars and jetties are typical sheepshead angling locations. Most jetties hold some sheepshead, with the best spots being low areas in rocks where ocean water seeps through. Current coming through rocks draws sheepshead, as it disorients the crustaceans upon which they feed.

In some areas, like coastal Georgia or along the Gulf Coast, near-shore reefs offer excellent sheepshead fishing in water 20 to 50 feet deep. In other locales, like Texas and Louisiana, oil rigs and platforms can be loaded with sheepshead, sometimes many miles offshore.

Other states, such as Florida, hold fish all year, with spring and fall normally offering the best action as runs of fish commonly occur around inlet jetties and near-shore reefs and wrecks.

## How to Catch Sheepshead

Still-fishing is most productive, but anglers also catch fish vertical jigging using bait or casting with a very slow retrieve. Chumming works well in attracting sheepshead and turning them on to feed. Often oysters or barnacles can be gathered from around dock or bulkhead pilings, placed in a bucket and crushed with a hoe or shovel. Tossing crushed crustaceans into the fishing area brings in sheepshead.

Sheepshead are also occasionally caught over shallow inshore grass flats, usually in spring or fall, when high tides push onto usually dry areas. Sheepshead move there to feed on crabs, so baits and lures imitating them do well for wade anglers stalking fish and sight-casting to them.

A medium-action spinning or baitcasting rod with a fast, sensitive tip enables anglers to "feel" or detect strikes much better than they can with the big tackle used to catch snook or tarpon. Typical largemouth bass tackle is suitable, with fast-taper graphite rods 6 to 7 feet long and lines in the 12- to 20-pound-test range.

A standard sheepshead rig consists of a sliding sinker (1 to 3 ounces in weight, determined by depth and current), a heavy-duty barrel swivel, a shock leader of about 30-pound test, and a short-shank bait hook. Thread the fishing line through the sliding sinker, then tie the fishing line to the swivel, attach 2 feet of shock leader to the swivel and tie the hook to the leader. Heavy wire, short-shank size # 1 to 3/0 bait hooks are used. Sheepshead are strong, determined fighters that do well at weaving lines through rocks and pilings and must be muscled away from cover once hooked.

Fiddler crabs are the number-one sheepshead bait, not only because they work well but because they're easy to catch, simple to keep alive and available at bait stores everywhere. Whole, live oyster crabs, mini-blue crabs, pieces of fresh dead crab and sometimes pieces of shrimp also tempt sheepshead.

Fiddler crabs store easily in a plastic bucket or cooler with no water (keep them out of direct sunlight). The large claw should be removed from the crab when putting it on a hook. Work the hook tip slowly through the spot where the second leg (from the crab's eyes) meets the crab's top shell. Wiggle the hook until the point of the hook pokes out the opposite side.

Sheepshead are tough to feel when they hit a bait because they don't actually eat it like other fish eat their food. Instead, they come to a bait like a crab, crush it in the back of their throat and swallow the meat and juices – but not until they spit out the shells, and often an angler's hook.

Sheepshead can be taken on small jigs or flies that mimic crabs or shrimp. Fish chummed to an area and put into a frenzy are particularly susceptible to artificials. Curlytail grubs in bright yellow or white are good, and are usually fished on a ⅛- or ¼-ounce jig head. Crab-imitating, bonefish-size flies have the best chance of duping a sheepshead, but be prepared for lots of casting between hookups.

Because sheepshead strikes are so difficult to detect, many experienced anglers prefer fishing for them during slow-running tides. Such minimal currents allow for better feel of baits and lures. Also, slightly stained water is often preferred as fish are less spooky and not as prone to seeing leaders and hooks hidden in baits. Most sheepshead of legal size are kept for the table, as they are excellent eating, particularly pan-fried or grilled.

—Bob McNally

# TRIPLETAIL

The unusual-looking and rather strange-acting tripletail (*Lobotes surinamensis*) resembles an oversize crappie or freshwater panfish. Found worldwide in tropical and subtropical waters, it's regularly caught in the Atlantic, Pacific and Indian oceans.

A tripletail varies in color from almost black to olive green, brown, light gray or rust. It can resemble a flounder when swimming on its side at the surface. Tripletail are deceptively quick and aggressive, even though most anglers see them as "lazy" floating fish. Nicknames for tripletail include buoy bass, snagdrifter, jumping cod and blackfish.

The tripletail's name comes from the fact that the fish's tail, dorsal and anal fins all extend to nearly the same length at the rear of the fish so they look like three tails. While they appear lethargic, hovering around flotsam and channel markers, tripletail are strong, hard-fighting light-tackle gamefish that frequently jump and run out plenty of line against a strong drag.

They commonly weigh 2 to 10 pounds, and fish to 20 pounds are caught seasonally. The world record 42-pound, 5-ouncer was taken off South Africa in 1989.

## Where to Find Tripletail

Tripletail can be caught anywhere from offshore weeds in billfish water to the mouths of inlets around tide rips. Like cobia, these fish have an affinity for shade, and can often be seen and cast to while they cruise near or under ocean pier pilings, range markers, buoys, oil rigs, floating offshore weeds and flotsam such as boards and trees. They sometimes seem to suddenly appear from nowhere under an angler's boat. Great action for tripletail can be found around large freighters and shrimp boats anchored offshore. The larger such

TRIPLETAIL
▨ RANGE
▧ PRIME FISHING

boats are, the better they are for catching numbers of tripletail.

Single, cruising tripletail are commonly seen along some beach shoal areas in late spring and summer. Anglers cruise along until they spot fish at the surface, in water sometimes only 5 feet deep, then cast lures and baits. The fish are believed to be staging for the spawn.

Scientists don't know much about tripletail migratory patterns, as very little tagging data is available. There does appear to be an interesting connection between Georgia tripletail and ones caught around Canaveral, Florida, a famed spot for heavyweight fish.

Florida guides have tagged fish at Canaveral and reported tag returns from Georgia. Georgia marine biologists did some tripletail tagging, and some fish were later recaptured off Canaveral, supporting the Florida-Georgia connection reported by Florida fishing guides.

Biologists believe Georgia summer tripletail may be spawning fish, and there are reports of coin-size juveniles found far inshore, floating with tides in salty rivers and creeks. Biologists say there may be a north-south seasonal migration of nearshore tripletail between the Carolinas, Georgia and Florida, but the extent is not known. Some liken tripletail to tarpon migrations, which move in much the same manner at the same time of year between the states mentioned.

## How to Catch Tripletail

Sight casting to fish spotted at the surface is very effective; so is blind casting to visible objects that tripletail may be holding under, such as buoys, crab trap floats and piers. Veteran anglers always wear quality polarized sunglasses and a brimmed cap to shade the eyes, which helps spot tripletail and make accurate casts. Calm, clear water is preferred for stalking tripletail.

Medium-action spinning or baitcasting tackle on the order of that used for largemouth bass gear is suitable for tripletail, with fast-taper graphite rods 6 to 7 feet long and lines from 8- to 20-pound test. Fly fishing for tripletail is great sport, and is feasible wherever fish are seen. Anglers use up to an 8- or 9-weight fly outfit in strong winds, which are common in tripletail country, especially in fall or winter.

A live shrimp cast with a small sliding float is the top tripletail producer. A 2- to 3-inch sliding float positioned on the line 2 feet above a bait is perfect. Then attach a small split shot or two midway between the float and a 1/0 Kahle hook.

Shock leaders from 15- to 50-pound test are in order, depending on the size of the fish in the area and the cover being worked. Tripletail will always take advantage of line-cutting snags, like the legs of range markers and buoy anchor chains. Small nylon jigs work well, especially when tipped with shrimp. Small plastic-imitation shrimp like the DOA Shrimp also are effective.

Because tripletail readily eat live shrimp, crabs and small fish, flies that imitate them work satisfactorily. Small bonefish and permit fly patterns score consistently. Epoxy bonefish flies and epoxy minnow flies can be deadly on finicky tripletail that refuse other offerings. A sinking fly like a Clouser often is needed to get down in the face of a tripletail that dives. Anglers often let flies sink, twitch them ever so slowly to draw attention to the lure, then let it rest. The strike usually comes as the retrieve is started again.

It's important that lures are presented slowly and carefully to tripletail, because the fish are very deliberate feeders. This is one reason streamer flies and small epoxy bonefish patterns work so well. The best technique once fish are spotted is to move slowly and quietly into casting position, then make a long, soft cast ahead of a moving fish. When fish are not spotted, cast beyond the object to which the tripletail is likely holding. If the fish is cruising, retrieve the lure until the tripletail is on a collision course, then halt the retrieve. The fish usually will do the rest. If casting to an object, bring the lure to it and pause. The fish should strike.

Sometimes, as a lure or bait is brought near a tripletail, it dives. Do not move the lure, as often the fish will rise again to take the offering. If a sinking lure is employed, a tripletail may strike as it sinks, so keep a tight line and be prepared to set the hook.

A landing net is helpful in boating tripletail. Be mindful of the gill plate, as it has a serrated, razor-sharp edge like a steak knife. Tripletail are outstanding on the dinner plate, and can be stuffed, baked, broiled or fried.

—*Bob McNally*

# WEAKFISH

The weakfish is referred to as a gray trout from Maryland south, mainly to separate it from the spotted seatrout (p. 36), which is found in the southern portion of the weakfish's range. Weakfish (*Cynoscion regalis*) look very much like a freshwater trout, although they exhibit few characteristics of those species. Weakfish are basically bottom dwellers, occasionally chasing bait to the surface.

While not fighters in the class of bluefish or striped bass, weakfish didn't get their name from a lack of fighting ability. It's the thin mouth membrane, from which hooks are easily pulled, that brought about their name. They are perfect light tackle opponents, as they're usually found in open water and don't demonstrate a tendency to dive for cover even when taken around structure such as bridges.

Weakfish have long been regarded as a classic cyclical fish, going from periods of incredible abundance to such scarcity that they virtually disappear. Yet the biology of the species hardly seems to support such vast swings. Weakfish grow quickly and mature by the end of their first year at only 10 to 12 inches in length. They also live reasonably long lives and grow to about 20 pounds. The main problem for weakfish populations has been that the fish are easily caught by a variety of commercial methods including gill nets, pound nets, and trawls.

Because of this tendency, populations were decimated in the early and mid-1900s. A revival started around 1970, but unfortunately, the same thing happened. This time the damage was done by gill netters who killed 8- to 14-pound spawners in May, while trawlers concentrated on the young-of-the-year weaks coming out of Delaware Bay in the fall. All to satisfy the Baltimore market for pan fish. Recreational fishermen also shared part of the blame as they observed no limits in the amount of weakfish they caught.

The Atlantic States Marine Fisheries Commission (ASMFC) finally passed a weakfish management plan during the 1990s. The plan stopped the worst commercial excesses, such as the fall small-mesh

**WEAKFISH**
RANGE
PRIME SUMMER FISHING
PRIME WINTER FISHING

trawling and winter trawling off North Carolina, where much of the entire population is concentrated for a few months. The result has been a resurgence of weakfish and recreational catches.

Weakfish are migratory fish that move up the coast in the spring before spawning in May, gathering in large bays such as the Chesapeake, Delaware, Raritan, Great South, Peconic and Narragansett. The largest specimens are usually roe-laden females in the spring. Some very large weaks are also caught during the fall as they start their southern migration.

## Where to Find Weakfish

Weaks favor relatively shallow waters and are usually caught near the coast or in bays. Occasionally, they may drop into deep holes within bays and rivers. Keep a sharp eye on your depth finder while traveling, as a big school of weaks will move up on the flats or bottoms of channels. The edges of channels are particularly attractive to them.

It is common for weakfish to spread over vast areas when they enter bays rather than congregating around structure. Do not rule out bridges, however, they are a powerful attraction, as bait is funneled through by currents. Also, weakfish tend to change locations during the day, and the same fish that feed in deep water during daylight may move onto the flats to pick off grass shrimp in the evening. As a rule, you won't go wrong by fishing deep all day unless you see some sign of weakfish moving up in the water column.

Weakfish frequently feed on the same baitfish being hounded by bluefish and striped bass. Blues will often feed on the surface. Their presence gives a hint of where to fish since weaks may feed underneath them. By letting baits and lures drop down, you're apt to catch weaks rather than hooking up to blues.

Creek mouths can be very productive at night for light spinning gear and offer the best shot at weaks with a fly rod. Small lures or flies retrieved very slowly on the outgoing tide are usually the key

to success. You'll often be able to hear the light "plops" as weakfish suck in small fish or grass shrimp.

## How to Catch Weakfish

Weakfish respond to a wide variety of live bait such as seaworms, squid, menhaden, shedder crab and grass shrimp. Water movement is important, even if it's very slow. Bait fishing is rarely good on slack tides even if fish are marking, but it improves as the current increases. In nearly all situations weakfish bite softly, so sensitive rods will help you detect strikes.

Seaworms are generally fished off a three-way swivel rig 1 to 3 feet off bottom. It is best to simply hook them once through the head so they trail out naturally. The length of the worm does not inhibit hooking since weakfish strike at the head. Baitholder hooks are often favored, and circle hooks should become more popular since many weakfish are now being released.

Weakfish love menhaden (bunkers) – particularly live peanut (baby) bunkers, which are common in the fall, or chunks fished on bottom. Small snapper bluefish also make prime live baits for large weakfish in fall.

Shedder crab is the best bait for weakfish from Barnegat Bay, New Jersey, south, but is rarely used north of there. The crab is cut up into small pieces and added to jigs, but can also be fished directly. Drift it out in the current or use a float to help keep it away from the boat and keep it off bottom in shallow waters.

Many types of jigs will catch weakfish. Use lead-head jigs from ¼ to 2 ounces or more are used depending on the depth of water and current. They may be tied with materials such as bucktail or utilized with various plastic worms or shad bodies. Jigs are often tipped with squid, shedder crab or a piece of worm to provide scent. In every case, jigs should be worked slowly for weakfish. During the great 1970s run in Peconic Bay, the primary producer was a 9-inch plastic worm on a jig head just heavy enough to stay near bottom. This type of rig can be slowly jigged off bottom or cast uptide and retrieved just fast enough to keep it moving. *Deadsticking* (drifting with the rod in a rod holder) is also effective.

Diamond jigs are also effective for weakfish. The trick is to hit bottom and then slowly reel up a few turns before pausing and dropping back again. Many strikes will occur on the pause or the drop. Diamond jigs are a good sand eel imitation and work best in areas where eels are present.

Plugs also attract weakfish, and as with all techniques, the secret to success is a slow retrieve. In addition, lures with relatively minimal action seem to work best. The tight wiggle of small minnow-like plugs such as the Bomber Long A, Gag's Grabbers, and Yo-Zuri Crystal Minnows will produce in surf and shoreline situations. Rat-L-Traps work well when peanut bunkers are the main quarry.

Trolling for weaks is not as popular as casting or jigging, but quite a few are caught in that fashion by anglers trolling for other species. Once again, slow, is the key. Small plugs, spoons, jigs and other lures can be trolled on monofilament line in shallow water areas or on wire line in deeper water.

Gear for weakfish varies from a lightweight 6-foot spinning rod for fishing grass shrimp with 6-pound test, to a medium-action casting rod and 12-pound-test line for trolling plugs or jigging.

Fishing for weakfish is pretty basic sport, and favored methods vary greatly in different areas. For instance, anglers in Raritan Bay swear by sandworms, while those at the other end of New Jersey in Delaware Bay prefer squid or shedder crab. The latter is also used to tip almost every jig in Chesapeake Bay.

—Al Ristori

# TAUTOG

This distinctive bottom fish can survive in the wide variety of temperatures found throughout its range from New England to South Carolina, but is generally regarded as a cool-water species. The tautog (*Tautoga onitis*) is one of only two temperate-water members of the extensive wrasse family, which includes many colorful tropical fish. The tautog's cousin, the cunner (called sea perch and choggie in New England and bergall in the Mid-Atlantic), is much smaller and shares the same rocky habitat. While cunners are fine fighters and food fish, they're usually disdained as bait stealers.

TAUTOG
▨ RANGE
▉ PRIME FISHING

Tautog thrive in southern New England waters and are abundant on the north side of Cape Cod, yet are rarely found farther north. Virginia is the southern end of the tautog's normal range and is also where most large tautog have been boated, primarily during the winter.

In 1998 the world record returned north to Ocean City, New Jersey. An angler fishing on a party boat landed a 25-pounder over a wreck while fishing in snow showers, 20-knot winds and 6- to 8-foot seas. The fish measured 34½ inches long and had a girth of 28½ inches. Average size for tautog is quite a bit smaller. Fish from 6 to 18 inches are common in bays and close to shore from spring to fall. Larger "tog" tend to hang over rough bottoms and wrecks a bit farther offshore, although some are taken from jetties. Three- to 6-pounders are considered good-sized almost everywhere, and those over 10 pounds are trophies. Very few tautog exceeding 15 pounds are caught each year.

In New Jersey and New York, tautog are almost invariably referred to as blackfish, although the old name "slippery bass" is still used occasionally in southern New Jersey. The name tautog, which has Indian origins, is common both north and south of these states and is the name recognized by the American Fisheries Society.

## Where to Find Tautog

Tautog are extremely slow-growing and long-lived fish. In the Mid-Atlantic and New England they winter in deeper waters a few miles offshore before starting an inshore movement in April and spawning in shallow waters during May and June. They become relatively inactive when waters warm during the summer, but bite well again in the fall before moving back offshore. Some of the deeper offshore spots, such as 17 Fathoms in New York Bight, have good December- to- January fisheries even as surface temperatures drop into the mid-40s. Winter is also a good time for wreck fishing for tautog from southern New Jersey to Virginia.

## How to Catch Tautog

While just about anything will attract tautog at times, they are basically crab eaters. Hermit crabs are the preferred food, but are rarely available for sale and must be obtained directly from lobster fishermen. Green and fiddler crabs are used primarily from central New Jersey to New England, while calico, blueclaw and fiddlers are more common to the south. Hooking tautog on such baits can be difficult, which is what separates tautog fishing from ordinary bottom fishing.

Tautog sport a set of buck teeth that are used to pick up shellfish before they're passed to crusher teeth in the throat. There the meat is extracted and most of the shell is spit out. The trick is not to strike on the first nibbles, but to wait for a steadier pull, which indicates that the bait has been passed back. Strike too soon and you'll pull the bait away. Wait too long and your hook will be expelled with the shells. More so than in any other type of bottom fishing, this sport requires a lot of attention, and even the best anglers miss bites.

Fiddlers are used whole, but other crabs are usually quartered or halved, depending on the size. Scissors have proven more practical than knives for this purpose. The top shell is normally removed; some anglers leave the legs on, while others eliminate them. The hook is inserted in a leg hole on one side and brought out through another. Some anglers prefer a single hook directly over the sinker, as hang-ups are frequent in this fishery.

Others fish two hooks, with one tied into the leader off the first hook eye. Those seeking only large tautog may fish a whole green crab with each hook of a two-hook rig on either side of the bait. This procedure discourages ravenous cunners and allows the angler to wait out a trophy tog.

In addition to hooking difficulty, tautog present another problem – they're very territorial. This is especially notable on party boats, where anglers in one section may be pulling tog steadily while others can't get a bite. This situation can also arise even with small-boat anglers, so you should move often.

Most anglers prefer 6- to 6½-foot heavy-action rods with some tip action for use when fishing on bottom with various types of sinker rigs. Small conventional reels are used in most cases, although heavy baitcasting gear works fine in shallower-water situations. Superlines are ideal for this type of fishing, as the near-zero stretch transmits the tautog's light bite and allows you to get fish off the bottom and away from snags quickly. Monofilament line or flourocarbon should be used as leader material.

*—Al Ristori*

# BLACK DRUM

**B**lack drum *(Pogonias cromis)* are popular bottom-feeding sportfish caught regularly along the inshore waters of the western Atlantic Ocean. Spring-run spawners can weigh 40 to 70 pounds, and are prized by some fishermen for their dogged, bottom-digging fight. Record-size fish over 100 pounds have been recorded from scattered spots along the Eastern Seaboard from New Jersey to Florida. The all-tackle IGFA record is a 113-pound, 1-ounce behemoth, caught in September 1975 off of Delaware.

Black drum have a silver-gray body, though in larger specimens the fish is dark in overall dorsal color, shading lighter to the belly. In some estuarine areas black drum can have a copper sheen. Smaller black drum (those under 15 pounds) have several wide and prominent dark vertical bars running down the flanks. Mature black drum have a high, arched back and 10 to 14 barbels under the chin.

Most black drum are caught near inlets and passes, around deep holes and shell bars, and sometimes on grass flats. Some of the biggest fish are taken near wrecks and reefs in water usually less than 80 feet deep, normally in winter when fish school deep. Black drum are shell-fish eaters, and often are found in deep holes adjacent to oysters.

Most drum are caught on bait by still-fishing. Chumming attracts black drum well and starts them feeding. Often oysters, barnacles and shrimp can be crushed with a hoe or shovel, then tossed overboard to attract drum. This technique works well in spring – particularly at night – in known black drum spawning areas, which are primarily rivers feeding the ocean. Such tactics often produce huge drum in the 50- to 80-pound range. For black drum under about 20 pounds, a medium-action spinning or baitcasting rod with a fast, sensitive tip is serviceable. Fast-taper graphite rods 6 to 7 feet long, used with lines 12- to 20-pound-test are ideal.

Fly fishing for black drum is specialized sport, but it's good in a few select areas, most notably in the Indian and Banana rivers on the east-central coast of Florida. Fly rod fishermen should use 8- to 9-weight tackle and weight-forward lines, with crab and shrimp patterns or silver-side streamers being best.

For giant drum – fish 30 to 80 pounds – much heavier tackle is required to leverage them out of holes and away from line-cutting jetties or shell bars. Tackle on the order of 30-pound-class trolling gear is not too stout.

A standard drum bait rig consists of a sliding sinker (1 to 8 ounces), a heavy-duty barrel swivel, a shock leader about 30- to 80-pound test, and a heavy short-shank bait hook. Whole, fresh shrimp, crabs, muscles, oysters, blue crab chunks and even fiddler crabs attract black drum. Sometimes a hook threaded with several different baits is used to fool hard-nosed drum.

*—Bob McNally*

BLACK DRUM
RANGE
PRIME FISHING

# SPANISH MACKEREL

Spunky and speedy Spanish mackerel are among the more popular and readily available sportfish found in the inshore waters of the Western Atlantic Ocean. Typically found in large schools in warm to temperate waters, Spanish are pursued by anglers because of their fight on light-tackle and because they are top table fare.

The primary range of the Spanish mackerel is from the Gulf of Mexico to Chesapeake Bay. The Gulf Coast mackerel and Atlantic coast fish are actually two separate populations that end up in southern Florida in the winter months. Then Spanish make large spring "runs" northward. Huge schools of fish can often be seen leaping and chasing baitfish and boiling the surface as they hunt down food fish such as glass minnows and menhaden.

SPANISH MACKEREL
■ SUMMER RANGE
▓ SPRING/FALL MIGRATION RANGE
■ WINTER RANGE

Most school-size Spanish mackerel run 1 to 3 pounds, with 5-pounders considered good-sized. Fish over 10 pounds occasionally are caught, and the world record is a 13-pounder, caught at Ocracoke Inlet, North Carolina, in 1987.

Spanish mackerel (*Scomberomorus maculatus*) are often confused with cero mackerel, which sometimes are found in the same waters and feeding on the same baitfish. Ceros run slightly larger in size than Spanish. Many fish in the 5-pound plus range touted as Spanish are in fact ceros.

Spanish are easy to differentiate from ceros and juvenile king mackerel in that Spanish have many rounded yellow spots and no stripes. The lateral line tapers gently from nose to tail with no quick dips like it has on king mackerel, and to a lesser extent on cero mackerel.

To be successful with cast lures, anglers must have either a large, competitive school of mackerel around them or a smaller school in a feeding frenzy. The best way to create either situation is chumming. Live baits can be set out in the chum to alert anglers when fish begin to show. Catch a Spanish or two with a menhaden, pilchard, or jumbo live shrimp and it's time to break out the lures.

Most casters opt for jigs, usually simple-style nylon or marabou, in white, blue and white, green and white or pale pink. Small, slender chrome spoons also work well, and minnow plugs and top-water lures like the popular Zara Spook are hit by frenzied Spanish.

Fly fishermen also do well with mackerel when they're sufficiently "chummed up." Small bucktail, marabou and Flashabou streamers tied in colors similar to those favored in jigs work very well, especially with sinking lines. Lead eye streamers, such as Clouser Minnows, also are great for Spanish.

Spanish tend to want a lure fished fast, either with long, sweeping strokes of the rod or a fast, straight retrieve. For this reason, when using spinning gear make sure the reel you employ has a fairly large spool and a high retrieve ratio. Fly-rod fishermen also should strip line quickly to make streamers scoot fast.

It's likely that more Spanish mackerel are caught trolling with spoons and jigs than any other method. Trolling works for many reasons, not the least of which is that the lures used are often flying through the water, which is what mackerel desire.

—*Bob McNally*

# Pacific Coast Fish

◆

SALMON · CALICO BASS · PACIFIC HALIBUT · BARRED SAND BASS · CALIFORNIA HALIBUT

· PACIFIC BARRACUDA · YELLOWTAIL · WHITE SEABASS · LINGCOD · ROCKFISH · STARRY FLOUNDER

· STRIPED BASS · WHITE STURGEON · SPOTTED SAND BASS · CALIFORNIA CORBINA

# SALMON

almon are a Northwest icon. Long before Lewis and Clark arrived at Astoria, Northwest native tribes subsisted on salmon, worshiped salmon and planned their yearly migrations to coincide with the return of the salmon. The Lewis and Clark expedition might have perished from starvation had local Indian bands not sustained them with dried salmon.

Today evidence of the importance of salmon is found everywhere one looks. Commercial fleets that exploit the salmon runs from Alaska to San Francisco form the economic backbone of many coastal communities. More than 100 salmon fishing resorts serve sport fishermen, some of whom travel thousands of miles to do battle with the broad-shouldered chinook and the acrobatic coho. Restaurants across America eagerly await the first salmon of the year, while hundreds of thousands of Northwest anglers await the opening of salmon season with the anticipation of a child awaiting Christmas.

There are six species of Pacific salmon, five of which are indigenous to U.S. waters. Anglers pursue all five species, but only two, the chinook salmon *(Oncorhynchus tshawytscha)* and the coho salmon *(Oncorhynchus kisutch),* are sought by large numbers of salmon-fishing fanatics. The chinook is undoubtedly the most prized of the salmon family due to its size and superb table quality, but the coho has a devoted following of anglers who treasure its spectacular aerial performance when hooked.

Chinook and coho are found all along the West Coast from northern California to Alaska. Chinook are abundant as far south as San Francisco Bay. Indeed, San Francisco anglers catch many thousands of chinook each year. The chinook range north as far as the Bering Sea and are also indigenous to Japan. Coho range from the Arctic to Baja and along the shores of Korea and Japan.

CHINOOK SALMON
RANGE
PRIME FISHING

Few sportfish go by such an array of names as do the chinook and coho. Their widespread popularity with sport and commercial anglers has resulted in a confusing range of local names. The chinook is also known quite appropriately as king salmon, an obvious reference to the fact that no salmon is larger. In addition, chinook are called tyee by many native bands, and inshore

COHO SALMON
RANGE
PRIME FISHING

**Chinook Salmon**

**Coho Salmon**

anglers now label any chinook in excess of 30 pounds a tyee. Commercial fishermen call any chinook in excess of 30 pounds a smiley. Chinook are known throughout Canada as spring salmon, as they are the first to return to the rivers each spring. Chinook can easily be distinguished from the other salmon species by their black gum line. Coho are usually called silvers in the U.S. Other popular nicknames for coho include hooknose (for the distinct hook-shaped nose on the males) and blueback. Coho also have needlelike teeth and a white gum line.

Chinook occasionally reach prodigious size. The current IGFA all-tackle record is an astounding 97-pound, 4-ounce monster taken in the Kenai River. The largest known chinook is a 126-pound fish taken by a commercial troller. The size and stamina of chinook salmon have resulted in many legendary battles. A Kenai River angler battled a huge

chinook for more than 22 hours before losing it at the net. Rivers Inlet, another locally famous spot for huge chinook, has been the scene of many battles that have lasted from 6 to 12 hours.

Coho, while not nearly as large as chinook, are still far from easy to land. The moment a coho slams a lure, it heads for the sky. It is not uncommon for a coho to tailwalk all the way around the boat, do a half-dozen complete flips, charge the boat and leave you with trembling hands and a slack line. Many avid salmon anglers believe the coho is the finest battler of all; others give the nod to the chinook. They both deserve special recognition among America's top gamefish.

Both chinook and coho rely on keen eyesight and an even keener sense of smell to guide them to their prey. Their vision is so extraordinary that they can home in on a 2-inch long herring from many yards away. Scientists believe that salmon navigate

from Arctic feeding grounds to their natal rivers by using their extraordinarily keen sense of smell.

Chinook and coho are opportunistic feeders. Herring, smelt, anchovies, candlefish and krill compose a large part of their diet. But both species have been found with squid, crab larvae, small salmon and other marine fishes in their stomachs. Naturally, herring and anchovies are top baits for both species. Many artificial lures, including Hoochies and lead jigs, are designed to imitate squid and candlefish.

## Where to Find Chinook and Coho

Chinook originating in rivers from Oregon to British Columbia tend to spend their ocean phase in Arctic waters. As they begin migrating back to their natal rivers, they pass through southeast Alaska, the waters of British Columbia's inside passage, and along the Washington coast. Top spots to intercept chinook include Alaska's Cook Inlet, Sitka and Ketchikan; British Columbia's Queen Charlotte Islands, Rivers Inlet and Campbell River; and Washington's Neah Bay, LaPush and Westport. The mouth of the Columbia River is often red hot in August. Oregon anglers find good numbers of chinook near Depot Bay, Newport and Brookings. California anglers do well at Eureka and San Francisco Bay.

In several areas hatchery-raised chinook are imprinted to stay near the vicinity where they were planted. Puget Sound is home to millions of such hatchery chinook, locally known as blackmouth. These fish stay in the sound their entire life, providing excellent fishing each year from November through April. While these immature chinook are small, averaging from 4 to 12 pounds, their abundance more than makes up for their size.

Coho tend to limit their migration to a few hundred miles from the river of their birth. Top-notch coho angling opportunities occur in Alaska at Seward, Cordova, Sitka, Ketchikan and all along Prince of Wales Island. Further south, anglers score great coho catches at Rivers Inlet and Port Hardy, British Columbia. Washington anglers do well all along the Strait of Juan de Fuca, as well as at Neah Bay, LaPush, Westport and the mouth of the Columbia River.

Chinook tend to follow the shoreline as they migrate. Consequently, the best fishing is often very near shore. Prime spots include steep rock walls that drop into great depths. At Rivers Inlet anglers fishing the wall often troll with their rod tip nearly brushing the rocks. The same technique is used all along the inside passage, where steep rock faces plunge into great depths.

Chinook love to hold on the down-current side of points and underwater structure. As the tide forces baitfish past, chinook dash out for an easy meal. Phenomenal chinook fishing can be had at Stuart Island, British Columbia, where the currents often run as fast as 10 knots. The surging water disorients small baitfish, bringing the waiting chinook an easy meal.

Coho tend to stay out in open water as they make their way toward the spawning grounds, and the best coho fishing is often as much as 10 to 20 miles offshore. Watch for seagulls and murlettes working to locate schools of coho. The coho will almost always be found near large schools of bait. If the bait is deep, birds may not be present, but you can see the bait balls on any good depth finder.

Coho will often tarry for days or even weeks if they encounter large school of baitfish. Since baitfish tend to stay near underwater plateaus and major structures, always target such areas to begin your hunt for coho.

Both coho and chinook congregate near the mouth of rivers as spawning time approaches. In every coastal community local fishermen will know when the fish are due and what rivers hold the most fish. While the chinook and coho may accumulate in large numbers near river mouths, they are often hard to catch. As the salmon begin the transition from salt to fresh water, they gradually stop feeding. Even when thousands of fish can be seen rolling on the surface, hooking them can be very difficult.

## How to Catch Chinook and Coho

The best way to attract either species is to match your offering to what the salmon are eating. Before you head out, ask the local anglers what type and size bait the salmon have been eating. Once you know that, you can begin narrowing your choices of bait or lure. If chinook or coho are present and you match the size, color and presentation of your bait or lure to their primary food source, success is assured.

Nothing imitates the real thing better than live bait. Chinook tend to respond to live bait better than coho, but both will inhale a well-presented live bait. It is essential that you fish live bait in areas with significant tidal flows. Try to find spots where baitfish are present, then estimate where the tide will sweep the baitfish.

Serious salmon anglers use pumps to keep sea water flowing through their bait tanks. Casual anglers simply rig an ice chest with an overflow pipe fitted near the top. New seawater is dipped into the tank before the herring are added and every twenty minutes or so all day long.

Herring will stay frisky for twenty minutes or more if you hook them gently and are careful not to drag them through the water too fast. It's important that your bait is lively.

For fishing live bait, a typical rig consists of a long 10- to 12-foot mooching rod, a level-wind reel, a swivel, a slip sinker and a two-treble hook harness. The best weighting system for live bait fishing is a round lead fitted with a hollow plastic center tube. The main line is inserted through the lead, which slides freely on the line. A swivel below the lead acts as a stopper. Eight to 12 feet of leader material is tied between the swivel and the bait harness. The best leaders are limp, small-diameter monofilament or fluorocarbon in the 12-pound-test range.

The top hook is placed through the clear membrane just in front of the herring's eye. It's important to keep this hook clear of the herring's lower jaw so it can breathe naturally. The back hook is slipped just beneath the skin near the dorsal fin, and must be inserted carefully to avoid injuring the herring (below).

For best results try to keep your bait directly under the boat. This assures that the herring has a slack leader, allowing it the freedom to swim naturally. If the line angles away from the boat significantly, you are trolling. Trolled baits do not swim naturally, and will die quickly.

When a salmon inhales a live bait, it often immediately swims toward the surface. The rod tip, relieved of the pull of the sinker, will suddenly spring up. The instant the rod pops up you must start reeling. The faster you reel the better your chances of getting a solid hook set. If you are fast enough you will soon feel substantial resistance. If you are into a chinook, it will almost certainly head back for the depths. A hooked coho will very likely head for the surface.

Fresh, bright baits are considerably more effective than the dull, soft baits most anglers use. Even if you do not intend to fish your bait alive, you should start your day with live bait. If you plan to fish with cut plugs or fillets, wait to kill the bait until you need it. Fresh baits are firm, have all their scales intact, and give off the most scent.

When using frozen bait thaw only a few at a time so that you are always using bait that is firm and fresh. Thaw your bait in fresh seawater and be careful not to disturb any scales when pulling the bait away from the packaging.

Take care to wash your hands in seawater before touching your bait. Once the bait is on the hook, never let it touch the floor of your boat, where it may pick up the smell of oil or gasoline. Be especially careful not to have strong-smelling scents such as sunscreen, gasoline or motor oil on your hands when touching bait. However, don't be afraid to use attractor or cover scents to increase the appeal of your bait.

Salmon are almost always where the baitfish are, so to increase your odds for success, constantly be on the alert for the presence of bait. A depth finder will show baitfish that are suspended in the water column, as will feeding seabirds. When you find bait stay near it and try to work lures or bait just above the baitfish. If there are no baitfish where you are fishing, there are probably no salmon. Don't be afraid to pick up and move until you find baitfish.

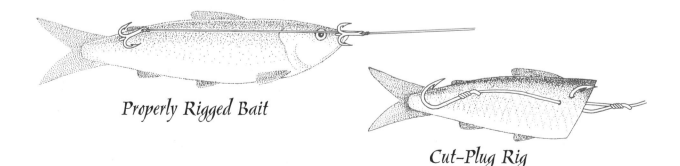

*Properly Rigged Bait*

*Cut-Plug Rig*

If herring are the salmon's primary food, stick with whole herring or try making cut plugs (opposite). These are made by slicing the herring head off at a double angle. The blade of your knife should cut from just behind the gills on an angle toward the tail and away from you. Getting a perfect angle can be tricky at first, but cut plug templates, which are available in many tackle shops, assure a perfect cut every time.

The bait should spin in a tight circle as it passes through the water. By experimenting with the placement of your hooks, you will learn how to increase or decrease the spin. Chinook almost always prefer a tight spin, while coho often prefer a big looping spin.

If anchovies are the preferred baitfish, use them as bait, although they tend to be too soft to use as cut plugs by themselves. Plastic holders can make it a snap to get a perfect roll on an anchovy, however.

To trigger more strikes from salmon you must do something to make your bait behave erratically. Steering a zigzagging course will make your baits slow down and speed up. The bait on the outside turn will speed up and lift toward the surface, while the one on the inside will slow and fall. Another excellent way to give your bait action is to slip the motor into neutral every few seconds. As the boat slows, the bait will drop. When you shift back into gear, the bait will lurch forward and begin to climb. That's usually when a salmon will attack.

Trolling speeds and depth for chinook are very different than for coho. Chinook like a slow-moving bait, and they often feed at depths of 40 to 200 feet. Mature chinook will seldom strike a bait trolled at more than two knots. Coho want a much livelier presentation. Optimum trolling speed for coho is between 2 and 5 knots. Coho are usually at depths of 10 to 30 feet.

One of the first lessons a salmon angler will learn is that salmon follow baitfish. Whenever experienced salmon anglers see bait scampering across the surface, they stop whatever they are doing and rush over to fish near the bait. The key to successfully finding bait balls and the salmon that often accompany them is to cover a lot of water, fast. This is best done by cruising as fast as possible without losing the signal from your depth finder. If you have a properly-mounted depth finder, you should be able to cruise at 15 to 20 knots while receiving an excellent signal.

With one eye on the depth finder screen and the other on the water, cruise until you find a school of bait. Don't worry about passing over the bait so fast that you miss it. The bait schools you are looking for are at least 10 feet in diameter. A typical school of baitfish will appear on the screen as a haystack shape.

If you do not see salmon under the bait, try slowly cruising around the school. Pay particular attention to the up-current side of the school. Strong currents often sweep baitfish along. When that happens, the school may form a shape like a comet. There will be a ball-shaped main body with a tapering tail consisting of straggling baitfish. Often the salmon will follow along, picking off stragglers near the end of the "tail".

In this situation, select a jig that is the approximate size and color of the baitfish present, and fish it through the bait to the depth where the salmon are showing up on the depth finder. If no strike comes, reel up rapidly and repeat.

A slack line is your sign that a salmon has intercepted the jig. A striking salmon will dash toward the surface to intercept a falling jig, and the momentum often keeps the fish moving toward the surface for several seconds after the grabs. When that happens, the line will go slack. A fast hook-set assures a hook-up before the fish can spit the lure.

Veteran anglers seldom make more than five unsuccessful drops before moving. If chinook or coho are feeding on the bait ball, strikes will come fast. If no fish are present, reel up and start looking for the next bait ball.

The ideal jigging setup includes a 6-foot, medium-action rod with a fast tip, a level wind reel and limp monofilament line. Use a top-quality level wind reel capable of holding 300 yards of 12-pound line. Lead jigs in the 1½- to 4½-ounce range are the best choice, depending on the depth of the bait.

Top jigs include Zzingers, Point Wilson Darts, Buzz Bombs, Crippled Herrings and Dungeness Stingers. Favorite colors include white, green and white, blue and white and chrome.

Many anglers have taken up the fly rod in pursuit of both chinook and coho. For years salmon anglers have targeted coho by trolling large bucktail flies designed to imitate herring. This technique, known as bucktailing, is great sport when large numbers of fish are congregated in a small area.

Recently, with the advent of fast-sinking fly lines, anglers have been successful in targeting both chinook and coho with flies. Flies used for both species are made of polar bear hair, deer hair and various artificial materials. The best patterns are 3- to 6-inches long with a blue, black or gray top and a white or light-blue bottom. The closer

**Lefty's Deceiver**

the fly comes to imitating the size and shape of the salmon's natural forage fish, the better the chances of success. Popular flies include Lefty's Deceiver (above) and Clouser Minnows.

For coho, fly casters can often use a floating line in conjunction with a weighted fly. The retrieve must be rapid and erratic to get the coho's attention. Those targeting chinook usually use heavily-weighted lines that will sink rapidly to get the fly down to where the chinook live. The best technique involves casting as far as possible and waiting for ten to thirty seconds to let the fly get to the desired depth. The best retrieve when targeting chinook is a series of short strips followed by a pause.

## *Other Salmon*

CHUM SALMON. The chum salmon (*Oncorhynchus keta*) has more names than any other Pacific salmon. Common names include chums, dogs, calico, tiger trout, keta and silver brights. Alaska natives call them dogs because they are often used to feed sled dogs. British Columbian

**CHUM SALMON**
■ RANGE
■ PRIME FISHING

anglers often call them tiger trout, a reference to the distinct purple bars that adorn the spawning phase of the chum's life cycle. In Japan, where chum roe is considered a great delicacy, they are known as keta. Chums are typically considered a valuable food fish, but are often disdained by sport fishermen. This is due more to their ghastly spawning colors than to any well-considered analysis of their sporting qualities. Any angler who has caught all five species of Pacific salmon will rate the chum as among the strongest and most tenacious of the bunch.

While many salmon species are in steep decline throughout their range, the chum salmon is thriving. This is due to dramatically increased

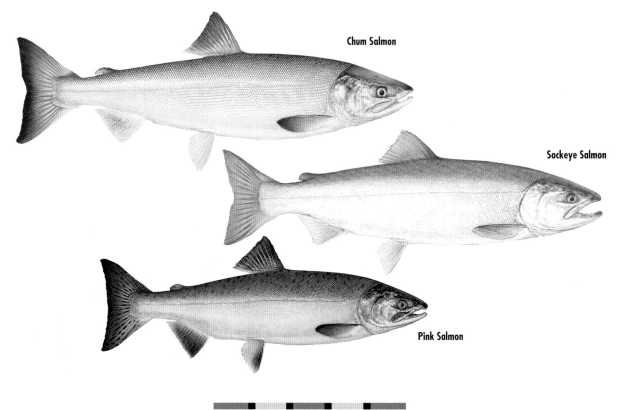

**Chum Salmon**

**Sockeye Salmon**

**Pink Salmon**

hatchery production as well as the chum's ability to successfully spawn under adverse conditions.

Once in salt water, chums migrate to the Arctic, where they grow fat on a diet composed largely of plankton and other tiny marine creatures. The chums strong preference for plankton is one reason anglers seldom do well trying to catch them with traditional baits. By the time they head back to their natal rivers, most chums average about 10 pounds. Twenty-pound chum salmon are common, and the current IGFA all-tackle record is 35 pounds.

Although chums are difficult to hook in salt water, anglers who slow-troll cut-plug herring near the surface often do quiet well. Guides in Campbell River, British Columbia, are now targeting the area's abundant chum runs with very good success.

Given its abundance and strong fighting characteristics, the chum is rapidly becoming a favorite among knowledgeable anglers.

SOCKEYE SALMON.
Sockeye are among the most abundant of Pacific salmon. Sockeye salmon *(Oncorhynchus nerka)* range from Japan to Alaska and as far south as Los Angeles, but few rivers south of the Columbia hold significant populations. Also known as reds and blueback, sockeye typically weigh 4 to 7 pounds

SOCKEYE SALMON
RANGE
PRIME FISHING

with the occasional fish as large as 15 pounds. Sockeye are by far the most valuable commercial salmon. Their bright red flesh brings a premium price in the market.

Unfortunately, sockeye are usually difficult to take in open salt water. Sockeye feed on tiny crustaceans and therefore are not often tempted by typical salmon baits or lures. On occasion, when sockeye are highly concentrated, anglers catch them using a flasher and a small red Hoochie or even bare hooks behind a flasher. Once in fresh water, sockeye often become aggressive and readily take flies, spinners and

spoons. Landlocked sockeye, also known as kokanee, are targeted in many areas. The landlocked sockeye readily take a variety of small spinners and spinner and bait rigs.

PINK SALMON.
Pink salmon *(Oncorhychus gorbuscha)* are the smallest and the most numerous of the Pacific salmon. The commercial harvest of pinks in Alaska and British Columbia numbers in the millions. Pinks, or humpies as they are also known, range from Japan to the Arctic and south to California. However, pinks are not common south of Puget Sound.

PINK SALMON
RANGE
PRIME FISHING

The pink salmon is unique in several ways. Unlike most Pacific salmon, it has only a two-year life cycle. This results in a relatively small salmon, typically 3 to 5 pounds, with occasional fish reaching as much as 12 pounds. Pinks are also unusual in that they only return every other year. In the northern part of their range pinks run in even-numbered years. In the southern part of their range they appear only in odd-numbered years. Near the Campbell River, in the center of their range, they appear every year.

Pink salmon are not highly regarded by many salmon anglers. This is a shame, as they fight very well on appropriate tackle, and the flesh, while a bit soft and light pink, is very good if properly prepared.

Pinks are so prevalent in southeast Alaska and northern British Columbia that most anglers don't bother fishing for them. In Puget Sound, where the runs are smaller and the number of anglers greater, pinks are prized. Thousands of Puget Sound anglers eagerly await the August return of pinks.

Pinks tend to school in huge groups, typically near the surface. They will readily take a trolled cut-plug herring or a Hoochie trolled on a short leader behind a flasher. Pinks seem to have a strong affinity for pink lures. A favorite lure is the ½-ounce pink Buzz Bomb.

—*Dave Vedder*

# KELP BASS (Calico Bass)

Ask almost any southern California salt water angler, and the first fish that comes to mind when you broach the subject of inshore fishing is the calico bass. These fish are technically called kelp bass, but this name is little used and hardly recognized along a waterfront that holds "calicos" in such high esteem. These salt water bass are not large and are slow to grow, yet over the last half-century, year in and year out, they have ranked among the top three species caught by the southern California party-boat fleet. As the southern California salt water bass fishing craze evolved, it expanded from the bays and harbors out to waters along the coast. Structure-hugging kelp bass became the primary target of a new breed of small-boat angler. These new anglers were willing to motor across the kelp beds and fish tight to the whitewater surge along boulder-laden beaches just to hook up with a monster "bull" calico.

The kelp bass (*Paralabrax clathratus*) is one of three related species of bass found along the southern California coast; the other two are the barred sand bass and spotted sand bass. Although these different species share some of the same habits and habitat, the calico is easily distinguished from the other two by a series of large white blotches or patches along its back and sides. The coloration of kelp bass, depending on their habitat, can vary from nearly black on the head and back to a greenish gray to a rusty copper-brown. Additionally, a golden hue will often highlight their face and underside from the lower jaw to the pectoral fins. Another distinguishing feature is that the kelp bass lacks the noticeably longer third dorsal spine characteristic of both the barred and spotted sand bass.

Reported as far north as the Columbia River (at the Oregon-Washington border), kelp bass are predominately found south of Point Conception and down along Mexico's Baja peninsula to Magdalena Bay. Considered a resident species, kelp bass tend to cling to the coastline, but unlike their sand bass cousins, calicos are also abundant around the offshore islands along the southern California and northern Baja coast. In fact, fishermen have reported observing schools of kelp bass swimming just below the surface in the middle of the Santa Barbara Channel, apparently migrating between the Channel Islands and the mainland.

Calicos grow slower than the two sand bass species, requiring about six years to reach their 12-inch legal size. (California regulations require fishermen to release any kelp bass measuring less than a foot in length.) They do grow a bit larger (nearly 15 pounds and 30 inches long) and live longer (at least 34 years) than their California cousins. Because of this slow growth rate the average kelp bass caught aboard southern California party boats often weighs just a pound or two. Private boat anglers who are more mobile catch more of the 6-pound-plus "bull" bass. A 14-pound, 7-ounce calico is recognized as both the California state and IGFA all-tackle world records.

## Where to Find Kelp Bass

As their name implies, kelp bass are often found around kelp – usually thick kelp forests, although an isolated kelp stringer will do at times.

**KELP BASS**
RANGE
PRIME FISHING

For young kelp bass, the canopy formed by the large blades of giant kelp waving in the coastal currents and pulsating tidal surge offers nourishment, protection from predators and a vantage point for ambushing prey. In general, the size of kelp-oriented bass increases as the water gets deeper. Larger fish, however, will occasionally come to the surface early and late in the day to feed. With age, older bull calicos tend to become solitary, sometimes leaving the kelp forests and orienting to food-rich rocky structure, moving seasonally between deeper water and the shallows, where tides surge against rock jetties and swells roll onto rugged stretches of coastline.

The best fishing for kelp bass coincides with their spawning season, which is rather long and stretches from May into the fall months, with June the peak period. This is also the period when water temperatures rise, energizing kelp bass and making them more active and aggressive. During the winter months, calicos are inclined to hold near the bottom as the cold water slows down their metabolism. However, well-presented baits and lures will still catch fish.

During these warm-water months look for periods of stable or slowly rising water temperatures. A sudden drop of even two or three degrees

CALICO BASS stalking a baitfish school

is often enough to shut off the bite. Tidal movement is also important in triggering aggressive behavior in bass. An exchange of 4 feet or more on the incoming tide is the most productive time to catch feeding calicos, particularly in the outer edge of kelp beds. Closer to shore, strong tides in combination with moderate swells tend to stir up the bottom, triggering a feeding frenzy by washing food loose from the kelp and rocks. The turbulent, off-color water assists the bass in ambushing their prey, and enables anglers to trick the older, wiser calicos into slamming artificial lures.

Anglers use a "tight to structure" approach along the coast in pursuit of larger bull bass. Here, the best action is often early and late in the day, when big fish typically move up into the surf zone to feed. Look for fish over shallow reefs and around *boiler rocks* (semi-exposed rocks just outside the surf zone).

From the Santa Barbara area south, inshore hot spots for calico bass include the numerous kelp beds and patch reefs found down the coast. Prime rocky shoreline areas can be found just north of Malibu and around the Palos Verdes Peninsula (Los Angeles County), along Laguna Beach (Orange County) and off La Jolla (San Diego). Also productive are most rock jetties and breakwaters at the entrance to southern California harbors, the most significant being a 9-mile wall of rock that separates the San Pedro/Long Beach harbor from the open ocean.

## How to Catch Kelp Bass

An increasing number of southern California anglers who target calico bass are switching from bait to lures to make it easier to release these fish which they have come to admire and respect. Kelp bass are anything but shy about eating live baits, with a particular affinity for anchovies. Larger bass eat live squid like they're candy and will horse down sardines, "brown baits" (queenfish and white croaker) and even small mackerels if given the opportunity. Be aware that calico bass dive for the protection of the kelp after grabbing a live bait. Again taking a lesson from party boat skippers, inshore anglers have learned to anchor up-current from kelp beds and use a chum line to draw the bass out and away from the hazardous kelp stringers.

Smaller kelp bass appear first in the chum line, often so close to the surface that an anchovy, fished weightless, collar-hooked on a #2 live bait hook is all the terminal gear you'll need to catch fish. For these smaller bass in relatively open water, a standard 7-foot live bait rod and 10- or 12-pound-test line spooled on either a spinning or baitcasting reel are adequate. However, when fishing big-fish areas such as one of the offshore islands during a squid spawn in the wintertime, anglers will want to be prepared. A sliding egg sinker positioned just above a 4/0 hook rigged through the tail end of a live squid (below) will attract larger calicos. A medium-heavy action rod and a baitcasting reel spooled with 20-pound test is a better combination for applying the brakes to a strong fish that's headed for cover.

As stated above, chumming brings the smaller calicos out into the open to feed. This does not mean there are no big calicos around, as the big bulls tend to hunker down deep or remain relatively close to the kelp stringers. Big bass specialists, aware of this fact, grab a jig rod and drop rigged baits down deep below the chum line. Others find the best technique is to yo-yo a jigging spoon, or slow wind a lead-head jig with a plastic trailer under the smaller fish. Still others cast lures or bait out to

*Sliding Egg Sinker and Live Squid*

20 lb. main line

1-ounce egg sinker

4/0 bait hook

the edge of the kelp beds. For this technique anglers rely on precision baitcasters, custom-made 10-foot rods, heavier line and a lot of skill to catch fish from longer distances.

Working lures near the surface is also a favorite approach of small-boat anglers, who motor along the coast casting to boiler rocks for big calicos. Retrieving just fast enough to make the jig wobble will often produce exciting surface strikes. Anglers should be alert when presenting baits in this situation, as big bass tend to hit quickly and bolt sideways into the structure. A heavy-action, 8-foot jig rod and baitcasting reel spooled with 30- to 40-pound-test abrasion-resistant line are used to leverage determined bulls out of these tough neighborhoods.

As exciting as surface strikes can be, inshore anglers who concentrate on calicos tight to the beach find their most consistent success when fishing versatile lead-head jigs rigged with soft plastic tails. Generally a shad-type, paddletail, or some form of curl-tail grub are the best options. A 6½- to 7-foot medium-heavy fast-action rod, with significant backbone and light tip, is ideal for this kind of fishing. Precision casting, quick, positive hook sets, and maximum leverage are all required to be successful. Baitcasting reels are preferred, with reliable, smooth drag systems, high-speed retrieve ratios (5:1 or better), and spools filled with 12- to 20-pound-test abrasion-resistant line.

Four- to 6-inch plastics, rigged on ¾- to 1½-ounce leadheads molded around hooks from 5/0 to 7/0 in size, are best. In general, use larger baits and a faster retrieve during the summer months, when the fish are most active and the water is off-color. Scale down in lure size and slow retrieve speeds as waters become clear and cool during the winter. Heavier lead is necessary where currents are strong or long casts are required. As a rule, use the lightest jighead that will still keep the bait in the strike zone along kelp stringers. When fish are biting lightly try using a stop-and-go retrieve, cycling 10 cranks followed by a two-second pause, to encourage a strike.

During the winter and early spring, when calico bass are less active, a single or double curl-tail grub, 4 or 5 inches in length, rigged on a ½- to ¾-ounce lead-head is best. Because curl-tails provide action with a very slow retrieve, they are ideal for stop-and-go techniques, vertical jigging or crawling along the bottom. Add a strip of squid to encourage strikes under very tough conditions. When

using soft plastics, choose color patterns that mimic live bait found in the area you are fishing. Keep in mind that bull calicos will often feed on small fish and other marine creatures that camouflage well around rocks and kelp.

Slow trolling with crankbaits (4- to 6-inch models in patterns that imitate baitfish) along the edge of kelp beds and breakwaters can trigger hard-hitting strikes from kelp bass. The same approach can be used along inshore reefs with deeper diving plugs. Electric trolling motors often perform best in these situations, as well as for maneuvering tight to the kelp and rocks along the beach. Caution is the word, as this kind of fishing can be dangerous. Keep the outboard ready to kick into gear for a quick escape from submerged rocks or surprise waves.

Big calicos ordinarily charge fast-moving baits hard, and inhale them on the fly as they keep coming toward the boat. Because of this tendency, it is important to reel fast until the line tightens up before you set the hook. This trait actually helps get bass farther from cover, thereby increasing your chances of landing the fish.

When you use finesse jigging techniques, calicos are prone to pick up lures on the drop, making it vitally important to watch for movement in your line or hold your line between your fingers to detect a subtle strike. On the other hand, calicos will usually slam live bait, making it difficult not to react by setting back hard. Prepared anglers spool with heavier line, have a tight drag, and horse the fish out and away from hazards. The trick to this method, however, is applying the right amount of pressure since big calicos tend to run harder for cover as more pressure is applied. Experienced anglers know the right balance of pressure to apply, but beginners have to learn through trial and error. A fish that seems hopelessly buried in the weeds or rocks can sometimes be coaxed to swim out if you let your line go slack.

Because "sub-legal" kelp bass (less than 12 inches) are so common along the southern California coast, anglers should be prepared to carefully release them with a minimum of handling. Clipping the line when a hook is swallowed is usually the best option. Scientists suggest that allowing older kelp bass to continue spawning helps preserve a stronger gene pool and a healthier calico fishery for the future.

—*Tom Waters*

# PACIFIC HALIBUT

The Pacific halibut holds the distinction of being the largest north Pacific gamefish, and many would argue it's the tastiest as well. Only the salmon has more devotees than the halibut, but even dedicated salmon anglers are usually delighted to hook into this battling behemoth. No other north Pacific gamefish holds such potential to break your line, break your rod and break your heart.

The Pacific halibut *(Hippoglossus stenolepis)* goes by different names depending on its size. Small fish, those between 10 and 50 pounds, are known as "chicken" halibut. The big girls (all trophy class halibut are females) are known as "barndoors" in reference to their size, color and shape.

No one knows how big Pacific halibut may grow. The IGFA lists the current all-tackle record as a 459-pound fish from Dutch Harbor, Alaska. Commercial fishermen have landed much bigger fish, and recreational anglers often tell tales of halibut so large that even the heaviest tackle would not budge them. Halibut exceeding 800 pounds have been reported. The truth is no one fishes with tackle heavy enough to land the largest halibut. This is a fish tailor-made for "the big one that got away" stories.

Pacific halibut range from Santa Rosa Island, California, to the Bering Sea. They reach greater size in the northern reaches of their range, but fish weighing more than 100 pounds are found throughout the range. From Washington south, 100-pound halibut are rare. Farther north, however, 100-pound halibut are common and 200-pound fish are often seen. In the Aleutian Islands 300- and even 400-pound fish are taken each year. Two men

PACIFIC HALIBUT
RANGE
PRIME FISHING

fishing from a small skiff, near Dutch Harbor, Alaska landed a barndoor over 400 pounds.

Halibut are migratory, often moving as much as 2000 miles. They spawn in deep water during the winter months. A 140-pound female may deposit as many as 2,500,000 eggs. The young fish live on the bottom of sandy inshore bays. As they reach adulthood, they migrate to deeper water.

While most large halibut are taken from water deeper than 100 feet, there are notable exceptions. A 400-pound halibut was taken from the boat harbor in Ninilchik, Alaska, and several 200-pound fish have been taken from boat docks at Alaska fish camps.

Halibut don't get that big by being dainty eaters. A check of the stomach contents of large halibut has turned up whole rockfish, Dungeness crabs, octopus and salmon. It seems clear that halibut will eat almost any form of protein they can find, and the bigger the better.

As halibut search the depths for squid, octopus, crabs and injured baitfish, they rely on a keen sense of smell, sharp eyes and an excellent lateral line. Halibut often home in on food with their sense of smell. They also use their lateral line sensitivity to detect vibrations, leading many anglers to purposely bang the bottom with downrigger balls or heavy weights to attract a halibut's attention.

## Where to Find Pacific Halibut

Noted hot spots for halibut include Newport, Oregon; Neah Bay, Washington; northern Vancouver Island; the Queen Charlotte Islands; southeast

Alaska and the Aleutian Islands. The Aleutians offer perhaps the world's finest halibut fishing. There anglers consider an 80-pound fish a "chicken." Aleutian Island halibut skippers routinely release fish weighing less than 50 pounds. When the weather lets the skippers get to the best fishing grounds, limits come easily and the average size of fish retained often tops 100 pounds.

Throughout their range halibut show a strong preference for relatively flat sand or mud bottom. Many of the best halibut-producing areas are underwater plateaus, also known as *banks*, with depths of 100 to 400 feet, a relatively flat bottom and sand, mud or gravel surface. Look for halibut in or near depressions or small underwater hilltops. Because halibut often move great distances, an area that was hot yesterday may be cold tomorrow. But halibut are creatures of habit. They will usually return time and again to a locale that meets their needs for habitat and food.

In late summer halibut congregate near river mouths to feed on the carcasses of spawned-out salmon. This is especially true of rivers with big runs of pink and chum salmon. These salmon tend to spawn in the lower reaches of small rivers. When a major rainstorm comes just after the spawn, halibut know an easy meal awaits near the river mouth. At this time salmon bellies are the best bait.

Because halibut tend to congregate in distinct areas, only a few consistently produce lunkers. Ask around to learn as much as you can about where local anglers took their trophies. If possible, getting the exact GPS coordinates to take you to the hot spots can be a big help. Often the areas where the big halibut roam are very deep, far from port and hard to find.

## How to Catch Pacific Halibut

Given the fact that halibut spend virtually their entire life with their belly touching the bottom, their food always comes from above. To be successful in catching halibut, your gear must be within a foot or two of the bottom.

It's not difficult to get a halibut to strike once it finds your bait or lure. Halibut have been caught on an amazing variety of lures and baits, including Zzingers, Spinnows and Scampi jigs. The best live baits include herring, salmon bellies and baby octopus. Although halibut inhale a lure with a vengeance, they will often nibble at a bait for a long while. Knowing this tendency, you need to wait until the rod is bent solidly before setting the hook.

Most halibut anglers know they must keep their lure near the bottom, but many make the mistake of leaving their gear motionless. You can greatly increase your odds of hooking a halibut by using a jigging motion with whatever lure you choose. An ideal presentation is to drop your gear to the bottom, lift it up a foot or so, then drop it back fast, letting it thump the bottom. This should be repeated every 10 seconds. This jigging action accomplishes three objectives. The sound of your gear thumping bottom will get the halibut's attention, the rapid falling motion of your bait will trigger an instinctive strike response and the movement of your bait or scented lure will help spread the scent trail throughout the water column.

After three or four jigging cycles let your lure rest just above the bottom for 15 to 30 seconds before beginning the cycle again. Halibut will strike a motionless jig if they have been watching it bounce along the bottom for a while. This is an effective variation on the non-stop jigging action employed by many, and it will help conserve your strength for the battle ahead.

Halibut skippers from Vancouver Island to Langara Island believe in big baits for big halibut. When guides target the big barndoors, they select baits in the 2- to 10-pound range. Whole salmon heads, salmon bellies, salmon guts and rockfish fillets are favorite baits of trophy tacklers. Again the bait is fished on some type of bottom rig or spreader bar (below).

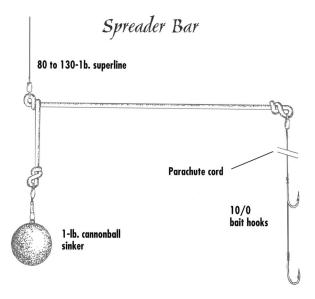

### Spreader Bar

80 to 130-1b. superline

Parachute cord

10/0 bait hooks

1-lb. cannonball sinker

Many expert halibut anglers use a "sandwich" of salmon guts, horse herring and cod fillets. Halibut will eat almost anything, including rotten salmon, but most experts agree the best baits are fresh. Fillets fresh from a cod caught that day are a top choice (right). If the goal is a barndoor of over 100 pounds, savvy skippers use an entire salmon or cod carcasses from which the fillets have been removed. They just put a hook through the lips and lower the whole bait to the bottom.

Bragging-size halibut swim with an undulating motion called galloping, and when you do hook a barndoor you will know it instantly. The first sign that you have hooked a monster comes when she "gallops" off in spite of all the drag your arms and reel can stand. Few angling thrills match the feeling of several hundred pounds of halibut galloping away at an unstoppable pace.

Landing a halibut is arm-wrenching work – slowly pumping the short rod skyward, then reeling in a few feet of line as you drop the rod tip toward the halibut. After what seems like a thousand pumps, after your forearms have been threatening to cramp for a half-hour, after the rod butt has turned your mid-section black and blue, a huge brown silhouette appears beneath the surface. Now is the crucial point of the battle. Landing a huge halibut is tricky and can be more than a little dangerous. The preferred methods for taming these bruisers are harpooning and gaffing.

Many seasoned halibut anglers carry a harpoon to subdue and tether huge halibut. Halibut harpoons have a sharp 6-inch metal tip that slips over the end of a wood or aluminum spear used to ram the tip through the halibut. Once the tip has passed through the fish, the handle is withdrawn, flipping the tip over much like a toggle bolt. A short length of steel cable connects the harpoon tip to a 10-foot length of nylon rope that is in turn attached to a large buoy. Now the halibut can dive and thrash until exhausted. The really big ones will

LARGE BAITS such as strips of cod meat work well for "barndoors."

dive for up to four minutes. But the harpoon wound and the inexorable pull of the buoy always force them to the surface. There is almost no chance of losing a halibut with this method because the angler's hook serves as an effective back-up to the harpoon line.

Halibut of up to 50 pounds can be handled with a traditional gaff hook. Fish larger than that need special measures. Professional halibut skippers often use a flying gaff. They attach a 10-foot length of nylon rope to a large shark hook. When the big halibut finally comes to the surface, the deckhand leans over and slips the shark hook through its jaw from the inside. Although this sounds tricky, it's quite simple. When the big fish opens its mouth to gasp, the deckhand strikes. Once the hook is securely in the halibut's lip the attached rope is tied to a cleat. For fish over 100 pounds halibut skippers use two or even three gaffs, each securely tied off to a cleat.

Halibut anglers prefer heavy standup rods. Reels need to have heavy gearing, butter-smooth drags and at least 300-yard line capacity. For the main line the best bet is braided Dacron or superline in the 80- to 130-pound range. Leaders should be 400-pound parachute cord attached to a 16/0-circle hook. (Commercial-long liners have proven that circle hooks are by far the most effective hooks for halibut.)

Halibut are among the toughest fish in the Pacific. Even after being harpooned or gaffed, these flatfish can still tear your boat apart. To be absolutely safe, and to assure top-quality table fare, bleed every halibut thoroughly. Slash the halibut's gills, then tow it behind the boat for at least 20 minutes before bringing it aboard. This isn't a sport for the timid or those with a queasy stomach, but if you are ready for a brawl, halibut will oblige.

—*Dave Vedder*

# BARRED SAND BASS

Although not the most glamorous of southern California inshore sport fish, the barred sand bass is among the most readily available. Sand bass are particularly plentiful from early to mid-summer, when they school up to spawn. This is when "sandies" become super-aggressive, quick to strike almost any kind of bait or lure, and often easy to catch. Because they are easy to catch and good to eat, sandies are the ideal target for a family fishing trip. They move between offshore waters and bays and harbors, and are pursued by boaters and shore-bound anglers alike because of their bulldog-like fighting qualities and the challenge they present on light tackle.

A close relative of both the kelp bass

(p. 106) and the spotted sand bass (p. 138), barred sand bass share some of the same habits and habitat of its two cousins. The barred sand bass *(Paralabrax nebulifer)* is distinguished primarily by its coloration and markings. Unlike the patches visible along each flank of the kelp bass or the prominent small spots characteristic of the spotted sand bass, the barred variety displays a greenish to gray to brownish back, a whitish belly, and a series of irregular vertical, somewhat angled, dusky bars along each side. Otherwise, a noticeably longer third dorsal spine distinguishes both barred and spotted sand bass from kelp bass.

Although barred sand bass range as far north

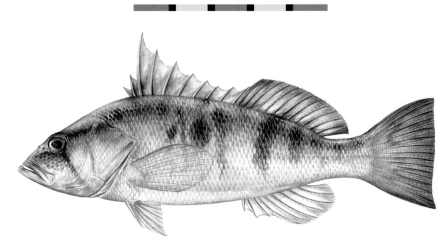

BARRED SAND BASS
RANGE
PRIME FISHING

as Monterey Bay, most are found south of Point Conception, with the largest concentrations found along the central west coast of the Baja California peninsula, as far down as Magdalena Bay. Researchers have theorized that some of these fish may actually migrate up the coast into southern California inshore waters each summer.

Although barred sand bass grow quicker than kelp bass and spotted sand bass, they still need four to five years to stretch 11 inches in length and reach sexual maturity. To ensure at least one opportunity for these fish to spawn, California regulations require that anglers release, unharmed, any barred sand bass measuring less than 12 inches in length. Sandies are known to live long as long as 24 years, reaching lengths in excess of 2 feet and double-digit poundage. The average catch, however, ranges anywhere from 1 to 3 pounds, with 5- to 7-pound "grumpies" being fairly common. The IGFA all-tackle world record catch for a barred sand bass stands at 13 pounds, 3 ounces, which is also the California hook-and-line record for the species.

## Where to Find Barred Sand Bass

Although known to range as deep as 600 feet, most barred sand bass are targeted by inshore anglers fishing in much shallower water. Like other salt water bass species, sand bass are inclined to orient to structure. But unlike kelp bass, which will burrow into the weeds and rocks, the barred variety tends to hover over sand and mud bottoms adjacent to reefs, rockpiles, grass beds and pieces of sunken debris. In the spring, in response to warming water temperatures, sand bass pull away from deeper water structure and move inshore to

congregate for summer spawning. They seek open-water areas over wide expanses of relatively flat bottom that range from 50 to 100 feet deep. Here the sandies feed and spawn vigorously for a two-month period.

This is prime time for sand bass fishing, with combative fish willing to grab almost any kind of bait or lure cast in their direction. Flotillas of watercraft will clearly mark the fishing grounds, where schools of aggressive sand bass often move vertically in the water column. Using your depth finder is the best method to pinpoint the location of suspended schools of sand bass. There is no faster action than when you locate a bunch of sandies working a school of anchovies.

Productive spots (from south to north) for fishing the summer sand bass spawn include the flats off Imperial Beach, the clam beds north of Oceanside (both in San Diego County), and Huntington Flats, a wide expanse of hard bottom between Huntington Beach and Seal Beach just south of the Los Angeles County line. To the north, the wide expanse of nearshore waters in Santa Monica Bay is often the best place to start.

Aside from the summertime spawning frenzy, large barred sand bass are most often caught around deep-water structure. Smaller sandies typically move into the bays, harbors and lagoons dotting the southern California coast, and offer anglers some excellent light-tackle fishing opportunities. Here, barred sand bass share habitat with spotted sand bass, though the barreds are more inclined to hug bottom in the deeper water along the channels, where there are clams and grass beds. Fishing is often best during a moving tide. The deep waters of San Diego Bay offer a terrific wintertime fishery for barred sand bass. Big sandies are also the target for small-boat anglers fishing "the wall," an extensive rock breakwater bordering the San Pedro/Long Beach harbor area.

## How to Catch Barred Sand Bass

The peak of the summertime sand bass spawn offers light-tackle salt water fishing at its best. Appropriate spinning or baitcasting gear includes, 6- to 8-foot live-bait or popping rods, and line from 6- to 15-pound-test. Anchovies are the most popular live bait, but sardines and small mackerels can entice strikes from bigger grumpies, as can whole squids and "brown baits" (queenfish and white croaker) when available. When the bass bite is really on, fleshy strip-baits will readily catch fish. Also effective are a wide range of artificial lures such as lead heads, metal jigs, spoons and plugs, which can be fished in any number of ways. Casting, cranking, yo-yoing, bottom bouncing and trolling are all effective methods.

For anglers targeting the flats for spawning sand bass, drift-fishing and anchoring are both effective. Drifting enables you to cover more area, but if a large school of fish is located, anchoring allows you to concentrate on a promising spot and possibly chum fish to the surface and into a feeding frenzy (Anchovies are a popular chum). For bait fishermen, catching sand bass at or near the surface often requires no more than fly-lining (casting with no weight attached) a collar-hooked live bait. If needed, pinching on a split-shot or small rubber-core sinker 12 to 18 inches above the hook encourages rigged anchovies to swim deeper.

When sand bass are down deep, use either a double dropper-loop, reverse dropper-loop or sliding sinker rigs for bouncing the bottom. Double dropper-loops (each 6 to 8 inches in diameter with a live-bait hook attached) are typically tied into the main line about 2 feet apart, with the bottom loop positioned another 2 feet above a snap that attaches to an interchangeable sinker (usually a pyramid style of 4 to 8 ounces, depending on depth and current). This is a good rig when anchored as it allows you to present multiple baits at one time. When drifting for sand bass, use the reverse dropper-loop, with a torpedo sinker attached to

a loop tied into the main line 18 to 30 inches above the hook, or a sliding egg-sinker rig. Both of these rigs are virtually identical to rigs commonly used for drift-fishing for halibut.

As a rule, match your hook size to the available bait (small hook, small bait) to allow the bait-fish to swim naturally. For sand bass use a #1 or #2 hook for rigging an anchovy, a 2/0 to 4/0 for rigging squid, and nose-hooking sardines or other oversize baits. Collar-hooking (right) can encourage anchovies to swim more erratically, though they tend to stay on the hook better when pinned through the snout. Snout hooking (right) is advisable when you need to drop a rig down fast and sneak past pesky mackerel that have invaded the area, or in heavy current. Anal hooking (right) encourages anchovies to swim downward.

Artificial lures at times attract more strikes from barred sand bass than do live baits. Among the most effective lures are leadhead jigs (½- to 2-ounces) rigged with soft plastic shad-type swimbaits, or single and twin curl-tail grubs. Color patterns that mimic live baitfish often produce best, particularly on the spawning grounds. Straight retrieves, stop-and-go, jigging and bottom bouncing can all be productive. Also effective for spawning sandies are shiny spoons and metal jigs (4- to 5-inch profiles) with bait-imitating colors being best. Work them at different depth ranges in the water column. Sweetening a jig with a squid strip will often enhance a lure's appeal; others use a 5-inch-long strip of squid on a plain lead head jig. For enticing larger bass near structure, hook the tail of a live or fresh-frozen squid on the treble hook of a metal jig. When yo-yoed, this "jig-n-squid" combination looks like mating squid and drives big grumps crazy.

Trolling with soft plastics or diving plugs (4- to 6-inch profiles in patterns that closely resemble live baitfish) can also be effective in catching summer sand bass. This also serves as a good way to cover a lot of ground when searching for concentrations of suspended fish. Early and late in the year, trolling deep-diving plugs can be a productive way of locating both

**Dropper–Loop Rig**

15 lb. main line

6-inch loop

#1 bait hook

18 inches

3-6 ounce torpedo sinker

## Anchovy Hooking Techniques

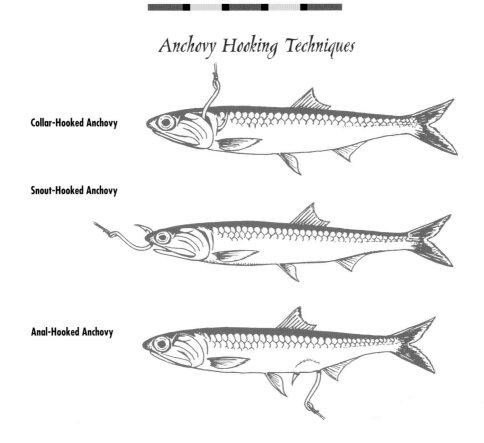

Collar-Hooked Anchovy

Snout-Hooked Anchovy

Anal-Hooked Anchovy

barred sand bass and kelp bass that hold tighter to structure. In bays and harbors, lures that troll just deep enough to nose into the mud can also be productive.

Although live bait catches plenty of barred sand bass in harbors, far more are hooked in bay waters by anglers bottom-bouncing lead head jigs (usually ¾- to 1-ounce sizes) rigged with soft plastics. Rather than the baitfish-imitating colors that are used on the open water flats, swimbaits and curl-tails in darker patterns usually best represent what sandies are feeding on. Because sand bass often hold along main channels where tidal flows run strongest, the trick is to keep the jig down in the strike zone. Along the deep-water channels of San Diego Bay, bass anglers find it necessary to feed up to 150 yards of line when drifting in order to hold bottom. Some experts drifting with plastics will hit bottom, then use a slow, steady retrieve until a bass "climbs on" their jig. Often they don't even need to set the hook. They simply crank the fish to the boat.

In contrast to the bay-fishing with jigs during the summer spawning frenzy, barred sand bass generally hit live anchovies with authority. In fact, when live-bait fishing for sand bass there is no need to freespool line so the fish can run with it, as they usually inhale such offerings and hook themselves.

*—Tom Waters*

# CALIFORNIA HALIBUT

For their food value alone, California halibut (*Paralichthys californicus*) rank as a favorite with seafood lovers in general, and with California's salt water fishermen in particular. However, the demand for their tasty flesh and the resulting pressure applied by commercial fishing interests were nearly the undoing of this popular food and game species. Only after gill nets were banned from inshore waters along the California coast did the state's valued California halibut and white seabass fisheries begin to recover from years of overfishing. No longer do anglers just catch halibut incidentally while targeting other species. With a renewed promise of success and the prospect of a delectable meal, anglers are once again targeting halibut.

Not to be confused with the much larger Pacific halibut (p. 111), the California halibut belongs to the left-eyed family of flounder (Bothidae), although nearly half of the Californias caught have their eyes set on the right side. An interesting note is that all flatfish, including halibut, are spawned with an eye on each side of the head. One of the eyes migrates during early developmental stages until both are positioned on the same side of the fish. The eyes are located on the darker, often mottled top side, while the underside or "blind-side" of the halibut is generally white. California halibut are distinguished from most other flatfish species by their very large mouth and numerous needle-sharp teeth.

Although occasionally found as far north as Vancouver Island, British Columbia, the largest concentrations of California halibut range from the San Francisco Bay area south to Magdalena Bay (on the west coast of the Baja peninsula), with isolated populations found in the upper stretches of Baja's Sea of Cortez. Studies have shown that these flatfish are inclined to move seasonally between deep water and shallow water rather than migrate up and down the coast.

Because California's halibut fishery has suffered through hard times, and because the fish are relatively slow growing, the state's regulations require that anglers release all California halibut measuring less than 22 inches in length (about 4 pounds). Catching "shorts" is quite common, and a legal fish is considered a prize. A *barndoor* (a California halibut over 20 pounds) is considered a trophy. In recent times more and more halibut in the 30- to 50-pound range are being caught, and records are being broken. The current IGFA all-tackle world record catch for a California halibut stands at 58 pounds, 9 ounces, which is also the state record. Halibut do grow larger than this, as a monster 72-pound, 8-ounce specimen was once speared in southern California waters.

## Where to Find California Halibut

Although sometimes harvested from offshore waters deeper than 300 feet, the majority of California halibut are taken by inshore anglers in less than 100 feet of water. At any depth, halibut hug what is usually a sand, mud or gravel bottom, and the pigments in their skin change to camouflage them with their surroundings. In some instances, halibut (often the larger specimens) will orient to structure and wait in ambush for unsuspecting prey that wash away from adjacent rock, weeds or kelp beds. Otherwise, halibut are content to congregate on flat

CALIFORNIA HALIBUT
■ RANGE
■ PRIME FISHING

sandy bottoms that play host to clams, sand dollars, shrimp, squid or small baitfish, all of which contribute to a halibut's diet. Oscillating the fins that border nearly the full length of both sides of their wide, flat torsos, halibut cover all but their protruding eyes with sand. Then they lay motionless, waiting to surprise-attack anchovies, sardines, smelt, grunion, lizardfish and squid.

The odds of finding willing halibut increase dramatically where an abundance of baitfish have been pushed into the shallows, or where bait balls can be located on your depth finder in deeper water. Most important to inshore anglers is the halibut's spawning cycle, which begins in the early spring as they move up into the shallows from their deeper winter sanctuaries. Studies suggest that halibut spawn just offshore in waters ranging from 40 to 60 feet deep, and continue to spawn

*Productive areas for California halibut*

Productive halibut areas

Pinole Pt.
Pt. San Pablo
San Rafael
RICHMOND
Bolina Pt.
Stinson Beach
South Hampton Shoals
BERKELEY
Rocky Pt.
Muir Beach
Pt. Bonita
OAKLAND
TREASURE ISLAND
North Bar
SAN FRANCISCO
ALAMEDA
Seal Rocks
Candlestick Pt.
Shallow Mud Flats
Mussel Rock
Oyster Pt.
San Bruno Shoals
Pedro Pt.
Coyote Pt.
Montara
Pillar Pt.

through the summer. Having spawned, adult halibut will often follow schools of baitfish into the bays and harbors, joining juvenile flatties that, for the first two years of their lives, seek these warm-water areas that offer an abundance of food and protection from predators.

From Bodega Bay, California, south to the Mexican border, any number of flat, sand-bottom stretches may produce halibut. Most halibut fishermen can be found drift-fishing with live baits over long stretches of hard sand bottom. Inside the bays, harbors and lagoons, sand-bottom areas adjacent to a channel are often the most productive location, particularly during the period from an hour before to an hour after high or low tide. Along the beaches, California halibut often congregate along the down-current side of jetties and piers, and surfcasters often find fish where there is a mix of sand and rock contours.

Larger "barndoor" halibut are caught from inshore waters of every kind. Most larger fish are taken by boaters that set up a drift or anchor up-current from likely structure and cast down current. In San Francisco Bay area, the waters just outside the Golden Gate Bridge, around well-known Seal Rock, routinely yield larger halibut for inshore anglers, as do the expansive waters of southern California's Santa Monica Bay. The structure-laden coastal stretch just north of Malibu is so productive for halibut that each spring the harbor at nearby Marina Del Rey is headquarters for a number of very popular halibut derbies.

## How to Catch California Halibut

For all-around halibut fishing, a 7-foot graphite rod with a substantial butt section (for leverage) and a relatively light-action tip (both for detecting subtle bites and for setting the hook without tearing it from the soft tissues of a halibut's mouth) is a good choice. Match this with a quality baitcasting reel with a smooth drag to accommodate the sudden and powerful runs of which big halibut are capable. For more hookups, some halibut fishing experts choose to replace traditional monofilament fishing lines with superlines and low-visibility fluorocarbon leaders.

Most anglers fish for halibut with bait, usually anchovies or sardines, although larger mackerel, "brown baits" (white croaker and queenfish), live squid and shiner perch often catch more barndoors.

California anglers have learned that live smelt, grunion and lizardfish work very well in some situations.

In San Francisco Bay, as well as along the southern California coast, drift-fishing while bottom-bouncing or dragging live bait rigs near the bottom is the most popular approach for halibut. For this technique a three-way rig is a popular choice. Typically a 15- to 20-pound-test main line is attached to one eye of the swivel. A foot-long, 10-pound "breakaway" line for the sinker is tied to another eye, and a 5-foot, 20-pound fluorocarbon leader with the hook attached occupies the remaining eye. Attaching a snap-swivel to the end of the breakaway line allows for a quick change in the amount of weight required (generally 4 to 8 ounces) as depth, wind and currents fluctuate.

Equally popular for drift-fishing live baits is the reverse dropper loop rig. Typically a short loop from 6 to 8 inches in diameter is tied in anywhere from 18 to 30 inches above the end of a 15- to 20-pound-test main line to which the hook is tied. To the loop you attach just enough weight to hold bottom (usually a torpedo sinker ranging from 3 to 6 ounces). This is a quick rig to make, and is very low maintenance. When drift conditions change, different sizes of sinkers can easily be interchanged on the loop, and if your hook breaks off, a new one can quickly be retied to the remaining line.

To encourage more hookups, some anglers have found success using a sliding sinker rig. Anglers fishing for halibut inside southern California's shallow back bays often use this approach by simply rigging a sliding egg sinker on the main line above a ball-bearing swivel, to which the leader and hook are attached. For drift-fishing along the coast, a plastic "slider-with-snap" unit (opposite page) can be substituted for the egg sinker. The snap allows for various styles and sizes of sinkers to be interchanged, depending on conditions. Four feet of super-tough, nearly invisible fluorocarbon leader will encourage more strikes and ultimately more hookups. The slider rigs allow halibut to grab the bait and take line without feeling resistance. This same setup works equally well for surf casters pursuing halibut along the beaches.

While most boaters will drift fish or anchor for halibut, others have devised deadly slow-trolling tactics using live bait. In the San Francisco Bay area, anglers have adopted a technique they call "motor mooching," where they slow-troll against winds and

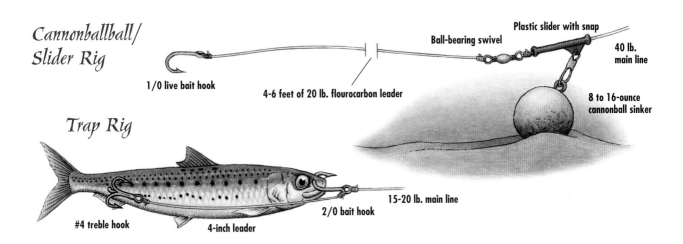

**Cannonballball/ Slider Rig**

Plastic slider with snap
Ball-bearing swivel
40 lb. main line
1/0 live bait hook
4-6 feet of 20 lb. flourocarbon leader
8 to 16-ounce cannonball sinker

**Trap Rig**

15-20 lb. main line
2/0 bait hook
#4 treble hook
4-inch leader

currents. This allows control over the way live baits are presented. Some troll with a three-way swivel setup, while others use the same plastic slider-snap rig previously described. However, the rig is modified with a heavier leader of 40-pound test and treble hook. Instead of attaching the sinker directly to the slider's snap, anglers snap on a swivel with a foot-and-a-half length of 30-pound-test leader. The leader terminates with a snap of its own for changing out cannonball sinkers. For small-boat anglers, up to four lines can be trolled at a time if the two front lines are rigged with heavier balls (up to 1 pound) and the two back lines with 6- to 10-ounce weights that allow them to drift back slightly.

A standard rig for live anchovies, smelt and lizard fish is a size #2 or #4 live bait hook rigged through the bait's lower jaw and up through the top of the nose. Sardines will often require a 1/0 or 2/0 hook, and mackerel up to a 5/0, with the single hook rigged sideways through the nose of these larger baits. For slow-trolling live baits for halibut, a size #2 or #4 treble hook is sometimes used, with one of the hooks rigged through the bait's nose.

Also popular with Southern California halibut anglers is a *trap rig* (above). Sometimes called a "stinger hook," the concept, when rigging a sardine, is to tie about 4 inches of fluorocarbon leader to the eye of the single or treble hook. To this leader attach a #6 trailing treble hook, then hook it in the tail section of the bait to help catch short-striking halibut. (Catching a big halibut on such a treble hook trap rig can disqualify the catch for IGFA world record consideration.)

Trailing "stinger" hooks can be very effective for catching halibut, which are notorious for the delicate manner in which they strike live bait. Because of this light-biting tendency, many anglers keep the reel out of gear and thumb the spool, feeding line to a nibbling halibut and refraining from setting the hook until the bait is inhaled and the weight of the fish loads up the rod. Use a tight drag and a firm sweeping motion when setting the hook, then back off the drag if needed and use a slow, steady retrieve. Be careful not to let the fish's head break the water's surface to prevent head-shaking and sudden runs that can break lines or tear hooks from a halibut's tender mouth.

California halibut are often caught on bait-imitating artificials, often incidentally by anglers fishing for other species. Lead head jigs rigged with soft plastics, sometimes "sweetened" with a strip of squid, are particularly effective for anglers who fish the harbors or work the surfline. Crankbaits that nose into the sand will also catch halibut inside the bays, and are especially effective when slow-trolled along the coast just outside of the surfline. In deeper water, metal jigs, including a plain chrome-plated torpedo sinker rigged with a hook, catch their share of halibut when rattled across the bottom. As in other types of halibut fishing, disturbing the bottom often triggers strikes.

Although California halibut have impressive teeth, they are conical shaped with no cutting edges and rarely slice through line. However, they are needle sharp on the tips and affixed in a vise-like jaw that can do serious damage to fingers. For this reason anglers should carry pliers for removing hooks. Large halibut should be gaffed when boated, but a net should be used for sublegal fish. If the hook has been swallowed, cut the line and release the fish. The hook will rust away. Efforts to return undersize fish unharmed will help assure that the once-depleted California halibut fishery will make a full recovery.

—*Tom Waters*

# PACIFIC BARRACUDA

The Pacific variety of barracuda may not be as big or strong as its subtropical counterpart, the great barracuda, (p. 76) but it is as spirited and aggressive. If barracuda walked the streets, it wouldn't be safe to go out at night!

As mean as Pacific barracuda *(Sphyraena argentea)* look and can be, they are a popular gamefish along the southern California coast and are good eating when quickly bled and prepared properly. Pacific barracuda are long and slender like their southeastern cousins, armed with a mouth full of sharp, canine-like teeth for foraging on small baitfish. The West Coast cuda is distinguished by its fine-scaled, brown to dark-grayish back, silvery to whitish sides and belly, prominent black lateral line and yellow-tinted, deeply forked tail.

Although cuda range as far north as Alaska, they are most often found from Point Conception south into Mexican waters. Pacific barracuda have been known to measure up to 5 feet in length and weigh over 18 pounds, but most caught by sportfishermen are much smaller, averaging 3 to 6 pounds. A 15-pound, 15-ounce fish stands as the California state record, while the IGFA all-tackle mark for the species (also

PACIFIC BARRACUDA
■ RANGE
■ PRIME FISHING

known as the California barracuda) is a 26½-pound monster caught off Costa Rica. Barracuda were fished heavily in the 1950s and 60s, and populations declined so drastically that in 1971 California instituted a 28-inch size limit for sport-caught cuda. Since then, they have made a dramatic comeback.

## Where to Find Barracuda

Typically, barracuda are first encountered in early spring by southern California boaters making the trek out to Catalina, San Clemente or Los Coronados islands, hoping to intercept the first runs of migrating yellowtail. Barracuda are swimming north from Mexican waters, and the offshore islands are usually their first stop on the way to the summer spawning grounds along southern California's coastal kelp beds.

Barracuda, also known as barries, scooters, logs (big brutes) and pencils (baby barracuda), rarely school at depths in excess of 60 feet, and, like other *pelagic* (open-water) gamefish species, are inclined to push schools of baitfish, usually anchovies, to the surface. Diving birds are often a clear indicator of barracuda or other gamefish feeding below, and in cases of a feeding frenzy, barries will sometimes appear as "missiles" being launched.

Though some migrating barracuda choose to take up residency in local waters and provide year-round sport, it is from early spring through

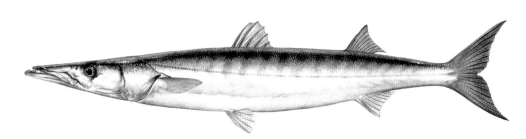

mid-summer that barracuda fishing is typically best. From north to south, productive inshore bites have traditionally been in Santa Monica Bay, around the Horseshoe Kelp (Long Beach), the Barn Kelp (Oceanside), and both the La Jolla and Point Loma kelp beds (San Diego), but schools of barries can pop up almost anywhere in between. Pier fishermen will intercept barracuda at times, and smaller barracuda will often enter the bays and harbors, providing action for boaters and shorecasters alike. Areas around docks and floating live-bait receivers attract cuda.

## How to Catch Barracuda

Usually, the best way to locate areas with barracuda is either by high-speed trolling (at 6 to 7 knots) bait-imitating plugs, or by drifting and chumming with live anchovies. In either case, the key to keeping barracuda schooled around your boat is to maintain a modest but continuous chumline. The idea is not to feed the fish, but to keep them interested.

When planning to fish live bait for barracuda, bring along patience and a lot of extra hooks. No matter how strong your favorite monofilament line is, barracuda can use their nasty dentures to quickly part ways. To combat frequent bite-offs, a common practice is to attach a 6- to 8-inch light wire leader between the live-bait hook and the monofilament. However, unless cuda are in a feeding frenzy, highly-visible wire leaders tend to deter strikes and restrict the movement of a live bait. Some veteran anglers switch to a heavy monofilament leader as long as 3 feet using 50-pound test, attached with an Albright Special knot to a 10- to 15-pound-test main line and a #2 or #4 live-bait hook. Depending on the size of the bait a 1/0 or 2/0 hook may be needed. The heavy mono provides reasonable protection from sharp teeth, and is less visible to wary barracuda. Securing the hook with a loop knot allows the bait to swim more naturally. To fish deeper, slide a ¼- to ½-ounce egg sinker up the leader

before tying the loop knot.

Cuda specialists choose a healthy bait and rig it sideways through the nose, keeping in mind that the liveliest baits (those that swim strongly down and away from the boat) are the first ones taken. After a gentle lob cast, keep the bail open on a spinning reel, or with a baitcaster, stay out of gear and thumb the spool. When the bait is picked up, freeline for several seconds to allow the fish to take the bait (twice as long with a big bait) before engaging the reel and firmly setting the hook.

Be sure the drag is set properly, as barracuda are inclined to make a series of short, fast runs. Once the fish is turned in your direction, retrieve line carefully. Erratic rod movements and heavy pressure encourage barracuda to vigorously shake their head and tear loose.

Barracuda favor bait-imitating lures, usually 4- to 6-inch profiles. Flashy metallic spoons, jigs, crankbaits and various forms of soft plastic baits all produce. Proven lure color patterns for Pacific barracuda include white, blue and white and chrome. Barries typically use short bursts of speed to attack lures, often from behind, and will inhale smaller lures and bite down on your line, which is why leaders are preferred. It's not unusual to feel or see your line go slack as a barracuda overtakes a lure on the retrieve. When this happens crank fast to pick up the slack before trying to set the hook.

Erratic retrieves are good for coaxing cuda strikes, as is dropping the lure to bottom and cranking it up. Many anglers prefer to fish barries with single-hook lures or replace trebles with a single hook because singles hook just as well, and are easier to remove from a tooth-filled mouth. Anglers fishing bait should clip the line on deeply-hooked fish that are going to be released rather than kill the fish trying to "dig" the hook out.

*—Tom Waters*

# YELLOWTAIL

Others in this group include amberjacks and crevalle jack (p. 82). The closest of its relatives, though, is the southern yellowtail, found only in the southern hemisphere of the Pacific. The southern variety grows a bit larger in size, but otherwise the two are almost identical in appearance. Both have two dorsal fins, are a metallic blue-to-greenish color above and silvery-to-white below, and have a brassy-to-gold horizontal stripe extending from the eye to their yellowish, deeply-forked tail.

Yellowtails typically range from Point Conception in California south into Mexican waters, and are often abundant along either side of the Baja peninsula. Most yellowtails caught inshore along the southern California coast measure less than 3 feet long and weigh under 15 pounds. However,

YELLOWTAIL
■ RANGE
■ PRIME FISHING

40- to 50-pound trophies are boated occasionally, and even larger yellowtails are caught along Baja's west coast. The long-standing California state record yellowtail catch is 62 pounds, while the IGFA all-tackle mark for the California variety is an 80-pound, 11-ounce monster caught in 1998 from Mexican waters. For California fishermen, the bag limit for yellowtails is 10 fish per day, only five of which can measure less than 24 inches (fork length).

## Where to Find Yellowtails

Yellowtail usually don't swim within range of southern California inshore anglers until summer arrives, after which the action can continue well into the fall. If the squid spawn is prolific off the southern California coast during the winter, yellowtails can linger year-round to feed, primarily out around the offshore islands (Catalina, San Clemente and Los Coronados). This is also where the first springtime

**P**ound for pound, there are few fish in any ocean that can "smoke" line off a reel faster and with more authority than a yellowtail. They range up to 40 pounds or more and are available to southern California anglers for both inshore and offshore fishing. Yellowtails are responsive to a wide variety of baits and lures, and are a delight at the dinner table. It's no wonder these high-octane tackle-busters rank as one of the most popular and challenging gamefish along the southern California waterfront.

The California yellowtail *(Seriola lalandi dorsalis)* is a member of the jack family.

yellowtail bites typically occur when water temperatures climb to 60 degrees. These fish are the first of many schools of yellows that migrate north into southern California waters from Mexico each spring.

While some migratory yellowtails congregate around the islands, others stay offshore to feed on small baitfish under floating kelp paddies, and yet others orient to deep-water pinnacles and ridges where forage is also plentiful. Yellowtails move freely between the surface and depths in excess of 200 feet, feeding on baitfish, squid and pelagic red crabs. By early summer, schools of smaller "firecrackers" (yellowtails of less than 10 pounds) move inshore and up the coast, where they're most often encountered by anglers fishing near the coastal kelp beds. Occasionally, an inshore angler will hook up with an old "mossback"(a large yellowtail) that has taken up residency in the kelp.

Beginning in the south, top spots for catching inshore yellowtail have traditionally been the La Jolla and Point Loma kelp beds (San Diego), the Barn Kelp (Oceanside), the Horseshoe Kelp (Long Beach), and Rocky Point (off Palos Verdes), but yellows can pop up almost anywhere in between, although rarely along the beaches or in harbors.

## How to Catch Yellowtails

Typically, from summer on into fall, southern California partyboat and small-boat anglers will encounter a fair number of yellowtail, often while fishing for bass, barracuda and bonito near kelp beds within a mile or two of shore. Most inshore yellows are caught on live baits (primarily anchovies and sardines), with the bite usually best when the boat is anchored and a chumline is maintained in an area where current is running.

When hard-charging yellowtails weighing 10 to 15 pounds or more crash the chum, it's best to be fishing with no less than 20-pound line and a baitcasting reel with a flawless drag system. A 7½-foot rod with a light tip but substantial butt section helps in both casting lightweight baits and leveraging strong fish. In many cases, anglers will simply *flyline* their bait (fish with no weight attached) or add a split-shot, or a ¼- to ½-ounce rubber-core or sliding egg-sinker above the hook. This can help the angler in more effectively work the water column.

When choosing live bait, remember that the strongest-swimming baits are the first ones bit, and no inshore baitfish swims harder than a mackerel.

Local small-boat anglers in the know will find schooling macks and jig some aboard before heading to the yellowtail grounds. In general, smaller hooks and lighter line encourage smaller baits to swim stronger and more naturally. A 3/0 to 5/0 hook is ideal for rigging mackerel. For rigging anchovies, use a #2 or #4 live bait hook, and for larger sardines use a 1/0 or 2/0 hook. Anchovies can be rigged through the nose or through the collar behind the gill plate, or anal hooked (p. 117). Sardines and mackerel are most often hooked sideways through the nostrils, a method also used by expert small-boat fishermen who have mastered the deadly approach of slow-trolling these larger baits for hard-to-catch yellowtails. The key here is to feed the bait 100 feet or so behind the boat, slow your trolling speed to a crawl, and keep the reel out of gear with your thumb lightly on the spool. As with any approach to live bait fishing, when a yellow strikes, let the fish run with the bait (usually to the count of five) and take it well before you set the hook.

Once a yellowtail feels pressure, it will explode on a sizzling, powerful first run. Although instinct tells you to slam on the brakes, the harder you pull, the harder the fish will run. This can prove disastrous if it's a big yellow and is able to dive deep into the kelp or across a rock reef. At times, the best approach can be to back off the pressure altogether. Suddenly, feeling little or no resistance, a yellowtail will often stop running and ultimately allow itself to be slowly finessed back to the boat.

Throwing the "iron" (die-cast, diamond-shaped metal jigs) is another favorite approach to catching yellowtails on artificial lures. With 8- to 10-foot jig rods and the proper casting technique, these heavy lures allow for long casts to the larger, boat-shy fish that are often circling along the outer perimeter of the chumline. Also effective for yellowtails is the use of a shorter, sturdy rod and up to 30-pound line when fishing jigs down deep. For inshore fishing where depths rarely exceed 100 feet, allow the jig to hit bottom, then retrieve it as fast as you can crank. Favorite jig colors for yellowtails include white, blue and white, blue and chrome, "scrambled egg," green and yellow, and mackerel patterns.

Although it is are only available to southern California inshore fishermen during certain times of the year, the yellowtail is both a challenging and hard-fighting species.

—*Tom Waters*

# WHITE SEABASS

I t wasn't long ago that southern California salt water fishermen worried that the white seabass might go the way of the dodo bird. Commercial fishing pressure, coupled with a complete collapse of the sardine fishery (a major source of forage for white seabass) relegated seabass to endangered species status. This prompted California fish and game authorities to mandate strict fishing regulations. The whites' great size, strong runs and superb eating qualities accounted for their popularity and led to their overharvest. But with the banning of gillnets from inshore waters, the return of sardines, and an ambitious fisheries restoration program in place, white seabass are making a comeback.

The white seabass (*Cynoscion nobilis*) is not a true bass but a "croaker," closely related to the corbina, weakfish and Gulf Coast spotted seatrout. In fact, juvenile seabass, frequently caught from southern California bays and harbors, are commonly referred to as "sea trout." Juveniles up to 2 feet in length have five or six dark vertical bars along their sides, which are commonly faded on larger adult fish. Adults are bluish above (with bronze to gold highlights) and frosted silver to whitish below. They turn to shades of gray minutes after being removed from the water.

Known to range as far north as the Gulf of Alaska,

WHITE SEABASS
▓ RANGE
■ PRIME FISHING

most white seabass are caught far to the south, from Santa Barbara down along the Baja coastline, including waters in the upper reaches of the Gulf of California. The IGFA all-tackle record for a white seabass is 83 pounds, 12 ounces and was caught in the Mexican gulf. In California, the hook-and-line record for the species stands at 77 pounds, 4 ounces. California state regulations require that any sport-caught white seabass measuring less than 28 inches be released.

## Where to Find White Seabass

As much as the availability of sardines as forage correlates with a healthy white seabass fishery, it's squid that really turn whites on. Where you find concentrations of squid, which move seasonally into southern California offshore waters to spawn from mid-winter into early spring, you'll find white seabass. Top spots to fish are usually out around the offshore islands with Catalina the most productive. And because squid don't often drift into nearshore waters, anglers should start with the islands. When squid are found near the coast, look for whites in deep-water canyons and dropoffs near (from south to north) La Jolla (San Diego), Laguna Beach, Palos Verdes Peninsula (where an 80-pound white was once speared), and the Deep Hole (north of Malibu). Anywhere there is a showing of squid, hungry whites will be nearby.

White seabass are most vulnerable to fishermen's hooks during the time their spawning coincides with squid spawning (the peak period being May and June). During this time California's daily bag limit for anglers drops from three fish to one fish. At times other than this spawning period white seabass fishing can be unpredictable. Smaller fish frequent the bays and harbors, often congregating around bait receivers. Occasionally a large white is pulled from the surf, yet rockfish fishermen have caught "king croakers" in waters 300 feet deep. During the summer and fall, seabass are typically an incidental catch for small-boat anglers fishing for other species over artificial reefs and around coastal kelp beds in 30 to 90 feet of water.

## How to Catch White Seabass

Live-baiting an anchovy, casting a spoon or swimbait, or trolling a bait-imitating plug in the vicinity of a live-bait receiver inside a southern California harbor is sometimes a way to target a white seabass. Although the odds are that it will be a smaller fish, 25- to 30-pounders have been taken this way. They are also taken on occasion by surf fishermen making distance casts with long rods, heavy sinkers and stout line. Discounting a 25-mile run out to the islands, though, the best chance for Southland small-boat anglers to score on sizeable seabass is to work deep-water, rocky shorelines or submerged reefs and coastal kelp beds.

Much can be learned from expert anglers who have spent years fishing the squid bite out at Catalina Island. The general consensus is that the best place to catch white seabass is over a sandy bottom in 90 to 150 feet of water. The best times are at dawn or dusk, especially when strong currents are pushing from at least a 5-foot tidal exchange. After the squid leave the area, small boat experts typically find big seabass foraging up in the "green" water of the shallows, around kelp beds and in the white waters up against the islands.

Anglers should keep in mind these seabass tendencies, along with the fact that whites rarely feed at the surface, and for the most part don't stray far from the bottom. Inshore boaters should concentrate their efforts over sandy areas adjacent to structure (rocks and kelp beds) that extend from deep water toward the shoreline. Whether live-baiting squids, sardines or mackerel, the same tackle and rigs that work near the bottom out at the islands are productive inshore as well.

Eight- to 9-foot live bait sticks and revolving-spool reels with reliable drags are favored by seabass experts, as is the lightest line weight that's practical. Twelve- to 15-pound test is preferred for line-shy seabass and allows a rigged live bait to move naturally, while 20- to 30-pound test might be needed to stop a big white from wrapping in nearby kelp. For rigging sardines and squids, a 1/0 or 2/0 live-bait or circle hook is appropriate. Going to a 4/0 for rigging multiple squids and a 6/0 hook for larger mackerels. In many instances, a sliding egg sinker from 1/4- to 1/2-ounce, positioned against the hook, may be all the weight needed to get your bait down into the strike zone. Almost as simple and equally effective is to tie a dropper loop into your main line 30 inches above your hook, then attach a torpedo sinker to the loop, using just enough weight to get down and hold bottom.

Jigs have also proven very productive in catching white seabass. Heavy, 5- to 6-inch diamond jigs, with white being a favorite color, can be dropped to the bottom, cranked upward three or four turns, and then yo-yoed up and down with the rod tip. Hesitate on the way down, as that's often when the whites grab the lure. Some anglers will rig a whole squid on the treble hook to enhance the jig's appeal. Also effective is a 1-ounce leadhead jig rigged twice through the tail of a fresh dead squid and jigged around deep structure.

Patience is often the rule when awaiting a seabass strike, then even more patience to allow a big fish time to take the bait before you set the hook. White seabass are notorious for making one or two strong, streaking runs (drags should be set light), after which they are often brought to the boat fairly easily. The trick is not to apply so much pressure that the hook tears out of the fish's soft mouth.

Anglers' release efforts, in conjunction with the intensive work of the Carlsbad White Seabass Hatchery and the volunteers who manage over a dozen strategically located southern California seabass grow-out facilities, can help assure a bright future for this species. The goal of this facility is to release more than 100,000 juvenile white seabass into local waters each year.

*—Tom Waters*

# LINGCOD

They will not make any top-ten lists for the most beautiful fish species, will attack almost anything smaller than themselves, and have a serious attitude problem. Lingcod *(Ophiodon elongatus)* apparently have little to recommend them. So why do West Coast anglers love these fish that even a mother lingcod doesn't love? (Female lingcod often eat their offspring!) The answer is simple: They are excellent eating and, when hooked on appropriate tackle, provide an exciting battle.

Lingcod are the most aggressive of all north Pacific salt water predators. Anglers battling rockfish and salmon often have their prize stolen by a hungry lingcod. Lingcod are so aggressive they will try to swallow fish that are nearly their own size. Many trophy-class lingcod are caught by anglers who hook a 5- to 10-pound lingcod, only to have it inhaled by a 30-pound-plus lingcod.

Lingcod are long and slender from head to tail, but their head and mouth are disproportionately large, with several rows of saber-sharp teeth. Their coloration varies from dark brown to pale green. The belly is usually lighter brown to cream colored. The entire fish is usually mottled with shades of brown or gray.

Lingcod inhabit North American waters from northern California to south central Alaska. The largest specimens typically are found in the northern part of their range.

Although lingcod rely primarily on keen eyesight to track their prey, a great sense of smell helps them home in on their victims. Anything that moves or falls rapidly will excite a lingcod's interest. Lingcod will eat almost anything, including other lingcod, rockfish, salmon, herring, candlefish and anchovies.

While the current IGFA record lingcod is 64 pounds, commercial longline fishermen routinely catch much larger fish, with 80-pound specimens being reported. Though the largest lingcod are consistently taken in the northern part of their range, northern California waters hold large numbers of 5- to 10-pound lingcod.

LINGCOD
RANGE
PRIME FISHING

## Where to Find Lingcod

Prime lingcod areas include the northwest tip of Washington state, the west coast of Vancouver Island, the Queen Charlotte Islands and southeast Alaska. Lingcod are always found near rocky reefs, seamounts and pinnacles. The steeper and rougher the underwater terrain, the more likely lingcod will be present. Lingcod love to hide in rocky crevasses and pounce on any meal that sweeps past with the tide. Ideal lingcod structure is steep, rocky and between 100 and 200 feet deep.

## How to Catch Lingcod

California and Oregon anglers targeting lingcod favor multiple flies or Hoochies attached to dropper loops above a heavy pyramid sinker. These rigs are fished on or near the bottom and account for many of the lingcod caught. From Washington to Alaska lingcod anglers tend to favor live baits, large chunk baits and a variety of leadhead jigs.

No matter what lure or bait is used, it must be presented within a few feet of the bottom. Lingcod will seldom leave the bottom unless in pursuit of a meal. Once in hot pursuit, however, a lingcod will follow its prey all the way to the surface.

The best time to target lingcod is an hour before and after slack tide. Because the best lingcod structure is typically 100 to 200 feet deep, it is imperative that you fish during periods of modest current flow. It is almost impossible to fish in 200 feet of water when the current is running hard.

Because lingcod are suckers for falling baits or lures, it always pays to keep all offerings in motion. Jigs are excellent lingcod lures because they flutter and spin as they fall through the water column. The best lingcod jigs imitate herring, candlefish or anchovies. The Zzinger, Buzz Bomb and Point Wilson Dart are proven lingcod lures. The best color choices are white, blue, green and black, with weights from 6 to 16 ounces.

A consistent jigging method is to raise the rod tip approximately 2 feet above horizontal, then rapidly dropping it back to the horizontal position. The drop motion should be rapid enough to allow your jig to flutter on a slack line. Be prepared to set the hook, as lingcod love to grab the jig on the fall.

Those who target trophy lingcod prefer to use live baits. Any small rockfish, lingcod or greenling will do, but most experts prefer to use greenling, which are a smaller cousin of lingcod. They are usually abundant in the areas lingcod inhabit, they have no large dorsal spines to wound anglers, and lingcod love them. If no live baits are available, frozen herring, rockfish fillets and pennants of lingcod skin all work well.

The best rig for live-bait lingcod fishing is a heavy banana sinker and a 14- to 30-inch leader snelled with tandem 9/0 hooks. Rig baitfish with one hook behind the dorsal fin, the other through the top lip. Lower the bait to the bottom in an area of rocky structure, and be ready. If an aggressive lingcod is in the area you will have a strike within minutes. After ten minutes without a strike, move to another rock pinnacle and try again.

Rods for lingcod should be 5 to 7 feet in length, fast-action and have a butt section with a lot of backbone. A top-quality level wind reel is a necessity. Your mainline should be braided Dacron or a superline, with the last 6 feet consisting of a leader tied with 30- to 80-pound-test monofilament. This setup allows a main line with the low stretch and sensitivity of braid and a leader with the abrasion resistance needed to stand up to the lingcod's sharp teeth and the rocky lairs they inhabit.

When landing lingcod, take care to keep your fingers away from their mouth. Many anglers have suffered nasty gashes from lingcod.

Because all lingcod weighing more than 20 pounds are females, try to keep only the smaller males for the table. They have better-textured flesh than the big females, and the breeding females are needed to keep populations healthy.

—*Dave Vedder*

# ROCKFISH

Rockfish are among the most abundant Pacific coast gamefish, with 68 known varieties in the genus *Sebastes* and a range that extends from Kodiak, Alaska, to Peru. Scattered populations also occur in the North and South Atlantic and the Western Pacific. On the West Coast rockfish are an important gamefish and a valuable commercial species. Rockfish range in size from less than a few ounces to more than 30 pounds. In addition, rockfish can be found in almost every color of the rainbow. While rockfish are not noted for their fighting ability, their abundance, willingness to bite and outstanding table quality make them a treasured species.

Rockfish come with almost as many names as colors. In the North Pacific they are often called rockcod, even though they are not closely related to the cod family. To confuse matters even more, the highly prized yelloweye rockfish (right) is often called red snapper even though it is no relation to the snapper family.

Rockfish are typically short and squat with a compressed body similar to a largemouth bass. They have large heads and huge mouths, typically lined with Velcro-like barbels rather than true teeth. They often have a single spiny dorsal fin with 13 to 15 spines. Rockfish come in every color from bright orange to black. Many species are similar, making exact identification difficult.

ROCKFISH
RANGE
PRIME FISHING

Rockfish are very slow growing. A 25-pound yelloweye rockfish is between 65 and 80 years of age. Due to their slow growth and willingness to bite almost any lure or bait, rockfish populations are in serious decline in Puget Sound and other areas that are heavily fished. However, open-ocean rockfish populations are generally in good health.

Rockfish are always alert for any moving object that might be food. Any dead or crippled fish that falls toward the bottom will trigger a rockfish strike. The fish also have a keen sense of smell and will track down a meal solely by smell, if necessary.

Rockfish are very opportunistic feeders. Almost any form of protein found near the bottom will attract their attention. Herring, candlefish, anchovies, smaller rockfish, squid and octopus are among their favorite foods. Best baits include herring and squid.

## Where to Find Rockfish

Rockfish are non-migratory. Many species live their entire lives within a few hundred yards of their birthplace. Some species can be found at depths as great as 3,600 feet, but most live at depths of 40 to 300 feet. The vast majority of rockfish species sought by sport fishermen spend their entire life within a few feet of the bottom. However, blue and black

A yelloweye rockfish

A China rockfish

rockfish are often found on the surface, and yellowtail, widow and canary rockfish may be found suspended in the water column. Most species of rockfish, as their name implies, live near steep rocky structure.

To prospect for top rockfish areas, use a detailed chart to find areas that drop off rapidly in the 60 to 300 foot depth range, or look for steep pinnacles in the same general depth range. Black and blue rockfish can often be found near kelp forests in water 20 to 40 feet deep. Look for the telltale small splashes that often signal a feeding school.

## How to Catch Rockfish

Rockfish will attack almost any lure that catches their eye and will eagerly eat most baits. Accordingly, your choice of lure or bait should be based on ease of use, cost and your ability to get it to the bottom and keep it there. The best rockfish lures are those that get down fast. For that reason, jigs and heavy jigging spoons in the 8- to 20-ounce range are ideal. The technique is simple. Lower your jig or spoon as rapidly as possible until slack line shows you have hit bottom. Once you hit bottom, quickly reel up 3 to 6 feet of line to keep your lure away from those grabby rocks. Every few seconds, play out a little more line. The instant your lure touches down, quickly reel up again.

For a less strenuous form of rockfish angling, you might want to consider bait fishing. Most bait anglers prefer herring, squid or anchovies for tempting rockfish.

Bait is usually fished beneath a spreader bar or as part of a sinker-on-the-bottom ganion rig. California anglers prefer the sinker-on-the-bottom rig with as many as ten hooks above the sinker. Northern anglers often choose spreader bars to get a single bait down quickly.

When prospecting for rockfish look for dramatic variations in depth, either by closely watching your depth finder or by previewing the area you intend to fish on a NOAA chart. For best results, use a chart that gives the greatest amount of detail.

Before you begin fishing that likely-looking structure, take a minute to figure out which way the wind and tide will cause you to drift. Tackle losses will be limited if you plan your drift to work your bait or lure down the slopes rather than up and into the crevasses. Good rockfish structure will grab lures, so you can count on losing tackle if you are fishing where these bottom-lovers live.

Selecting the right rod is the most important tackle choice facing the rockfish angler. Whether you're jigging with lures or bait fishing, a short, stiff rod can save you much work and will impart better action to your offering than a long soft rod. Bass flipping rods work very well. For deep-water angling try a heavy one-piece muskie rod rated for 20- to 30-pound-test lines.

Your main line should be braided Dacron or a superline. These lines are extremely sensitive and their low stretch will allow you to dislodge snagged lures much more easily than you can with monofilament.

The best lures for rockfish include Buzz Bombs, Zzingers, Point Wilson Darts, Crippled Herrings and lead-head jigs with plastic tails. The best live baits are herring, squid, anchovies and chunk baits of rockfish and greenling.

When it comes to taste and attitude, no other West Coast sport fish can compete with the yelloweye rockfish. Unfortunately, the rapid ascent from the bottom is often fatal to rockfish. Somewhere on the way up their swim bladder ruptures, effectively ending the battle and their lives. For that reason, rockfish are not a good choice for catch-and-release angling. When you are lucky enough to find a good rockfish hole, take a few for dinner and move on. It would be a shame to overharvest these user-friendly bottom fish.

—*Dave Vedder*

# STARRY FLOUNDER

The starry flounder *(Platichthys stellatus)* is a flatfish common to the West Coast. Starries are found from Santa Barbara, California, to Arctic Alaska on flat sandy or mud bottoms. This flatfish can be identified by its dark brown back, which is covered with rough, star-shaped *tubercles* (modified scales), and by the alternating light orange or white and black bands on the dorsal and anal fins. The starry has been reported to reach up to 20 pounds and 3 feet in length, although most specimens average around a pound. They are opportunistic feeders and eat a variety of bottom-living food items such as shrimp,

STARRY FLOUNDER
RANGE
PRIME FISHING

crabs, clams, marine worms and mussels. At times starries will come off the bottom and feed at mid-level on shrimps or small baitfish. They are most common in bays and estuaries and are a fairly common catch for winter or spring inshore anglers.

## Where to Find Starry Flounder

The starry flounder is a very popular fish, especially in the San Francisco Bay area of California. It is excellent to eat and fairly easy to catch. Although not as plentiful as in years past, the starry is a welcome catch for anglers. Most anglers catch starries using baits fished on the bottom.

To begin looking for flounder, try flat mud or sand bottom or shell banks in 5 to 30 feet of water located near the mouth of any small slough, creek or river. Flounder will bite on any moving tide. As a rule, if the tide is strong, concentrate your fishing in shallower water; and on weak-moving tides, head out to deeper water. The types of bottoms mentioned are common in San Francisco Bay and San Pablo Bay. One of the most popular areas, located near the northeast side of San Pablo Bay, is the Napa River. This area produces good numbers of pan-sized flounder for pier and small-boat anglers.

Once a good-looking area is located, the boat is anchored and the rigs are cast out and allowed to sink to the bottom. Make sure the bait stays flat on the bottom; if it planes up in the current, increase your weight until it stays down. Starries bite very delicately, so anglers fishing for them should use rods with a sensitive tip to help them read the bite.

If flounder are present, it doesn't take long to get a bite. If no action occurs in fifteen minutes or so, move to another location until you start getting bites. Starry flounder tend to be grouped up, so when you catch one, you can usually catch several more in the area. Starries bite with a series of sharp taps. Wait for the rod to load with weight before setting the hook.

## How to Catch Starry Flounder

A 7-foot medium-action rod and baitcasting reel loaded with 12- to 20-pound test are more than adequate for these flatfish. Many anglers opt for this slightly heavier outfit simply because areas where you can catch starry flounder also offer a good chance at a big bruising sturgeon or striped bass. In fact, many of the flounder captured by sport fishermen are a welcome incidental catch made by anglers pursuing other species.

Terminal tackle for flounder fishing consists of a standard slip-sinker rig. Make sure the sinker (preferably pyramid style) is large enough to keep the gear on the bottom. Next, a swivel is attached and a leader is attached to that. The leader will be 2 to 3 feet long and consists of 40- to 60-pound-test monofilament or plastic-coated wire. Starry flounder are not leader shy, and anglers often use heavy stuff to make sure they don't have any problems should they hook into one of the big guys. Hooks are secured to the end of the leader; 3/0 to 6/0 Octopus hooks are preferred.

Hooks can be baited with any natural bait. Favorites include grass, ghost or mud shrimp, and pile worms. Flounder will also take baits such as sardine, anchovy or herring cut into bite-sized chunks.

Anglers who prefer to cast artificial lures or flies can catch starry flounder under the right conditions. In the clear tide waters of small coastal creeks and rivers it is not uncommon for starries to grab a small, brightly-colored shrimp pattern of the type cast for salmon and steelhead. If a fly crosses a flounder's nose it will bite. If you want to target flounder on a fly, make sure to use a sinking fly line and any bright shrimp-type pattern tied on a #4 or #6 hook. Make sure to allow the fly to sink close to the bottom before starting a slow retrieve. Light-action 5- to 6-foot spinning outfits loaded with 4- to 6-pound-test monofilament are perfect. Small $1/16$- to $1/8$-ounce, brightly-colored marabou tail or rubber grub body jigs work well when hopped across the bottom.

For a small flatfish, the starry flounder gives a good fight for its size. And as far as table qualities are concerned, starries are great when coated with flour and sauted in garlic and olive oil.

—*Angelo Cuanang*

# STRIPED BASS (Pacific Coast)

Since its introduction into San Francisco Bay in the late 1800s the striped bass *(Morone saxatilis)* has established itself as one of the West Coast's premier gamefish. Although stragglers are found from British Columbia to northern Baja, and a small fishery exists in Oregon, the San Francisco Bay region has the largest population and is the heart of West Coast striped bass activity.

In the late 1900s striper populations faced major problems due to environmental issues such as drought conditions and manmade water-diversion projects. The fishery made a tremendous upward surge after several high-rainfall years, as high rainfall aids tremendously in young striper survival.

Another major reason for the upswing in striper activity was a recovery program that saves young striped bass from the deadly delta-water pump screens that have killed millions of young stripers in the past. This "net pen program" takes young stripers off the screens and raises them in grow-out pens in the bay. When they reach 8 to 10 inches

STRIPED BASS
■ RANGE
■ PRIME FISHING

in size they are released back into the fishery. Fish this size have an excellent survival rate, and the program, which is run by the Fisheries Foundation, has released close to a million stripers. This program has been a tremendous boon to dedicated Bay Area striper anglers, who love stripers for their handsome look, hard fighting ability and excellent eating quality, and for the fact that they can be captured using a wide variety of methods. Stripers can be caught by live-bait fishing, trolling, casting lures, vertical jigging, fishing cut and rigged baits on the bottom, and fly fishing.

## Where to Find Striped Bass

West Coast striped bass fishing takes place just about year-round, and anglers can usually locate fish throughout the year and expect to catch a striper or two. Near the first of the year the majority of adult stripers spend much of their time in the lower Delta region. As the season progresses towards spring, many of the adult fish head up into the Sacramento River region to spawn. By the time spring and early summer roll around, adult fish head down to the main part of San Francisco Bay to feed on the large schools of anchovies found there.

Some stripers become residents in the river systems, while others move up and down the coast. Immature stripers, or *schoolies*, are spread throughout the bay-delta system. Spring and fall bring some of the best action for these younger fish.

In spring and early summer schools of anchovies and sardines start to migrate into the bay as they feed on rich plankton. Any rock, reef, or firm bottom where the main currents flow will attract baitfish, which feed actively. Not far behind, hungry stripers gorge on the concentrated forage. As stripers enter the bay system the schools will first be found in the northern part of the bay; then they quickly filter through the system. North bay anglers can find a mixture of adult and schoolie stripers at the Sisters Islands, the Brothers Islands, also the nearby Whiting and Invincible reefs, and Red Rock. In these areas anglers can toss lures, vertical jig or drift live bait to catch stripers. South Hampton shoals is also good for live-bait drifting and trolling. To the west the small points along the Marin shoreline, Raccoon Straits and the points along Angel Island will produce fish for anglers casting jigs or drifting live bait.

When stripers are feeding in the main bay, the areas west of Alcatraz such as the Rockpile, Harding Rock, and the south tower of the Golden Gate Bridge can hold large schools. Other areas such as the Bay Bridge, the waters outside Alameda, and west to Candlestick Point and the San Francisco Airport can be great areas to find fish.

## How to Catch Striped Bass

When casting lures or vertical jigging in the bay, anglers can use spinning or baitcasting gear. A 6- to 7½-foot rod capable of handling jigs up to 2 ounces, matched with a reel loaded with 12- to 20-pound-test, will do the job. Anglers will want to make sure make sure to have plenty of ½- to 2-ounce jigs in white, chartreuse or combinations of colors. (Add a 3- to 5-inch curly-tail worm for attraction.) Other jigs that work well are the soft rubber-body Fish Traps on ½- to 2-ounce heads in natural baitfish colors. For plugs, anglers should have ½- to ¾-ounce Rattle Traps, Bombers and Rebel Minnows

in natural colors. For vertical jigging in the shallower portions of the bay, Luhr Jensen Crippled Herring, stinger jigs, Hopkins spoons and Kastmasters in the 1- to 3-ounce sizes all work well.

Live-bait drifting probably takes more fish than any other method in the main bay. The basic live-bait outfit consists of a 7-foot sensitive-tip rod capable of handling 1 to 8 ounces of weight. The reel should have a smooth drag and hold 150 to 200 yards of 12- to 25-pound-test line. Most anglers use monofilament, but superlines may give you a better feel of the bottom and light bites. This same outfit can be used for vertical jigging in the deeper parts of the main bay.

Live bait rigs consists of a #1 three-way swivel, 18- to 20-inch sinker dropper and a snap for the weight, a 4-foot section of 25- to 30-pound test and a size #1 to 2/0 live-bait hook tied to the end. This is an easy rig to make, or it can be purchased at most tackle stores. This rig is designed to be fished on or close to the bottom as you drift.

During the summer, when adult stripers leave the bay and head out into the ocean, the majority of the fish head to the south. Here anglers can wade in the surf and cast Krocodile or Hopkins spoons, Miki Jigs, bucktail jigs, pencil poppers and Rebel or Bomber plugs. Seagulls, terns, shearwaters and pelicans will dive and pick off baitfish forced to the surface by stripers feeding below. When things are hot and heavy, stripers can be seen breaking the surface as anchovies spray across the surface like rain.

During late summer and early fall, stripers head back into the bay and offer fly casters a chance to get into some hot action. Anglers prefer a 9-foot, 8- to 10-weight fly rod matched with a quality fly reel, loaded with 150 to 200 yards of backing with a shooting line and a fast-sinking shooting head. A short 5- to 6-foot leader with a 12-to 20-pound-test tippet works well. Preferred baits are white 2- to 4-inch bucktail and hackle streamers tied on stainless 1/0 to 3/0 hooks. Cast near structure and points along the Marin shoreline or along the points near San Francisco Airport. Use a stop-and-go retrieve – and if the fish are there, it only takes a few casts to find out.

If you are lucky enough to get into a hot striper bite, keep only what you need for a meal and release the rest to help ensure that this great fishery stays strong into the future.

—*Angelo Cuanang*

# WHITE STURGEON

Despite its ancient appearance the white sturgeon (*Acipenser transmontanus*) has become one of San Francisco Bay's most popular winter game-fish. While it may look slow and cumbersome, the white sturgeon is a superb fighter, has great strength and endurance and can jump with amazing agility. It is little wonder why this unusual fish has become such a highly sought prize throughout the bay area.

White sturgeon are *anadromous*, which means they are born in fresh water but head into the salt to live most of their lives. When the urge to spawn comes, White sturgeon return to fresh water rivers. The white sturgeon is the largest fish that enters fresh water in North America; specimens of well over 1,000 pounds have been caught. Besides the delta and San Francisco Bay, there are healthy populations of these fish in the Columbia River in Oregon. The sturgeon is a popular game-fish there as well, although fishing for them is heavily regulated. Anglers should check into regulations prior to fishing.

Generally, in the bay area sturgeon fishing begins in the late fall and extends to early spring. During this period storms and heavy rains can be prevalent. Such inclement weather acts as a vital catalyst because it creates a downstream flush of fresh water that brings sturgeon schools into the bay to spawn.

As they enter the bay system sturgeon fan out across its vast expanse. The first major body of water they enter is the San Pablo. From there they continue to move south, eventually passing through the middle bay and finally traveling into the south bay waters. All three of these major regions feature shallow mud and shell banks, with deeper water along the edge of shipping channels.

## Where to Find Sturgeon

One of the quickest ways to locate sturgeon is by watching for jumpers. Jumping sturgeon will reveal themselves with a heavy splash, or you may see their white belly flash in the sunlight. If you see many jumpers in one locale, it's a good indicator of a concentration of fish.

If you find a group of sturgeon that is holding in shallow water, approach the area slowly to avoid spooking the fish. Once you are in their general line of movement ease the anchor overboard. Sturgeon will also congregate along channel edges and shell mounds. The best way to locate these fish is by watching your depth finder closely. Sturgeon will appear as large, distinctive arches on the screen. As with jumpers, when you find an active lane of fish, anchor on that spot.

Sturgeon can also be found feeding near bridge abutments, particularly on the down-current side and in spots where the bottom features sloping depressions. These fish can also be located with a depth finder.

WHITE STURGEON
RANGE
PRIME FISHING

Tide lines generally indicate the initial push of the tide whether it's incoming or outgoing. They'll often appear as a choppy, active surface highlighted with plumes of mud and debris. During the calm tide the surface will feature a flat face, indicating minimal current movement. When you see these tide lines, anchor on the active side, as that's where the sturgeon will be feeding.

## How to Catch White Sturgeon

A good rod for fishing sturgeon from a boat will measure 7 feet. It should have a sensitive tip to detect for the gentle bite of the sturgeon, but it must also have stiff backbone for lifting a heavy fish. A rod rated for 20- to 40-pound-test line would be a reliable choice. Match the rod with a reel with a smooth drag system and load it with a minimum of 200 yards of 30- to 50-pound-test line. Anglers can use monofilament line, but superlines are excellent for this kind of fishing. Superlines feature a thin diameter and minimal stretch, which give the angler tremendous feel for light bites and quick, positive hook sets.

Sturgeon feed on the bottom, so terminal gear must keep the baits down but still allow the angler to feel the delicate bite. Basic sturgeon terminal gear starts with a sliding sinker sleeve slipped onto the main line. The snap on the sleeve will hold your sinker. Next the leader is tied on, with the most common type constructed of 24 to 36 inches of braided 60-pound plastic-coated wire with a 1/0 swivel attached to one end and two 6/0 to 8/0 Octopus-style hooks attached to the other end. Both connections are secured via size A5 sleeves. When tying superline to the swivel on your leader, use a two-strand knot such as a double improved clinch knot.

Anglers need to use a sinker that will hold bottom well. Pyramid-style sinkers are preferred because they hold bottom well, but cannonball sinkers can also be used in sturgeon fishing. To cover a wide range of depth and current conditions, carry sinkers weighing from 4 to 16 ounces to keep the rig on the bottom.

White sturgeon evolved as bottom feeders, and their mouth is underslung like a vacuum tube that drops when browsing along the bottom. Sturgeon have a highly developed sense of feel and smell. They prey on specific baits and can be quite selective at times. Because of this selective feeding behavior, anglers will do best using fresh or live local baits. In San Francisco Bay, mud, ghost and grass shrimp will consistently take sturgeon. Another effective bait is fresh herring.

Generally, the best fishing in the bay is generated by strong tides, either ebb or flood. The strong currents kick up the bottom and cause sturgeon to begin feeding actively during the first push of the tide and about one to two hours before the top. On the ebb side, the first push and then near the bottom of the low are the best.

White sturgeon, regardless of their size, bite very delicately. Also, skates, rays, sharks and white croakers will compete for the bait. Because of these two factors, an angler must watch the rod tip constantly as well as check and re-bait the hook often. Sturgeon will often initiate the first bite with a quick tap that shows on the rod tip, followed quickly by a series of slow, pronounced pumps. As the rod tip begins to load, set the hook hard. Should you make a solid connection with the fish, keep in mind that it will often have extra companions swimming with it. If at all possible keep the other lines in the water for a chance at another quick hookup.

When fishing in a boat with a group of anglers, make sure that casts are made in different directions off the stern and bow, and stagger casts both long and short. By doing this you cover all of the potential avenues the sturgeon may take as they pass the boat.

Relentless rod pressure must be applied to get the fish to the surface without the line getting tangled or line being cut on the keel or prop of the boat. Follow the line wherever it goes. In California it is illegal to use gaffs or guns to capture sturgeon. Smaller sturgeon can be easily landed with a net, and larger legal fish can be landed using a snare. The snare is slipped over the sturgeon's head and secured behind the pectoral fins or at the base of the tail.

White sturgeon comprise a unique fishery, and anglers should check regulations before pursuing them. If you are lucky enough to catch a sturgeon you can set it free. If you decide to keep a legal fish, the table qualities are excellent. They have a firm white meat that can be grilled, fried, baked or smoked. Any way you prepare it, a white sturgeon is always delicious.

—*Abe Cuanang*

# Spotted Sand Bass

Curiously, the origins of the popularity of salt water bass fishing along the southern California coast can be traced directly to the diminutive spotted sand bass. Back in the early 70s, these tough little bay residents were the first bass species to catch the attention of fresh water bass fishermen. After making the easy transition to fishing salt water, these anglers organized the still-popular bay fishing tournaments, and ultimately inspired the development of a whole series of southern California-based lure manufacturing companies. The popularity of spotted sand bass stems from the fact that they are willing biters and strong fighters that live in easily accessible but tough habitats.

Spotted sand bass (*Paralabrax maculatofasciatus*) are more similar to the barred sand bass (p. 114) than to the calico bass (p. 106) and are distinguished by their broad, dusky vertical bars and the small brown spots that cover all but their gray bellies. During the summer spawning season the lower jaw and underside of the gills of some specimens take on a yellow to orange cast. Although they range as far north as Monterey Bay, spotted sand bass are most prevalent from the Long Beach area south to San Diego. Healthy populations of these fish can also be found in the bays and lagoons along the west coast of the Baja Peninsula south to Magdalena Bay, as well as in the upper reaches of the Sea of Cortez.

Although the IGFA all-tackle world record catch for the species is listed at only 2 pounds, California

SPOTTED SAND BASS
RANGE
PRIME FISHING

recognizes an impressive 24-inch, 6¾-pound specimen.

Spotted sand bass (often referred to as spotted bay or simply bay bass) rarely venture out of southern California bays and harbors. They sometimes share habitat with barred sand bass, but being highly territorial, bay bass will usually occupy the shallower areas of the bay. They prefer to be close to structure features like dock pilings, bridge abutments, rocky points and beds of eel grass and kelp. There they wait to ambush crabs, shrimp, small baitfish and any other edible morsel that drifts by with the currents. When pickings are slim, bay bass will dredge up clams or pull barnacles off the pilings.

Rigging a live anchovy and dropping it to the bottom adjacent to structure in shallow bay waters is a good way to hook up with a spotted sand bass. At times, drifting with the wind or tide while bouncing a jig along the bottom can yield big dividends, as can slow trolling with small diving plugs that nose into and stir up the bottom sediment.

In general, spotted sand bass are more aggressive and easier to hook than fresh water bass. Bay bass anglers are typically armed with sturdy 6-foot medium to medium-heavy "bass gear" and 10- or 12-pound-test lines.

After setting the hook on a spottie, get ready for a contest of strength versus strength as you try to turn the hooked fish away from the hazardous structure this species inhabits.

—*Tom Waters*

# CALIFORNIA CORBINA

The California corbina *(Menticirrhus undulatus)* is the one fish most sought after by southern California surfcasting enthusiasts. Averaging just 2 to 3 pounds (18 to 21 inches), corbina are not "big" by any standards. However, once they are hooked up on light tackle in shallow water, and explode on blistering runs – not unlike those of bonefish – the small size is forgotten. Couple such aggressive behavior with the corbina's finicky feeding habits and the fact that fillets of these torpedo-shaped croakers are similar in flavor and consistency of crab meat, and you have one of the most exciting inshore gamefish to be found anywhere.

Ranging from California's Point Conception (just north of Santa Barbara) down along the Baja California peninsula and over into the upper reaches of Mexico's Sea of Cortez, corbina have been found at depths of up to 45 feet. Most are encountered in the very shallow waters of the surf zone (where they voraciously feed on sand crabs), and to a lesser degree in the coastal bays and harbors. Among surf fishermen, a 5-pounder is a trophy, but corbinas have been reported up to 30 inches in length and 8-plus pounds. The California state and IGFA all-tackle world records officially recognize a 6-pound, 8-ounce trophy.

The traditional approach to catching corbina is to use heavy tackle for casting baits well beyond the shorebreak. At low tide, anything from sand bottoms to grass beds to rocky reefs or ledges can lie within range of such casts. Achieving such distance requires long rods (10 to 15 feet), mounted with revolving spool or large line-capacity spinning reels spooled with 20- or 25-pound-test line and sinkers as heavy as 6 ounces. When

CALIFORNIA CORBINA
RANGE
PRIME FISHING

mounted nearly vertical in a sand spike, the long rod keeps the line above the pounding of incoming breakers, which otherwise tend to drag baits back toward the beach.

Besides sand crabs, natural baits like ghost shrimp, bloodworms, razor clams, mussels and innkeeper worms can also lure corbina from the deeper outside water. Present these baits on a rig consisting of dual leaders positioned above a pyramid sinker (usually from 1 to 4 ounces); each foot-long leader is attached to the main line with dropper loops and has a hook on the end. Also effective is a slider rig, which consists of a sliding plastic sleeve with flat-sided sinker attached, positioned above a barrel swivel to which a 12- to 18-inch leader with a bait hook is attached.

Gaining popularity is the light tackle approach to catching corbina. This method is most effective during the summer months when the larger female fish are up feeding in the shallows.

A 6½ foot medium-light rod and a spinning reel with a smooth drag, spooled with 6-pound-test line is the ideal combination for this type of fishing. A split shot positioned a foot or so ahead of a #4 to #8 baitholder hook is often the only rig needed. Simply walk the beach, casting ahead to any dark areas, which are indicators of troughs or holes and tend to attract fish.

Whatever the approach, be prepared for some strong, sometimes lightning-fast runs when you hook up. A big corbina on light tackle can be a real workout as you sprint up and down and along the beach just trying to keep up!

—*Tom Waters*

# Index

141

Creative Publishing international, Inc. offers
a variety of how-to books.
For information call or write:

   Creative Publishing international, Inc.
   Customer Service
   5900 Green Oak Drive
   Minnetonka, MN 55343
   1-800-328-3895

Or visit us at:
www.howtobookstore.com

# Author Biographies

**John Brownlee** is a native Floridian who grew up fishing the waters of the Gulf of Mexico north of Tampa for king and Spanish mackerel, speckled trout and redfish. He has since expanded his angling horizons to include fishing excursions throughout the coastal United States, Mexico, Central America, the Caribbean and the Bahamas. A dedicated conservationist, Brownlee and his family moved to Islamorada, Florida, to indulge themselves in the incredible fishing opportunities available in the Florida Keys. He currently serves as the Upper Keys IGFA representative, the sportfishing representative on the Florida Keys National Marine Sanctuary Advisory Council and as a Senior Editor for *Salt Water Sportsman.*

**Abe Cuanang** is a 47-year-old freelance outdoor writer and photographer. He has fished almost his entire life, pursuing all of the major gamefish on the West Coast. In those pursuits he has learned the ins and outs of catching West Coast fish and has also compiled a huge photo library of those fishing exploits. He has written three books —*San Francisco Bay Striper, San Francisco Bay Sturgeon* and *Sturgeon* — and also has two videotapes, *Saltwater Secrets: Salmon, Stripers, Sturgeon* and *Saltwater Secrets: Rockfish*. Abe does most of his fishing from a 17-foot Boston Whaler.

**Angelo Cuanang** is the 44-year-old San Francisco Bay Regional Editor for *Salt Water Sportsman* magazine and has fished for, photographed and written articles on a large variety of popular salt water gamefish. His photos and features have appeared in all the major West Coast fishing publications. Although he enjoys fishing other great locations like Baja, Alaska and Costa Rica, Angelo does most of his fishing in the San Francisco Bay area for stripers, salmon, halibut and sturgeon. And like his brother, he does most of his fishing from a Boston Whaler.

**Barry Gibson** is the long-time Editor of *Salt Water Sportsman* magazine. He has been a charter boat captain in Boothbay Harbor, Maine, since 1971, and currently guides exclusively for striped bass and bluefish from his 24-foot center-console. He has served as a government fishery manager, has fished extensively in North and South America, and contributes to a variety of outdoor publications.

**Bob McNally** has been around fishing and the outdoors all his life. He caught his first sailfish at age 9, his first tarpon and bonefish at age 10. His first magazine feature on fly fishing was sold to *Sports Afield* at age 18. He is the author of 11 outdoor books, including his definitive, best-selling *Fishermen's Knots, Fishing Rigs, and How To Use Them.* Bob has fished throughout Canada, Mexico, Central and South America, Europe, Cuba and the Bahamas. He lives near Jacksonville, Florida, with his wife Chris and three children, Eric, Matt and Lindsey.

**Tom Richardson** is Managing Editor of *Salt Water Sportsman* magazine. In addition to his photo and article contributions to *SWS*, Richardson is a freelance writer and photographer, as well as a contributing writer to the on-line fishing magazine *Reel-time*. Tom pursues a number of salt water fish species and spends most of his time on the waters of southern Massachusetts, Cape Cod and Rhode Island.

**Allan J. (Al) Ristori** started salt water fishing 55 years ago and began writing about it for national and regional magazines in 1965. He has written thousands of articles and is in his 17th year as Salt Water Editor of the *Newark Star-Ledger*. His books include *North American Saltwater Fishing, The Saltwater Fish Identifier* and *Fishing for Bluefish* in addition to sections in *Striped Bass Fishing: Salt Water Strategies*. Ristori is a charter captain who fishes out of Point Pleasant, New Jersey for everything from stripers and blues to tuna and sharks. He currently serves as *Salt Water Sportsman's* New York/New Jersey Editor.

**Dave Vedder** is a lifetime resident of Washington state. Raised on the Olympic Peninsula, he began salmon fishing with his parents at Sekiu while he was still in diapers. Dave's love of fishing has taken him to every part of Washington, Oregon, Alaska and British Columbia and to such foreign angling destinations as Africa, Cuba, the Marshall Islands and Mexico. His special loves are salmon, trout and steelhead fishing. He has authored two books on steelhead fishing and has written hundreds of fishing articles for many national and local magazines. Dave's writing and photography have won him numerous awards, and his photos have graced the covers of more than 40 magazines.

**Tom Waters** is Southwest Regional Editor for *Salt Water Sportsman* magazine. Tom is an accomplished writer, artist/illustrator, photographer and lecturer who specializes in sportfishing and has fished Pacific waters from Alaska to Mexico and Hawaii. He was a fishing lure manufacturer for nearly a decade and has served as an editor to four different sportfishing magazines. Tom and his wife Sherry enjoy travel, fishing and photography and also operate their own graphic design studio.

# Photo & Illustration Credits

## PHOTOGRAPHERS

(Note: T=Top, C=Center, B=Bottom, L=Left, R=Right)

**Joel Arrington**
Oriental, NC
© Joel Arrington: pp. 13, 14, 78L, 91, 93

**Ron Ballanti**
Westlake, CA
© Ron Ballanti: back cover C, p. 118

**John Brownlee**
Islamorada, FL
© John Brownlee: pp. 5R, 95

**Hanson Carroll**
Islamorada, FL
© Hanson Carroll: p. 72B

**Angelo Cuanang**
South San Francisco, CA
© Angelo Cuanang: pp. 132, 134, 136

**Marc Epstein**
Titusville, FL
© Marc Epstein: p. 22

**Jim Hendricks**
Downey, CA
© Jim Hendricks: pp. 106, 124, 126

**Richard Herrmann**
Poway, CA
© Richard Herrmann: pp. 107, 122

**Innerspace Visions**
Kailua-Kona, HI
© Doug Perrine: p. 73

**Gary Kramer**
Willows, CA
© Gary Kramer: cover background photo, pp. 130, 131

**Larry Larsen Photography**
Lakeland, FL
© Larry Larsen: p. 39

**Bill Lindner Photography**
St. Paul, MN
© Bill Lindner Photography: cover BR, back cover L, pp. 3T, 4L, 18 both, 44, 60, 76 both, 81, 82, 86T

**Bob McNally**
Jacksonville, FL
© Bob McNally: back cover R, pp. 27, 75, 86B

**Dick Mermon**
Spring Hill, FL
© Dick Mermon: pp. 68, 71R

**Brian O'Keefe**
Bend, OR
© Brian O'Keefe: pp. 4R, 5L, 21, 26, 30, 58, 59, 100, 110

**John E. Phillips**
Birmingham, AL
© John E. Phillips: pp. 42, 72T

**Tom Richardson**
Brookline, MA
© Tom Richardson: pp. 3BC, 8-9, 15, 50-51, 52, 78R, 79

**Al Ristori**
Manasquan Park, NJ
© Al Ristori: pp. 33, 77

**Neal Rogers**
Butte, MT
© Neal Rogers: p. 28

**David J. Sams**
DavidJSams.com
© David J. Sams/Texas Inprint: pp. 3B, 24, 84, 88, 94

**Tom Stack & Associates**
Key Largo, FL
© Mark Stack: p. 45

**Doug Stamm**
Prairie du Sac, WI
© Doug Stamm/ProPhoto: p. 64

**Walt Stearns**
Boca Raton, FL
© Walt Stearns: pp. 56, 70

**Sam Talarico**
Mohnton, PA
© Sam Talarico: pp. 3TC, 32, 35, 36-37, 71L

**Dave Vedder**
Woodinville, WA
© Dave Vedder: cover BL, pp. 98, 129

**Tom Waters**
Carlsbad, CA
© Tom Waters: pp. 113, 114, 138, 139

## ILLUSTRATORS

**Chris Armstrong**
Jacksonville, FL
© Chris Armstrong: pp. 12, 15, 41, 69B

**John F. Eggert**
Marstons Mills, MA
© John F. Eggert: p. 67 both

**Diane Rome Peebles***
St. Petersburg, FL
© Diane Rome Peebles: pp. 10, 19, 29, 37, 45, 50, 57, 61, 65B, 69T, 74, 76, 78R, 78L, 81, 82, 84, 86, 89, 90, 92, 94, 95, 107, 111, 115, 119, 123, 124, 126, 128, 130, 133, 134, 138, 139

**Don Ray**
Vero Beach, FL
© Don Ray: cover painting

**John Rice**
New York, NY
© John Rice: p. 63

**Dave Shepherd**
Narragansett, RI
© Dave Shepherd: p. 48

**Jim Singer**
Kirkland, WA
© Jim Singer: pp. 102 both, 112

**Fred W. Thomas**
Shoreline, WA
© Fred W. Thomas: pp. 3BC, 96-97

**Joseph R. Tomelleri**
Leawood, KS
© Joseph R. Tomelleri: pp. 65T, 99 both, 104 all, 136

**Tom Waters**
Carlsbad, CA
© Tom Waters: pp. 108, 116, 117 all, 121 both

**Wild Wings, Inc.**
Lake City, MN
© Mark Susinno: pp. 6-7

*\* some of Diane Rome Peebles illustrations are provided by the Florida Fish & Wildlife Conservation Commission*